For the
Next Generation

For the Next Generation

A Wake-Up Call to Solving Our Nation's Problems

Debbie Wasserman Schultz

with Julie M. Fenster

St. Martin's Press

New York

www.stmartins.com

Library of Congress Cataloging-in-Publication Data

Schultz, Debbie Wasserman.
   For the next generation : a wake-up call to solving our nation's problem / Debbie Wasserman Schultz, with Julie M. Fenster.—First edition.
      pages cm
   ISBN 978-1-250-00099-6 (hardcover)
   ISBN 978-1-250-02177-9 (e-book)
  1. Schultz, Debbie Wasserman.   2. United States—Politics and government—21st century.   3. United States. Congress. House—Biography.   4. Women legislators—United States—Biography.   5. Women legislators—Florida—Biography.   I. Fenster, J. M. (Julie M.)   II. Title.
   E901.1.S38A3 2013
   328.73'092—dc23
   [B]

2013002627

St. Martin's Press books may be purchased for educational, business, or promotional use. For information on bulk purchases, please contact Macmillan Corporate and Premium Sales Department at 1-800-221-7945, extension 5442, or write specialmarkets@macmillan.com.

First Edition: October 2013

10 9 8 7 6 5 4 3 2 1

TO SAINT STEVE, WHO IS THE REASON I
TRULY "HAVE IT ALL"
and
REBECCA, JAKE, AND SHELBY,
WHO ARE THE "ALL" I DREAMT OF HAVING

Contents

For the
Next Generation

The Future Our Children
Deserve

The work that would define my life began shortly after my twenty-sixth birthday. I had become the youngest woman ever elected to the Florida Legislature, and though I had yet to have kids of my own, I was determined to be a children's advocate in government. In the years to follow, I drafted and passed legislation that would enhance child safety around pools—drowning is the leading cause of accidental death for children under five years old in Florida. I fought for more funding for Florida schools and against wrongheaded education reforms championed by Jeb Bush, then the state's governor. And I reached across the aisle to work with Republican leaders on a program that teaches parents how to be their child's first teacher.

As doggedly as I worked to improve the welfare of children, my pursuit of these goals was based on intuition, the sense that kids were the most vulnerable members of our society and so they needed legislators like me to look out for them. But they were not a direct part of my daily life—during my first seven years in public office, my encounters with children were limited to those who belonged to my friends and constituents. Friends and constituents would share with me the hopes, dreams, and anxiety they had for their kids. But while I could certainly empathize, I suppose these parents sensed that I couldn't entirely relate to their point of view. "When you become a parent," they often said, "you'll understand."

They were absolutely right. Becoming a parent changes you forever. I gave birth to my twins, Rebecca and Jake, in my eighth and final year in the Florida House of Representatives. Suddenly, I could see in sharp relief the way my adult decisions affected my kids—and by extension how every adult's decision had implications for the young people who would inherit this nation from us.

As a parent, you can guide your daughters and sons along a path that will allow them to be safe, healthy, and knowledgeable, with a moral compass that navigates them through life's most treacherous terrain. I share this profound responsibility with my husband, Steve, and I am very proud of the children we are raising—Rebecca, Jake, and Shelby. My love for them is the most powerful, all-consuming force I've known. They remind me every day that the sacrifices I make are investments in their future. There is absolutely no question in my mind that being a mother has made me a better legislator, because I bring that unique perspective to bear on every decision I make.

I wish there were more legislators in Washington who could relate to a parent's point of view. After all, Congress is designed to reflect the diversity of perspectives within our nation. But since the founding of this republic, mothers with school-age children have been woefully underrepresented. Through the centuries, there have been more than 12,000 members of Congress, but only 267 of them have been women. Most of the women who were also moms joined Congress *after* their kids had grown, as was the case for the first woman Speaker of the House (now Minority Leader) Nancy Pelosi (D-CA), who explained to *USA Today*, "When my children were small, I barely had time to wash my face." In the session of Congress that took office in January 2013, there were only eight female members of Congress with children under the age of ten.

Mothers have a distinctly intimate, emotional stake in policies that directly affect kids, just as they have a sensibility for anticipating how policies will affect kids indirectly. Other adults can use their intuition to empathize with mothers, but as my friends used to tell me, you have to be a parent to truly understand.

For instance, on the days when I am not in Washington, when I wake up in my own home in Weston, Florida, and eat breakfast with my three school-age children, I am reminded how different the experience of living their daily lives is to them, compared to adults. For every adult, there is both a past and a future. Because our pasts are enriched with the lessons that come from life experience, we can apply those lessons in a way that shapes our individual futures. By the time we've become adults, we've also accumulated knowledge of how to work with others in a way that will affect the future that we share collectively. For me that work takes place in Congress and on the campaign trail, while other Americans go off to teach a class, or treat patients, or police a town. Whatever it is we adults do, most of us are informed by an awareness of the past and a desire to improve the future, not just for our families but for the country and the world.

For children, there is little regard for the past, only an eye toward immediate gratification. They are charging into the future so eagerly, so hopefully, that they have little use for regret or nostalgia. Most of their wisdom has been acquired on a subconscious level—they learn caution toward a hot iron and to eat their ice cream *slowly*, lest they get a brain freeze. The rest of what they will need to know, they can only learn from their parents and from other adults who will have a role in the formative years of their childhood. There are precocious children who have a blooming interest in politics, but still, those children have no power to vote. They have no means for organizing the way other interest groups can. They cannot drive to a job and with no independent income they have little power to effect change through spending.

In short, the Americans who have the greatest stake in the future of this world—children—have the least capacity to control it. They are *totally* dependent on adults, with no choice but to hope that as we adults go through our daily lives, applying our life's experience in making decisions that affect the future, we are mindful of our responsibility to them and *their* future. Children can only hope that we are being unselfish and conscientious.

The best way that we can show our love for our own children is to do our utmost to secure the future for *all* young people, because our kids today will be tomorrow's adults, inhabiting a world populated by their children, and then their children's children. For instance, given the role we adults have in shaping that world, we have an opportunity to promote a more sustainable environment for those future adults. Education can steer them toward high-paying, professional careers and away from crime. We can promote the ideals of equality and demonstrate how the most complex, polarizing debates can be settled with respectful discourse. If we want this future for our children, then we have to take action on all children's behalf.

Within a democracy, change does not come easily. And there are some days when even the most commonsense reforms seem like a mirage, an illusion of water to a weary traveler crossing the desert. In those moments, I think back to the hopes I had twenty years ago when I first allowed myself to dream of being elected to the state legislature. I confided these ambitions to one of my mentors, and he told me that before I launch a campaign, I should sit down to make a list of the reasons why I want to serve in government. Not only would it help provide clarity of purpose in my pursuit, it would help me stay focused through the trials and tribulations of holding public office.

At the top of that list were these priorities:

1. Improve the quality of our children's public education
2. Expand access to quality, affordable health care
3. Make government more responsive to people's needs

More than twenty years have passed since I made that list, and I still keep it in mind. If I'm still fortunate enough to be holding elected office twenty years from now, I want to be judging my performance according to those three objectives.

But the single objective that cuts across all three is children. They are the ones who profit from our investments in education, just as they are the ones who have the most to lose from gaps in health-care coverage, and because they can't organize to demand these policies, government must be proactive, with each elected leader being "lobbied" by her or his own conscience to intercede on behalf of children.

I would encourage every American, even those with no plans to run for office, to make a list like I did. Consider how the issues on that list relate to children. If we look at the world from the perspective of doing right by our kids, then we will stay true to our original goals, and we'll be making progress every day. It is a matter of applying what we have learned from recent events, then letting those lessons inform our attitudes and actions going forward. For example, it is my fervent hope that my children will never again witness an event as fraught with peril as the Great Recession. With them in mind, I cast votes in support of regulations for the banking and housing industries, measures that will minimize the risk of another subprime mortgage meltdown. As a way to promote job growth and greater income equality, my fellow Democrats and I are taking a hard look at the tax code, making it more likely that the wealthy pay their fair share of taxes and easier for middle-class and low-income families to pay for necessities. We invested in our long-term infrastructure needs through the American Recovery and Reinvestment Act by expanding the funding for smart electrical grid technology and by beginning to modernize badly deteriorated roads and bridges. We began to address an appropriate amount of regulation on the financial services industry by passing the Dodd-Frank Wall Street Reform and Consumer Protection Act to fill in tremendous gaps that contributed to the worst economic crisis America had experienced since the Great Depression.

But every American can do his or her own part to enhance our nation and world for future generations. For example, we can improve our country's economic stability by making responsible choices with our money, a habit worth passing down to our kids. Previously we have had too much of boom and bust. Rather, we must be committed to reliable, steady economic growth, the kind that is leading us out of a recession and to a recovery. If we can stay on track, then future workers will have an opportunity to choose among a wide array of jobs, allowing them to find the one that best suits their unique talents.

But first we have a solemn responsibility to prepare our kids for promising professional careers. Education has always powered economic growth in this country, and it always will. In the classroom, we will discover future leaders, entrepreneurs, and scientists. Every child should have equal opportunity to realize those goals through education, which is why it's up to us to work with public school teachers and administrators to foster a learning environment driven by students' genuine intellectual curiosity, rather than one dictated by scores on standardized tests. We must take individual action to improve our children's future: Parents, especially those who organize through groups like the PTA and school advisory councils, can have an impact on the curriculum and policies of their children's school. Their activism can lead to educational improvements across the school district and beyond.

Of course, child safety is a prerequisite to child learning—and too often children have been victims of adult violence. Imagine the despair and anger felt by the parents whose children were victims of the shootings at Sandy Hook Elementary, especially knowing that the military-style rifle used in the assault was purchased legally. I know that improving mental health services is a key component of reducing the incidence of gun violence, but for the safety of schoolchildren and the general public, we must take commonsense measures to keep guns out of the hands of those who shouldn't have them. Requiring background checks before any purchase of a gun is one of those necessities, which has the overwhelming support of the American public. Banning high-capacity magazines and assault-style weapons, in addition to strengthening our National Instant Criminal Background Check System database to ensure that anyone who shouldn't be able to purchase a weapon is in the system, are just a few of the other essential reforms that common sense requires.

Children understand that actions speak louder than words, so if we strive to avoid bloodshed around the globe, then we will have more authority to discourage bloodshed within neighborhoods. I am proud of the relative peace we knew during the Clinton administration, and I'm glad that another Democratic administration led us out of Iraq and will do the same in Afghanistan. But in between, I regret the violence that my children have witnessed in the news during their young lives, from the 9/11 attacks to the daily reports of U.S. soldiers killed in conflict. It bothers me that they can't remember a time when Americans weren't occupying a foreign country. Eventually, I want those to be distant memories, of a time before this country understood the full scope of its power to defuse foreign conflict through diplomacy. There should be no doubt when it comes to America's willingness to use force, but I hope that my children and their generation inherit from us the sense that it is an object of last resort, available only to contain a severe threat to national security against us or our allies.

If we can bring up our kids in a safer, more secure world, with access to health care, clean air, clean water, and a job that provides for the comfort and stability of their families, then we have every reason to hope that this future society can work toward achieving higher ideals of equality and justice. In the last few decades, we have witnessed people bound by their identity rally for their collective good. Whether it's gay Americans making their case to be legally married to their partners or undocumented workers organizing to oppose exploitation or disabled Americans insisting on access to public places and protection from discrimination, they all deserve to be heard. I have faith that children who came of age during this dynamic time in civil rights will be more sensitive to their struggles. That empathy will lead to policy that fosters goodwill and diminishes bigotry. As a woman committed to trailblazing, I look forward to seeing the progress that women's rights groups will make in the century to come, in reproductive health and in seeking to balance the demands of being a mother with the rigors of a professional career. I know how hard that is for me, and I hope it's not nearly so hard for my two daughters.

This child-centric perspective has always guided me in my work as a legislator, first in the Florida Legislature and now in the U.S. House of Representatives. When I arrived in Washington in 2005, I was determined to find allies in this cause, members I could unite with and fight for legislation that would positively change the lives of the next generation.

That previous year's presidential campaign was the first one of which my five-year-old twins, Rebecca and Jake, were consciously aware. To them, John Kerry was just the biggest deal in the world. The junior senator from Massachusetts, Kerry had been nominated to head the Democratic ticket, and in their own way, my twins were thrilled by the prospect of him being President. Senator Kerry's unfortunate defeat did little to diminish their regard for him. As soon as my kids visited me in Washington, all I heard was, "Can we meet John Kerry? Can we meet John Kerry?"

I had campaigned with Senator Kerry, joining him in fly-arounds through Florida, introducing him to crowds of Democratic supporters. Still, as a newly elected freshman House member, I thought it might be difficult to get a stop-by on the calendar of a senator who remained one of the busiest on Capitol Hill. Knowing how much it meant for Rebecca and Jake to meet the man they had heard so much about and whom their mom had been working so hard to try to elect, I asked my scheduler to call over to his scheduler. (Members of Congress would be lost without the people who keep track of our days, hours, and in some cases, minutes.) We asked if he could spare a few moments so that Representative Wasserman Schultz from Florida could introduce her kids to Senator Kerry. The answer came back: "Of course."

As we boarded the train that snakes through a tunnel underneath the Capitol, I did my best to manage my star-struck twins' expectations. I knew Senator Kerry would greet them kindly, but I assumed it would be a quick encounter. We'd snap a picture and be out the door. I didn't want them to be disappointed because I knew how busy the senator must be.

When we were ushered into Senator Kerry's office, he greeted my kids with a broad, genuine smile, like an uncle reunited with his niece and nephew. After we'd taken some pictures and had a brief chat, I was careful to hasten our exit, so that the senator could get back to work. But to my astonishment, he wasn't quite done showing the kids around. He brought them into his personal office, bending down on one knee to talk to them. Then the threesome walked around his office, getting to know each other, while he showed them his amazing mementos chronicling his career as a soldier and then a senator. Thanks to Senator Kerry's generosity, my twins have a memory that will last a lifetime.

As I look back on it now, having accumulated nearly a decade of service in Congress, I can understand why Senator Kerry—now Secretary of State—made an extra effort: I believe he realized that this would be a formative experience for two very young Americans who were still developing a sense for what government was and how it related to them. By seeing Senator Kerry as a real person who acted sincerely, out of kindness, my twins would know that it was possible for such people to rise to places of power in this country. The hope that springs from this memory can endure, even as they grow up to encounter politicians whose positions infuriate them. They can call upon that experience when they might otherwise give in to cynical attitudes toward American politics. And they can spread this message among their peers as they all grow toward adulthood.

I think of that afternoon when I consider the vast amount of good that can be accomplished through small acts of unselfish regard for children. But you don't have to be a U.S. Senator to have a lasting impact on a child's perspective on government and the world. Children are in awe of adults. They hang on our every word and follow our every action, forming impressions that will become permanent features of their characters.

So it is up to us as adults, individually, to examine our own words and actions: Are we doing everything we can to lift up the next generation? Our nation and the world face challenges on many fronts. Given that our children will inherit the world we leave them, we cannot afford to take a narrow view of what constitutes our responsibility to them. It is not enough to simply go to work, help our kids with their homework, and go to the polls on Election Day. We must do that *and* we must demonstrate our willingness to take action that will change this country for the better.

If we look within our own histories, we can see that the challenges that face us today are no more daunting than those faced by previous generations. I believe that within every American family, there is an American story that speaks to this nation's bedrock principles, binding us not only to our ancestors but to other living Americans whose ancestors had experiences similar to the ones that forged our own family's identity. Like many others, I am living proof of one of its innate characteristics, the spirit of generosity. I am a native-born American, but still I feel a powerful connection to ancestors who came to this country out of hope for a better life. My paternal grandmother was born in Poland and came to America as a child, right around World War I. My maternal grandfather came from Austria, when he was about nineteen. Going back another generation, all of my great-grandparents were born either in Russia, Bulgaria, or Poland and they were all Jewish.

Eastern Europe was by no means a hospitable place to be Jewish in the first half of the twentieth century, with numerous forms of institutionalized prejudice. The persecution of Jews by other citizens was not just tolerated but even encouraged. In Russia, there were pogroms: outrageous bursts of mob violence against Jewish people, their homes, and their businesses, all sanctioned by a police force that neither investigated nor prosecuted these crimes. Like so many Eastern European Jewish families who came here, my family desperately needed a haven.

They found it. My Grandma Helen, from Poland, married my Grandpa Harry and they lived the American Dream, working hard and earning an upper-middle-class lifestyle. Grandpa Murray, the Austrian, became a pharmacist after graduating from Columbia College. That's where he met his future wife, my Grandma Lily, who also became a pharmacist, which is a pretty amazing accomplishment for a woman in the 1930s. As owners of their own drugstore, they also attained their dream. For millions like my Grandma Helen and my Grandpa Murray, America opened a world of freedom and economic opportunity. This nation didn't shun those who were weak and vulnerable. On the contrary, it took them into its embrace, giving them a chance to grow strong. This is America at its best. It is how this country renews itself.

Yet that same instinct of generosity is falling short with America's own children. They are absolutely not the high priority that they should be. To rectify this, let us recognize that every citizen shares the heritage of this ever-evolving nation, and we are united by our desire to make improvements to the quality of life of all citizens. Americans who are currently in the workforce were fortunate enough to have had their careers nurtured by a confident nation still ascending to the peak of its strength. We have long been the world leader in finance, innovation, diplomacy, and hundreds of specific fields, not the least of which is the propagation of democracy. I believe it's safe to say that everyone, even the most self-concerned, wants the United States to be even more potent and prosperous in the future than it is now. If so, then we must be generous and attentive to children. Yet there are so many people in public office who talk about the future without talking—or even *thinking*, it seems—about children. This should concern all of us.

In the chapters to come, I will talk in more detail about the obstacles to progress within major national policy areas, looking toward history for clues about how to overcome them, while suggesting direct actions that we can take to enhance the quality of life in modern America. Some actions will require our personal efforts and others will necessitate resources from the government and the private sector. Both are vital to securing the next generation.

This book is not written for political insiders who know the issues backward and forward and think they have all the answers. It is written to give everyday Americans the information, tools, and insight to ensure that decisions we make today are made with an eye toward our children's future. Hopefully, it is a wake-up call, a reminder that we must resist the lure of cynicism, knowing that we can achieve our goals only if we make a commitment in this moment to keep focused, to not be discouraged by occasional setbacks. We can and should accomplish it with grace and civility, attracting allies to our cause by treating even our fiercest opponents with respect. If we should waiver from this purpose, then the sight of children ought to be a source of inspiration. Let all our future endeavors be worthy of them, proof of the depth of love we have for them and the conviction we have for their health, happiness, and prosperity.

ONE

Strengthening the Economy
(So Our Children Don't Have To)

The New Year's Eve that preceded 2013 was certainly memorable, but not in a good way. My staff and I spent the holiday in Washington, D.C., to deal with the dreaded "fiscal cliff."

That grim phrase had been on everyone's lips for the previous several months. Of course, it referred to the December 31 deadline for Congress and the President to reach an agreement on the budget to avoid sequestration, a set of across-the-board spending cuts that would be automatically triggered at the same time that tax breaks expired. Economists warned that the failure to reach a deal would disrupt the markets, leading to job losses and quite possibly another massive recession.

On the evening of that deadline, I was in the rotunda of the National Archives Building where Democratic Leader Nancy Pelosi and nineteen other members of Congress were attending the 150th anniversary of the Emancipation Proclamation, the document that marked the beginning of the end of slavery in the United States. The irony was inescapable: We celebrated a historic act of courageous leadership as we faced the prospect of witnessing a historic failure of leadership that very same night.

If so, that failure would belong to House Speaker John Boehner

(R-OH), whose usual policy was to only allow bills to reach the floor if they were going to get votes from the majority of his Republican members, also known as the "Hastert Rule," after the previous speaker who adopted the practice. With one eye on the Emancipation Proclamation and the other on our mobile phones, we learned just before ten o'clock that Senate Republicans had reached a deal with the White House that would increase tax revenues from the wealthiest Americans and postpone the sequester cuts for two months. As details of that deal emerged, scores of House Republicans made it known that they would reject it. Members of the party's Tea Party Caucus even left Capitol Hill in hopes of blocking a House vote through their absence. In effect, they had decided to put their personal ideology above the national economy.

Ultimately, Speaker Boehner realized that the only way to avoid triggering sequestration was to abandon his party's majority. He recruited eighty-five Republicans to join him, and along with myself and other House Democrats, we finally passed the legislation, which was then signed by the President. We avoided going over the fiscal cliff, barely.

This close encounter begged the question: Had we learned so little from the last recession that we were ready to risk a new one? We teach our children to learn from their mistakes, yet the very leaders elected to represent us had not learned from their own. The mistake was not the decision to bail out the banks, or the American Recovery and Reinvestment Act, as Tea Party Republicans believed. Rather, the mistake was all the wild, unpaid-for spending that came before. And it was the attitude that we'll worry about the future when it arrives. In this instance, even though we avoided going over the fiscal cliff, we did so by pushing back the sequester by two months. Another can kicked a little farther down the road.

We can no longer afford to put off the tough, practical decisions that must be made to stabilize the economy. They will only grow in magnitude, and if we fail in this regard, those decisions will be thrust upon our children. That is unacceptable. Our children deserve to grow up in a national economy that offers them a fulfilling career, with income sufficient to raise a family of their own and then to retire in comfort. I share conservative Republicans' concern about the national debt, but the debt we owe to the next generation is the greatest, most demanding one of all.

The first order of business is to make sure that we have learned from the financial follies of recent years. Like all political events, the Great Recession's origins are open to interpretation. So let's stick with the facts. We know that in the fall of 2008, the national economy shrunk by nearly 5 percent. It was by far the biggest financial collapse since the Great Depression. Prior to this crisis, banks had been approving mortgages for homes to buyers that just a few years before would have been declined, based on the risk that those buyers would default on their payments. Rather than preach financial prudence, lenders often encouraged borrowers to take out a larger loan than they could afford, or that they needed.

At the other end of the spectrum, Wall Street investment firms bundled these mortgages into investable products—mortgage-backed securities—and sold them to investors, who often had little idea of what it was that they were actually investing in. Meanwhile, rating agencies like Standard & Poor's, Moody's, and Fitch did not adjust their ratings to reflect the risk these investment firms were taking. This signaled to others in the market that mortgage-backed securities were safe investments. The housing industry had been booming for years, but history shows that this market always goes through cycles. The boom was unsustainable.

While this disaster was brewing in the private sector, the public sector was being battered by the economic recklessness of President George W. Bush's administration. The spending spree started with the post-9/11 invasion of Afghanistan. There's no question that pursuing Al Qaeda was the right policy; the tougher question was how to pay for it. Past wars had been financed either through the issuance of war bonds or through increased taxes. President Bush didn't propose any method at all.

Nor did President Bush have a method for dealing with the expenses of another war, in Iraq. This one was based on faulty, trumped-up intelligence and it came with no exit strategy. Indeed, as then Defense Secretary Donald Rumsfeld said at an October 2003 press conference,

"The bulk of the funds for Iraq's reconstruction will come from Iraqis—from oil revenues, recovered assets, international trade, direct foreign investment, as well as some contributions we've already received and hope to receive from the international community."

Like most of Rumsfeld's predictions, that didn't quite happen. Both foreign conflicts added greatly to the national deficit. The Iraq War alone cost about $800 billion. If you factor in long-term benefits to be paid out to U.S. troops either killed or wounded in battle, the final tab for the Iraq War is projected to be roughly $1 trillion, a bill that belongs to U.S. taxpayers.

As if it wasn't enough to put two wars on what amounted to a credit card, President Bush insisted on sweeping tax cuts in 2001 and 2003. Those cuts were skewed toward the wealthiest Americans, dramatically reducing the amount of revenue the government had for improving our children's education. It would make it harder to modernize our national health-care system. We would be unable to make investments in domestic infrastructure and innovation. At the same time, we racked up record budget deficits.

To add one final insult to these injuries, President Bush made one more massive purchase: In 2003, he extended Medicare coverage for prescription drugs. It was an important and worthwhile investment; but it was the responsibility of the President and the Republicans in Congress to find a method to pay for Medicare's drug coverage, known as Part D. Again, they failed to do so. It was little more than a cynical maneuver to win votes among seniors before the 2004 election. And it blew another gaping hole in our deficit, plunging the country further into debt. The record budget surplus that the Bush administration inherited from President Clinton was a distant memory.

Having been sworn in to Congress in 2005, I wasn't there for those far-reaching Bush spending decisions. But the overwhelming majority of my Democratic colleagues opposed President Bush's out-of-control spending spree with criticism that now seems prophetic. In 2003, then Senate Majority Leader Tom Daschle called for a "return to fiscal responsibility" and warned about the dangers of running deficits instead of paying down the debt.

✦ ✦ ✦

For all these reasons, the federal government was in no condition to "bail out" anyone in the fall of 2008. But there was no other solution. Allowing those banks and investment firms to fail would have frozen the credit markets, making it virtually impossible for families to get loans for cars and homes. In fact, in October of 2008, I recall sitting in a meeting in which House Democratic Leader Pelosi recounted her conversation with then Treasury Secretary Henry Paulson. He reportedly told her that we had to pass a bank bailout bill "immediately" and the situation was very dire.

Without the government's intervention, interest rates would have shot up on everything from construction bonds to credit cards. Many businesses would have been unable to even make payroll. Paulson himself later told CBS News that without congressional action to stop the slide, unemployment would hit 25 percent, putting the crisis on the scale of the Great Depression. These were the Main Street consequences of Wall Street financial institutions being overwhelmed by "toxic assets"—that is, investments that had lost value they would never recover. This classification included an exotic array of formerly obscure financial products like mortgage-backed securities, collateralized debt obligations, and credit default swaps.

In response to this catastrophe, the Bush administration sent Congress a three-page bill that proposed to bail out the banks, but the bill came with no consumer protections and no accountability for the banks whatsoever. Given the role that lack of regulation played in bringing about the crisis in the first place, this was clearly unacceptable, even as a short-term solution. Through negotiations between Speaker Pelosi and Secretary Paulson, the Democratic Caucus had committed to providing the voting majority needed to pass the bill; still, we insisted that the legislation contain measures for holding the failing banks accountable, along with language that required taxpayers' money to be paid back, with interest.

I vividly remember the House debate on September 29, 2008. As members vowed to vote against the Emergency Economic Stabilization Act, a $700 billion purchase of financial firms' "toxic assets," the Dow

Jones tumbled. Minority Leader John Boehner had fallen short of delivering the 100 Republican votes he had committed to, and as a result the measure was defeated. The Dow Jones lost nearly eight hundred points—the largest one-day drop in U.S. history. Later that week, we brought forward another piece of legislation that contained the same basic provisions as the EESA (Emergency Economic Stabilization Act), along with a number of "sweeteners" designed to win over reluctant members of the House to vote for the bill. It would become known as TARP—the Troubled Asset Relief Program, and the market regained much of what it lost, but for how long? No one knew. The world's most eminent economists each seemed to have a different answer.

It was one of the most frightening and disturbing moments I can remember in my lifetime. I had never seen such an immediate connection between the votes we took in Congress and events in the real world.

The bailouts were not popular among voters, of course, and I definitely had my own misgivings about the legislation we approved that day. The easy thing to do would have been to vote against TARP, then go home to the cheers of those constituents who wanted to see the banks punished.

But it was also one of those moments that reminded me about the responsibility that comes with being elected to public office. Sometimes, the right decision is not the popular one. I certainly remember hearing about it later in town hall meetings. By the same token, I'm fortunate: So many of my constituents who may oppose a piece of legislation like the bailout still trust that I have done my due diligence, then made an informed decision for what's best for the district and the nation. They want someone who will make that decision and then meet with them to explain all the considerations that went into a vote.

I understand why Tea Party protesters would be enraged by government bailouts and stimulus spending, just as I appreciate the "99 percent" activists' fury over the financial elite's disproportionate control of the nation's wealth. Make no mistake, the executives at Fannie Mae, Freddie Mac, and AIG were not sympathetic "victims" of misfortune—they were architects of their own disaster. Still, there were millions of Americans whose financial well-being was, unbeknown to them, intertwined with these enormous institutions. These were the people who would truly suffer, and my vote for TARP was cast with them in mind.

Legislators on both sides of the aisle recognized this, which is why TARP even garnered a vote from a Tea Party darling like Rep. Paul Ryan. (Of course, that vote didn't stop him from railing against the program in the years to follow.)

By late 2008, the automobile industry was also on the brink of ruin. For years American automakers had faced increased competition from foreign companies, who had long succeeded in making their cars cheaper than American manufacturers, and had become increasingly competitive in matching the quality and innovation, not to mention fuel efficiency. This placed considerable strain on American auto manufacturers whose workforce and infrastructure still reflected the bygone days when they made the vast majority of the cars sold in the United States.

Among the Big Three automakers, Ford fared best, largely because the company had turned to the private market in 2007 for $23.5 billion in finance restructuring. When the financial crisis struck in 2008, it collapsed the capital lending markets, meaning that when GM and Chrysler needed finance restructuring packages of their own, they could not get a loan on the private market. So at the same time as they were hit with a massive drop in revenue from domestic car sales, they didn't have the capital needed to sustain operations.

If those companies were to survive, the government would have to bail them out—except the notion of rescuing car makers was even less popular among Americans than the bailout given to Wall Street executives. Understandably, taxpayers were in no mood to reward auto CEOs who had failed to adapt their companies to a changing marketplace and who seemed woefully out of touch, flying to congressional hearings in their corporate jets.

As President Obama took office, he faced the terrible prospect of watching two of the largest, oldest manufacturers in the country go out of business, an outcome that would cost more than a million Americans their jobs, harming the American economy both psychologically and operationally.

Again, the unpopular decision proved the correct one. Under the terms of their loans, GM and Chrysler were forced to agree to a fundamental restructuring that would make them more competitive. It worked. They were able to pay back the loans just two years later, in 2010, and were soon turning profits again. Not only did that intervention save over a million jobs, but the revived auto industry has added roughly a quarter million new jobs in the last few years. Considering all the Republicans—including Michigan native Mitt Romney—who wanted to let the automakers fail, this episode was a vivid demonstration of the difference in vision between the two major parties.

The next urgent piece of legislation, of course, was the American Recovery and Reinvestment Act of 2009—the federal "stimulus bill" that invested capital to jump-start the national economy. The Act would legislate a combination of tax cuts and targeted spending on historically neglected issues like infrastructure, alternative energy, and health information technology. There was no doubt the economy needed a kick start. The question was how much of an infusion was necessary.

It was the subject of ferocious debate. The Tea Party had organized to oppose this policy on the grounds that it would lead to more debt and higher taxes, while rank-and-file Republicans stoked the usual fear over big government. These critics overlooked the fact that the legislation included generous tax cuts amounting to approximately 36 percent of the cost of the legislation. Those tax cuts were to be enjoyed by 98 percent of Americans. The stimulus was both a badly needed tourniquet to stop the hemorrhaging of jobs from our economy and an injection of capital into the economy via tax cuts.

Based on what was known then about the scale of the financial crisis, the Obama administration's Council of Economic Advisers concluded the stimulus should amount to roughly $2 trillion. But those advisers knew that it would be difficult to design a foolproof method for recovering the investment. They also realized that such an outlay had the potential to spook the financial markets and trigger a political meltdown on Capitol Hill by

Republican legislators. Ultimately, Obama's financial team proposed an $850 billion stimulus, and in order to earn votes from Senate Republicans, that amount was whittled down to $787 billion, passing by the slimmest of margins against GOP resistance.

I recall thinking that the Republicans' opposition to this spending smacked of hypocrisy, because so many of those same Republicans had blown through the record budget surplus that had been handed to President George W. Bush by President Bill Clinton. Many of the Republican opponents of the Recovery Act had voted for the 2001 and 2003 Bush tax cuts, the wars in Iraq and Afghanistan, and the Medicare Part D plan, all unpaid for. Led by Representative Ryan, Republicans favored a crash diet of spending cuts along with the always fashionable tax cuts skewed toward the wealthiest Americans.

Guess what? The stimulus should have been larger—much, much larger. The Obama administration was reacting to the worst-case scenario as portrayed by the Bureau of Economic Analysis, a nonpartisan agency within the Commerce Department, which projected the economy was shrinking at an annual rate of 3.8 percent in the last quarter of the 2008 fiscal year. That worst-case scenario was wrong. In actuality, the economy that quarter was shrinking at an annual rate of 8.9 percent.

Nevertheless, it was the biggest stimulus that Democrats could pass through Congress in the face of opposition from Republicans who favored Ryan's austerity measures—to slash programs for seniors, children, the poor, and the middle class. Even if the independent analysts had produced a more accurate projection of economic shrinkage, I seriously doubt that congressional Republicans would have agreed to a larger stimulus than was passed.

In 2011 and 2012, the House Budget Committee, of which I was a member at the time, held multiple hearings about the state of the economy, providing me the opportunity to ask leading authorities on fiscal policy whether TARP, the Recovery Act, and the auto bailout helped, or whether we should focus on a cuts-only approach. In particular, I recall putting these questions to then chairman of the Federal Reserve, Ben Bernanke. He told me the same thing that I heard from then Treasury Secretary

Timothy Geithner and the director of the nonpartisan Congressional Budget Office (CBO), Douglas Elmendorf: The stimulus most definitely did help the economy and Ryan's plan would harm the economy, disrupting the recovery.

So there is no credence to the Republican refrain that "the stimulus didn't work." When Fox News Channel personalities brought me on the air to defend the stimulus, they took this refrain as gospel, despite all the evidence to the contrary. The Bureau of Economic Analysis statistics show that America's GDP had been declining dramatically over the previous four quarters and that almost immediately after the signing of the Recovery Act the national economy stopped contracting, then began to grow again by the middle of 2009. It always takes a little time for economic growth to produce higher employment numbers, but the same trend occurred there: The rate of job losses slowed shortly after the stimulus, continuing on that path until about a year after the stimulus, when the United States finally showed net job growth.

The stimulus has not permanently fixed the economy—and no Democrat, including the President, ever said it would. But it has undoubtedly succeeded in averting a far more spectacular economic meltdown. If the stimulus hasn't been as effective as we might have hoped, the primary reason is that Republicans insisted on it being smaller than it should have been and because the increase in federal spending has been neutralized by decreases in spending at the state level, where conservative principles are being applied.

The Great Recession was triggered by a reckless tax policy and a "fox guarding the henhouse" approach to regulation by a Republican President who was aided by Republican legislators. Their policies were both the cause of the problem and the obstacle to the solution.

For better or worse, our society is more aware today of the importance of economic policy and financial literacy. I hope that this results in more lasting, commonsense reforms. My husband, Steve, is a commercial banker, and he's always told me that his community bank prefers to work out a

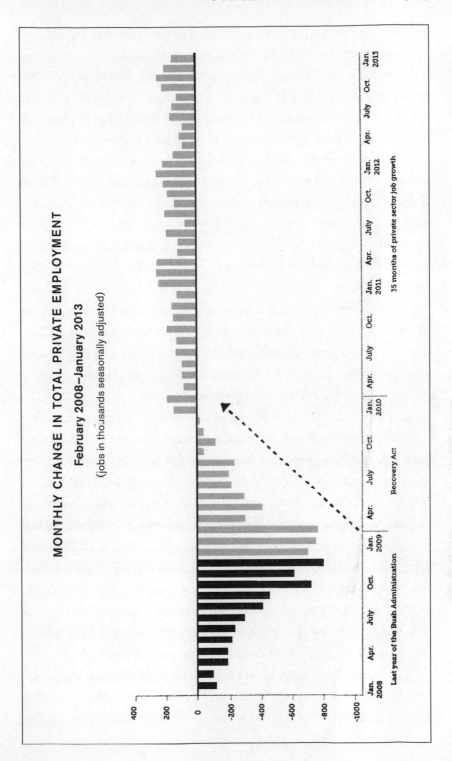

MONTHLY CHANGE IN TOTAL PRIVATE EMPLOYMENT
February 2008–January 2013
(jobs in thousands seasonally adjusted)

payment plan with a customer as opposed to going through the arduous foreclosure process. The difference is that Steve works at a community bank, which is small enough that a client can speak directly to his or her lender, then negotiate terms that make it possible for the loan to be worked out and brought current under mutually agreed upon terms. With a bank so close to its clients, common sense can be applied to every transaction.

The problem at the nation's biggest banks was not only that they were too big to fail; they were too big to bother talking to their clients. Within these massive financial institutions, the entity you received the loan from may not own it anymore, because those mortgages were resold so many times. My congressional office has received numerous calls from people trying to reach someone at their bank to talk about the status of their loan. My district staff does its best to help my constituents get their banks on the phone, but there are so many layers of bureaucracy, no one at the banks even seems to know where to start, and some have deliberately attempted to avoid resolving mortgagees' problems. It's infuriating that these banks received TARP money, which spared them from going under, and yet they still refuse to work with people.

The same can be said of efforts to reform the too-big-to-fail culture on Wall Street. Much like the stimulus package, the Dodd-Frank Act is a flawed piece of legislation that doesn't quite go as far as it needs to in response to the economic crisis—the same banks are still too big to fail— but it's the most our party could get in a Congress where too many Republicans refuse to acknowledge the dangers of a deregulated market. It protects consumers from predatory lenders and ensures that bankers can't make the same reckless investments. It's not perfect, but it's progress; and yet the majority of Republicans campaigning in 2012 vowed to repeal it and return to the days of Wall Street self-regulation that got us into this mess in the first place. Rather than repeal it, the two parties should be working together to refine and improve Dodd-Frank.

The system has clearly run amok, and it goes beyond just the banks. In my first year in Congress, I remember getting a tour of the New York Stock Exchange (NYSE) with the rest of the freshman class serving on the House Financial Services Committee. We had a meeting in the boardroom. The principals of the NYSE were proud to tell us that their system was essentially self-regulating, and that struck me as risky for consumers and for the stability of the financial system. Clearly, the Securities and Exchange Commission failed to exercise its regulatory authority as well, and one of the lessons of the recession was to empower that agency, which was one aspect of the Dodd-Frank Act of 2010.

Another aspect of the legislation was the creation of the Consumer Financial Protection Bureau (CFPB), which is tasked with looking out for Americans who venture into markets for consumer financial products and services. That activity may take the form of a mortgage application or a credit card contract, among others. Given the way financial services firms violated the trust of American consumers in the years leading up to the crisis, consumers were absolutely entitled to more security. Prior to Dodd-Frank, there was no federal agency that specifically looked out for the consumers' interests in the financial sector.

Yet that same financial services industry whose greed triggered the meltdown had the nerve to fight these commonsense reforms, and the GOP was there to do their bidding. A group of forty-four Senate Republicans vowed to oppose nominations at financial regulatory agencies—unless those agencies agreed to changes in structure that would make them completely powerless in regulating the financial industry. These same senators blocked President Obama's initial selection to head the CFPB, the woman who developed the concept, Elizabeth Warren. Ultimately, she set up the agency without being nominated and President Obama nominated Ohio Attorney General Richard Cordray. The Republicans in the Senate stalled his nomination for months and the President eventually used a recess appointment to install him. After his reelection, President Obama renominated Richard Cordray to head the CFPB, setting the stage for another potential clash with Senate Republicans. It is frustrating to have to deal with these obstructions, but it shouldn't discourage us from our objective: to put America's economy back on the right course.

+ + +

We must take the same commonsense approach to reforming our nation's tax code. It must ensure that everyone pays their fair share in order
to reduce our deficit and invest in future economic growth. Unfortunately,
Washington has become so paralyzed that in the past few years, there
has been little room for even commonsense reforms. Republicans have
become absolutely enraged about the raising of the debt ceiling. For all
the political strife in Capitol Hill's history, a party had never refused to
raise the debt ceiling as a negotiating tactic, because the consequences of
refusing were so unthinkable: America would default on its bills and ruin
its credit. Our entire economy relies upon the premise that the United
States stands behind the value of its currency and will repay any debts
incurred. If the United States suddenly stopped paying its bills, no one
would want to loan us money, the value of the dollar could collapse, and
foreign investors would be running for the exits. There would be economic chaos not only in this country but worldwide. In other words, it
would be crazy to do this to ourselves.

The first sign of trouble came in the summer of 2011 as President Obama
sought a deal to raise the debt ceiling. Republicans in Congress refused to
grant their support unless the President met their demands: draconian budget cuts aimed squarely at programs that benefit the middle class, seniors,
and the poor. In effect, they were playing a high-stakes game of chicken with
the economy.

President Obama and congressional Democrats wanted a more balanced approach to deficit reduction, which would include both spending
cuts and raising revenue by eliminating tax breaks for individuals whose
income placed them among the top 1–2 percent of U.S. households. Ultimately, in August 2011, with the economy hanging in the balance, Republicans got their "cuts-only" deal.

I have spent my career opposing cuts like those that came with that
legislation. I hated the deal, but I voted for it, because unlike Republicans I wasn't willing to let America default on its bills. I also knew that
we couldn't engage in a "my way or the highway" approach to governing

that the Republicans, radicalized by their Tea Party members, had adopted. It was my responsibility to go back home to Florida to explain the debt ceiling crisis and my vote to my constituents.

Of course, one of the reasons we have a debt problem in the first place is that deficit reduction and tax cuts are often at odds. A good example of this can be seen in the demise of the Budget Enforcement Act. Signed into law by President George H. W. Bush in 1990, it was a way to stop the growth of the colossal deficit created under President Ronald Reagan. This legislation introduced the practice of "pay-as-you-go," also referred to as PAYGO, which made it necessary for Congress to increase taxes or make spending cuts if it wanted to fund a new program. The idea is, you pay as you go, just like in a household budget where you try not to spend more than you take in. But when that rule expired in 2002, it was Democrats who sought to renew it completely. Republicans, on the other hand, did not—unless Democrats agreed to exclude the need to pay for tax cuts. Of course, this would take the teeth out of the Act, because tax cuts reduce the government's revenue, meaning they must either be paid for by severe cuts to government services or by running up enormous debt. Democrats insisted that any tax cuts would have to be paid for, and in return Republicans kicked PAYGO to the curb, because it stood in the way of passing tax cuts for the wealthiest 2 percent of Americans, not to mention that it would have forced Republicans to figure out how to pay for the war President George W. Bush was looking to wage in Iraq.

So it was surreal to watch the 2012 Republican National Convention and hear a procession of speakers blaming the sluggish economy on the so-called liberal spending of President Barack Obama. Some may have even believed he was at fault. But the truth is that every major policy contributing to the growth of public debt since 2001 was either directly initiated by President Bush (such as the tax cuts and the Iraq War) or initiated in desperate response to a financial collapse that began during his administration.

I'm sure most Republicans would agree that the annual rate of growth in federal spending is an excellent way of judging a President's commitment to conservative principles. If so, they may be surprised to know that

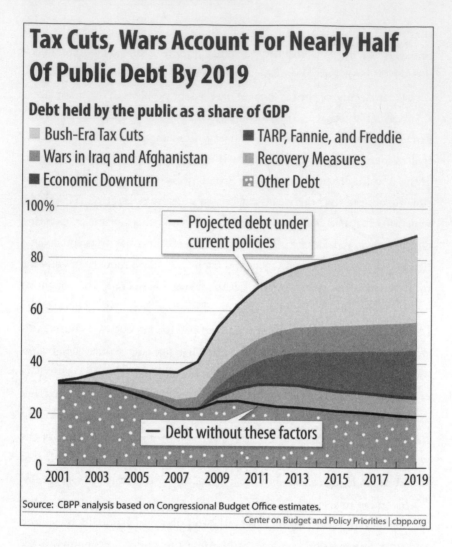

Tax Cuts, Wars Account For Nearly Half Of Public Debt By 2019

Debt held by the public as a share of GDP

- Bush-Era Tax Cuts
- Wars in Iraq and Afghanistan
- Economic Downturn
- TARP, Fannie, and Freddie
- Recovery Measures
- Other Debt

— Projected debt under current policies

— Debt without these factors

Source: CBPP analysis based on Congressional Budget Office estimates.

Center on Budget and Policy Priorities | cbpp.org

the most conservative President over the last thirty years is the much-maligned Barack Obama. The most "liberal" with spending was Ronald Reagan. President Reagan let government spending grow by nearly 9 percent each year during his first term, while in Obama's first term, spending has risen just 1.4 percent. That includes the stimulus package. The next most "conservative" President? Bill Clinton, who never let government spending grow by more than 4 percent in any of the eight years he was in the White House.

So either our Democratic presidents are closeted fiscal conservatives, or

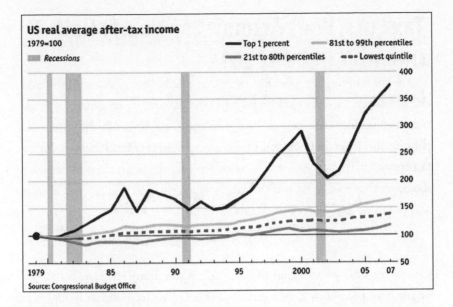

US real average after-tax income
1979=100
Recessions
Top 1 percent   81st to 99th percentiles
21st to 80th percentiles   Lowest quintile
Source: Congressional Budget Office

the Republican presidents are really, really bad at staying true to their sup-posed conservative principles. Whatever the case, I would ask the truly conservative voters in America, with legitimate concerns about our nation's debt problems, to consider whether the Republican Party has proved itself trustworthy.

In addition, it is time for registered Republicans and fiscally conserva-tive independents to demand that the GOP make a more meaningful commitment to serving voters in every income bracket, as opposed to the recent trend to serve the narrow interests of the nation's wealthy.

According to the Congressional Budget Office (CBO), income inequal-ity in America has stayed relatively constant over the last twenty years for 99 percent of the population. By contrast, the income of the top 1 percent has grown dramatically—especially since 2001. Adjusting for inflation, the after-tax income of middle Americans grew by a modest 40 percent be-tween 1979 and 2007, according to a CBO analysis. It increased by 65 per-cent for upper middle-class Americans. But for the richest one percent, income skyrocketed 275 percent over that twenty-eight-year span. And as the chart above makes clear, those inequalities became even more pro-nounced after 2001, when Bush rolled out his first round of tax cuts for the wealthy. This single truth blows a gaping hole in "trickle-down economics," the idea that the benefits of tax cuts for the wealthy would trickle down to the middle class.

I'm not vilifying the wealthy—there are plenty like Warren Buffett and Bill Gates who are activists for income fairness and make generous donations to humanitarian causes. Nor do I mean to diminish the success of those in the 1 percent. In fact, I represent a congressional district with a fair amount of "1 percenters." Rather, I'm asking the wealthy to consider the harm that will be done if the gap between the rich and the rest of us is allowed to widen.

One of the only good things to come out of the financial crisis is that we finally have the political momentum it takes to address the widening gap. The refrain of "We are the 99 percent" is really an outgrowth of frustrations by the middle class. To me that expression is symbolized by working families, and they're right to complain about policies that appeal to that powerful, privileged 1 percent.

During his reelection campaign, President Obama frequently said that America prospers when everyone does his or her fair share, plays by the same rules, and has the same shot at success. For this to be the case, the wealthiest Americans should not pay a smaller share of their income in taxes than middle-class families pay. Given the importance of the economy in the 2012 campaign, the voters' decision to reelect Barack Obama gave the President a fresh mandate to put these principles of income fairness into effect. It should have come as no surprise, then, when he insisted that a balanced deficit reduction package include an increase in taxes on the wealthiest 1 percent of American taxpayers.

Yet Republicans seemed indignant that the President was unwilling to yield to their demands of a cuts-only approach to deficit reduction. By refusing to compromise, they were holding the American economy hostage, preferring to go through with the massive, across-the-board cuts that came from sequestration rather than raise taxes on the wealthy. It took the assistance of Vice President Joe Biden before Republicans finally reached a compromise with the President, and in January 2013 tax cuts were allowed to expire on Americans making more than $450,000 a year.

While this was indeed a step in the right direction, it should be seen as only the beginning of long-overdue tax reform. It is time to close tax loopholes, ensure that everyone pays their fair share, and begin to restore a measure of equality of opportunity to attain a decent standard of living in this nation, so that we can all enjoy success. But House Republicans' refusal to close those loopholes led to even more clashes with the White House, culminating in the $85 billion in sequester cuts that were triggered on March 1, after the two sides failed to reach a deal.

One President and one party in Congress are not enough to overcome the lockstep obstruction of today's GOP. Congressional Republicans and presidential candidates are happy to tell voters what they want to hear, how cutting taxes and cutting spending while scaling back government regulations is a panacea; but they refuse to acknowledge the necessity of a balanced approach to government that allows us to continue our economic vitality by investing in education, innovation, and infrastructure.

The time has come for registered Republicans to demand that their leaders be responsible stewards of the national economy. It's a party that today is focused more on getting elected than on the responsibilities of governing. America is strongest when both parties are engaged in a good faith effort to create jobs for all Americans.

I think of my legislative occupation as an extension of my familial job, being a mother to my three young children. And I can't imagine jeopardizing their economic future for a short-term political reward. To do what's right, you have to be willing to risk losing. We must move beyond pure party loyalty and be willing to come together, spend some of our precious political capital, and take risks that can benefit the next generation.

After all, the courage to risk failure in pursuit of success has been a defining feature of the American character since the Declaration of Independence. We must never lose that force of will. At this crucial moment in our nation's history, the middle class needs strength. These hardworking folks have been battered by more than a decade of war. They have suffered under the weight of tax policies tilted in favor of the rich.

And they have been demoralized by the looming presence of an enormous national debt. These American families deserve a path forward and the peace of mind that comes with knowing that their children will be allowed to compete on a level playing field, with a fair shot at achieving lifelong financial security.

TWO

Safety Nets, Built to Last

When I think about federal programs like Social Security, it brings to mind people like Paul Snow. Paul is seventy-six years old, and he moved to South Florida in 1991, having spent most of his life in New England, where he was a restaurant owner. Paul was determined to use his retirement to work toward an admirable ideal: feeding the poor. A lifelong Methodist, Paul forged an alliance with the Haitian United Methodist Church, which gave him the use of a storage space in Hallandale Beach, in my congressional district in southeast Broward County. That's where Paul founded a food pantry, using a combination of grants and donations. In the first week, he handed out groceries to eleven struggling families. In 2013, the pantry was in its twenty-third year of operation. The previous year, Paul and his seventeen volunteers had handed out some thirteen thousand packages of canned goods, produce, and dry food.

Over that time, Paul has seen former volunteers return to the pantry as beneficiaries, often because their retirement savings had run out. They told him that the expense of buying medication made it impossible to afford food.

On those occasions when the private donations and public grants weren't enough to sustain the pantry, Paul dipped into his own savings—he estimates that he spent roughly $65,000 of his own money, exhausting his 401(k). If it weren't for Social Security, Paul would be on the streets. And the poor people he serves would be that much hungrier and more desperate.

Social Security is a vital program for the Paul Snows of the world, as it is for the rest of the nation's elderly and disabled. Its importance transcends politics, serving a purpose that is fundamental to any definition of human morality: that one should treat others as he or she would like to be treated. Around the world and through the centuries, cultures with distinct customs and languages have all independently arrived at this same principle. The concept is so universal that we refer to it, simply, as the Golden Rule. It is a code of social responsibility that leads us to look out for our neighbors. It pervades the texts of every organized religion and lies at the heart of every altruistic cause. This social compact is the foundation of the safety-net programs—not just Social Security, but also Medicare and Medicaid.

We did not come by these programs easily. They are the product of lessons learned through arduous periods in U.S. history, filled with poverty and illness. And they are reminders of how sincerely past generations of Americans cared for one another.

The Social Security Act, signed in 1935 at the behest of President Franklin D. Roosevelt, was our nation's response to how poorly equipped the nation's elderly were to deal with the ravages of the Great Depression. That year, more than 65 percent of seniors were living in poverty. These were Americans who toiled in factories and mines, building railroads and growing crops, but who in old age had no choice but to beg in the street. They had earned the right to retire with a modicum of comfort, which is why a younger generation was willing to accept a payroll tax that funded a public pension fund, which paid benefits to those eligible seniors.

Thirty years later, President Lyndon Johnson's "Great Society" brought us Medicare and Medicaid, a bold response to a fearsome crisis: the cost of medical care had been rising much too fast for those who were too old to work, as well as for low-income families. Again, these programs would mean that working Americans pay slightly more in taxes, but it was a modest sacrifice compared to the payoff: security not just for their own parents and grandparents but for all the less fortunate members of society.

Social Security, Medicare, and Medicaid may not always work perfectly, as no human endeavor ever does, but there is no disputing that these programs bring our communities closer together. Retired Americans feel gratitude to those who work, as do those who are poor or disabled. If it weren't for these programs, there would be more people on the street forced to take desperate measures to survive. The young who couldn't afford to place their frail parents in a nursing home would have to choose between going to work and caring for those parents.

So when politicians talk about privatizing these safety-net programs, the question is whether our generation wants to be the one that severs a tradition for empathy established by previous generations of Americans. Are we still a nation that will ensure those who worked their whole lives will be treated with dignity in their remaining years? Or are we concerned entirely with our own self-interest?

To really drive home a valuable lesson to our children about the merit of helping one another, we must demonstrate it with actions. My children are growing up watching me fight hard to protect these safety-net programs that prevent our elderly from falling through holes that some politicians want to cut in them. We must stay true to the commitment we made to aging members of our community and to others who depend on us.

If the Great Depression compelled our nation to create Social Security, then the more recent Great Recession has reminded us why it is an essential program. With all the shocks the national economy has endured, it is a comfort to know that our seniors have at least one steady source of income. The Center on Budget and Policy Priorities found that in 2010 during the height of the recession, over twenty million Americans would have fallen below the federal poverty level if not for Social Security payments. On average, that income is two-thirds of the total income for recipients over sixty-five. For one-third, Social Security is at least 90 percent of their total income.

Some argue that Social Security is broken, that it should be scrapped and privatized. There is no doubt that demographic changes in our nation present a challenge for the program. For example, retirement of the Baby Boomer generation, seventy-six million strong, has been and will continue to be a stress on Social Security. Demographic projections show that there will be more Americans entering the program as beneficiaries than those paying into it as workers, and life expectancy has grown over the years. But Social Security was designed to weather these challenges. According to administrators, the fund has accrued a surplus over each of the past twenty-five years. It now has in excess of $2.6 trillion in reserve. The program is equipped to pay full benefits to eligible Americans through at least 2036. Advances in technology are likely to make workers even more productive in the next fifty years, which could increase the nation's economic output, thereby increasing the flow of contributions, just as we've seen in the previous fifty years. Many in the Republican Party have long had an ideological objection to Social Security, regarding it as a public handout, or welfare. It is neither of those things. It is a social compact guaranteeing that if you contribute to society in your life, then society will be there for you when you need it. As President Obama said during his January 2013 Inaugural Address,

> We do not believe that in this country freedom is reserved for the lucky or happiness for the few. We recognize that no matter how responsibly we live our lives, any one of us at any time may face a job loss, or a sudden illness, or a home swept away in a terrible storm. The commitments we make to each other through Medicare and Medicaid and Social Security, these things do not sap our initiative, they strengthen us. They do not make us a nation of takers; they free us to take the risks that make this country great.

Shoring up Social Security, Medicare, and Medicaid is a political problem that can be ironed out if the two parties work together, as opposed to huddling in their respective war rooms to draw out battle plans. The entitlements issue has been particularly explosive over the last several years, and I have no doubt that voters are eager to see their representatives in Washington work more collaboratively.

I recall exactly when the first shot of the modern era was fired across the bow. Shortly after I was sworn in to the House in Washington in early 2005, I attended a lunch hosted by President Bush at the White House for the freshman class. The new members were seated at small, round tables. At each table there was a top-level staff member from the administration. I was seated at the President's table with my Republican colleague from Florida, Connie Mack. The conversation turned from small talk to issues, and I remember being shocked when the President told our table that he intended to take on the issue of privatizing Social Security. He said, "I earned some political capital in this election and I intend to spend it."

I remember thinking to myself that this wasn't a very prominent part of Bush's reelection campaign, so how could he think voters gave him political capital to spend on removing seniors' safety net? After the lunch, the buzz among my Democratic colleagues was intense. This was such a nonstarter for Democrats, and especially for a legislator like me, given all the seniors in my South Florida district. Not only would the notion of privatizing Social Security be an extremely volatile issue, but the President's ham-handed approach obliterated any opportunity there may have been to build a bipartisan consensus.

This is why Minority Leader Nancy Pelosi made it known that House Democrats ought to be unified and immovable in our opposition to President Bush's proposed dismantling of Social Security. I was in full agreement with this strategy because while I believe we must take steps to shore up Social Security so we don't reach a point where the trust fund is exhausted, President Bush went too far, declaring that Social Security was in "crisis" and required drastic action. In actuality, the Social Security Board of Trustees, which issues an annual report on the solvency of the program, at the time predicted insolvency around 2041, hardly a "crisis." I recognize that we did need to address the long-term problem, but not by ending Social Security's guaranteed safety net.

Two of my Democratic colleagues in the Florida delegation, Allen Boyd and Robert Wexler, defied the minority leader. Boyd actually signed on to the Republican bill to privatize Social Security while Wexler proposed a separate bill that he thought would split the difference, making the idea more palatable to Democrats. Pelosi was livid. From that point forward, both Boyd and Wexler were personae non gratae with her and her leadership team, and the clash with Pelosi diminished their power in the Democratic caucus.

I strongly supported Minority Leader Pelosi and joined the messaging team to oppose Republicans' move to yank the safety net out from under our seniors. I certainly don't regret voting against privatizing such an important federal program, but I do regret that President Bush failed to create an atmosphere of bipartisanship that would have enabled both sides to come together and find a solution to a problem that needs one.

There were other ways this issue could have been handled: President Bush could have waited until the heat of what was a very intense election had dissipated before broaching the subject of Social Security, and then he could have extended more of an olive branch than a hammer. Even if it was wise to flatly reject privatization, rather than digging in, Leader Pelosi could have taken the longer view and reached out across the aisle to find Republicans willing to work toward compromise.

Of course, compromise requires both sides to share common ground and common purpose. So if the goal of one side is simply to dismantle a program rather than improve it, compromise is not achievable.

Two years later, we won multiple seats in Congress, resulting in Democrats retaking the congressional majority, in part because of our effective opposition to Republicans' support for privatizing Social Security. That class of incoming Democrats had a clear mandate from voters: safeguard Social Security.

Still, after all the partisan sniping was finished and the smoke cleared, the problem of Social Security's long-term solvency was still there, gnawing at us for a bipartisan solution.

Sadly, rather than come to the table to work on a bipartisan solution, the GOP doubled down on their "my way or the highway" approach, launching another attack against these safety-net programs. In 2008, Republicans on the House Budget Committee crafted the first version of what they dubbed a "Roadmap for America's Future," which included the very same reckless experiments that voters rejected, like a proposal for giving workers private accounts for investing more than a third of the payroll taxes that would have gone into Social Security. In 2011, the Republicans in the House passed a budget that called for $1.7 billion in cuts to Social Security's operating budget, which would have decreased services to seniors and led to delays in receiving benefits. Fortunately, congressional Democrats were able to restore that funding in the final version of the bill.

It seems House Republicans had forgotten the message that voters sent in the 2006 mid-term election that Social Security must be protected. Americans have witnessed the chaos that's occurred on Wall Street over the last several years, the way major financial institutions went hog-wild for subprime mortgages, crashing the international economy. What rational person wants to put all of their eggs in one basket, trusting Wall Street with all of his or her retirement money over a program as stable and successful as Social Security? Indeed, the *Los Angeles Times* reported in August 2012 that "the crash of 2008 would have stripped nearly 60 percent from retirement investors' stock portfolios."

The Social Security Administration follows investment mandates that reap a dividend of about 4.4 percent, derived from U.S. securities backed by the Treasury. In the investment industry, these are widely considered the safest vehicles available in the world. If we allow people to make their own investment decisions on what would then be their own accounts (the amount they've contributed to Social Security through taxes), they might just do very well. But they might not. Playing the market is a tricky business, full of temptations to invest in riskier vehicles. Performing one's due diligence takes research that's often very time-consuming. What happens when you have a stock market crash or just a long, stubborn bear market? What happens if we have volatility like we've had recently? If you're very near retirement and your portfolio suffers a downturn, then you are potentially facing no income for the rest of your life. What happens then?

The Republicans don't really have an answer.

The bottom line is that Social Security works. There's nothing wrong with investing some of your disposable income in stocks, bonds, and other securities. But when it comes to retirement savings, a wise investor realizes the value of a guaranteed return on investment.

As a representative of a congressional district with one of the highest percentages of seniors in the nation, I know only too well that seniors are the population most frequently victimized by con artists. I've held numerous anti-fraud senior workshops in my congressional district to minimize the likelihood of my constituents falling susceptible to these scams. Unfortunately, there are roughly five million cases of financial exploitation of the elderly in the United States each year totaling more than $2.9 billion annually. Encouraging seniors to privately invest their Social Security funds would make them even more inviting targets. As for current workers who would allegedly have more to gain from the private accounts, they would also have more to lose. Americans who are already spending long hours at their job shouldn't be required to also spend time researching investment funds, trying to identify one that will yield a rate of return at least equal to or greater than what they already have with Social Security.

The message from American voters is unambiguous: Social Security is a critical program that should be protected, not dismantled.

Of course, Republicans haven't only focused on dismantling Social Security as we know it; they've also set their sights on Medicare and Medicaid, two programs on which millions of seniors and children rely.

During the debate over health-care reform, Republicans used their media machine to traffic the myth that the Affordable Care Act would destroy Medicare. Since Obamacare was signed into law in 2010, I have spent much of my time trying to calm fears among my senior constituents by explaining that the reforms actually expanded Medicare benefits in various ways. Obamacare also put the program on better financial footing, strengthening it for today's seniors and future generations of retirees by extending its life by an additional eight years. Medicare has been a lifeline for America's seniors since 1965, and for all of that time, Democrats have been staunch supporters of the program.

Like Social Security, Medicare is expected to face increased financial stress in the future: starting in 2024, according to recent estimates. Led by Paul Ryan, Republicans have proposed turning Medicare into an annual lump sum payment, termed a voucher. So instead of it being a guaranteed insurance policy for our seniors at the time they are usually having their most significant health problems, they would receive a voucher that may or may not cover their actual medical expenses, one that would not keep up with the rate of inflation. As they get sicker, they're going to face astronomical increases in health-care costs—without insurance. Who would end up paying for millions of destitute seniors whose vouchers can't cover their medical expenses? It's a shortsighted proposal that would leave millions of seniors without the resources needed to cover their medical costs, and it would return us to the health-care system seniors faced before Medicare, when medical bankruptcy was a common occurrence for families with seniors.

Members of Congress should sit down together and look at the possibilities for shoring up Social Security and Medicare, without changing the programs' intent or scope. These successful programs, upon which millions of Americans rely, need to be modified for financial security, not scrapped altogether.

The House Republicans' 2012 budget claimed to keep traditional Medicare as an option, while expanding the role of private plans. Peter Orszag, former director of the Office of Management and Budget, pointed out in a *Washington Post* op-ed that the plan is similar to existing Medicare Advantage plans, which give beneficiaries the option of selecting private plans. Medicare Advantage plans were implemented in 2003 by

Republicans with the expectation that bringing in private insurance as an option would drive down costs through competition. In reality, these private plans have proved to be 17 percent more costly than Medicare. (In fact, Obamacare ends these wasteful subsidies to private Medicare Advantage plans while lowering their costs and improving or maintaining their benefits and in doing so adds eight years of solvency to Medicare.)

Republicans attempted to sell their plan by saying it would not affect anyone aged fifty-five or older. This simply isn't true. By repealing Obamacare, the Republican plan would have reopened the prescription drug donut hole coverage gap for seniors who are on Medicare. It would also eliminate the preventive health-care available without a copayment or deductible to seniors on Medicare. Finally, by allowing younger, healthier patients to opt out of Medicare, the program would disproportionately be comprised of older and less healthy individuals, dramatically increasing Medicare's expenses, which would shorten the life of the program.

Presidential candidate Mitt Romney avoided going into great detail about his plans for Medicare, but campaign sources told *The Washington Post* he intended to give beneficiaries a voucher they could use to purchase traditional Medicare or a private plan, just like congressional Republicans' plan. That kind of competition might seem like it would reduce costs for consumers, but it ignores decades of history showing the meteoric rise of health-care costs despite our free-market approach involving private insurers.

We have already known a world where Medicare doesn't exist: Prior to the program's inception, some 51 percent of seniors went without health care. In an advanced country that is the undisputed leader of the free world, that level of negligence is unconscionable. Fortunately our nation has committed itself to ensuring our seniors have income and affordable health care to allow them to age with dignity. We must be resolute in this commitment.

The Republican leadership saved its cruelest round of entitlement reform for Medicaid, apparently having calculated that the nation's poor are a politically impotent constituency. The program provides health coverage for sixty-three million low-income Americans, including thirty-one million children and ten million people with disabilities.

Like Social Security and Medicare, Medicaid may not be a perfect program, but it is one that Americans rely on for critical services. So it's our responsibility as policymakers to do our best to make improvements within the program, as opposed to simply scrapping it. At the very least, anyone with such a radical plan for changing an essential government program has the burden of proof: Any new system must be demonstrably better than the existing one.

Nothing Republicans have offered to date has met that standard.

The most recent attack on Medicaid came from House Republicans' 2012 budget proposal, which intended to slash $1.4 trillion from Medicaid over a decade. The plan proposed to achieve this by shifting costs from the federal government to state governments. Under the Republican proposal, the program would no longer be funded by matching grants that are adjusted according to actual market rates for health-care services. Instead, Medicaid would be funded via block grants, with individual states having to decide whether to kick in their own funds to make up the difference between the federal grant money and the actual cost of providing care to low-income patients.

This simply punts a complex political issue from the nation's capital to state capitals, where governors would each have to make painful choices. There are certain issues that demand a federal response and access to affordable health care is one of them. As the CBO analysts concluded, the outcome would be "reduced eligibility for Medicaid and CHIP [Children's Health Insurance Program], coverage of fewer services, lower payments to providers or increased cost sharing by beneficiaries—all of which would reduce access to care."

What many people do not realize is that, nationally, Medicaid pays for the care of more than half the seniors in nursing homes, meaning that the Republican plan to starve the program would cause many low-income elderly to either be stranded in their homes or, more likely, cared for by younger generations of their family. That obligation would be an additional burden to working people who may already have trouble covering their own household expenses.

That is why I get angry when I hear Republicans like Representative Ryan cite their plan as part of his "duty to leave our children with a better America." If that's the case, then Ryan should have voted for Barack Obama! Republicans should not be dismantling these programs; rather, they should be working with their Democratic colleagues to strengthen them. Children and young adults would also be affected by the Republican plan to repeal Obamacare, a move that would cost thirty-one million Americans their health coverage, would kick many young adults off their parents' health insurance, and would allow Americans to once again be dropped or denied coverage for preexisting conditions.

Clearly, our society must do something to help low-income families, and when Republicans talk about the savings in their plan, they leave out the societal cost of not providing comprehensive and preventive care. The undeniable impact, if not the direct intention, of these so-called reforms would be to make the most basic human rights a privilege reserved for those who can afford them.

It's hard to move forward as a nation when we expend so much energy trying to avoid taking two steps back. Rather than working together to try to extend the life of these programs and improve outcomes through the addition of features like preventive care, we end up getting bogged down in attempts to end or severely restrict these programs. The rule for tinkering with Social Security, Medicare, and Medicaid should be the same as the Hippocratic Oath sworn by physicians: "First, do no harm."

We must concentrate on revisions to each program that will keep its essence intact. For instance, Social Security currently caps contributions at $106,800, meaning the wealthy pay a much smaller portion of their annual income in payroll tax—that is, the deduction from a worker's wage—while still collecting the program's full benefits. Senator Bernie Sanders of Vermont has pushed for eliminating the payroll tax cap, such that everyone who earns a wage pays the same percentage of their income into the program. If so, this would extend the solvency of Social Security for seventy-five years. A long-term fix could really be that simple.

Given the political risks of making reforms to Social Security, however, this kind of legislation must be forged in a bipartisan fashion, with both Democrats and Republicans having equal skin in the game. For all the political rancor of the last several years, I hope that it's still possible for the two parties to work together the way that Ronald Reagan, Democratic House Speaker Tip O'Neill, and Republican House Minority Leader Bob Michel hashed out modifications that gave Social Security an extra twenty-five years of solvency.

Finally, we must do even better as a country to recover the billions of dollars lost annually to fraud. Social Security disability fraud is a particularly frustrating expense—and yet in 2012 the House Republican budget appropriation for 2013 proposed to slash $752 million that went toward "program integrity," a division that paid for itself by busting con artists. The Social Security chief actuary, Stephen Goss, estimated that the cut would increase the annual program costs by up to $6 billion due to additional undetected fraud. In one recent case near Dallas, Texas, a single provider named Dr. Jacques Roy allegedly pocketed $375 million in Medicare reimbursements. According to federal investigators, Roy recruited homeless people to pose as patients, then billed Medicare for services those patients didn't need or that were never delivered. If those allegations are true, it would be the biggest Medicare fraud case ever uncovered. Roy has denied the charges.

If proved, the Roy case would be only the tip of the iceberg of the fraud committed nationwide. In fiscal year 2010 alone, the government estimated spending $125 billion in fraudulent payments from safety-net programs. Truly, cuts to fraud detection are penny-wise and pound-foolish.

In the last two years, there has been progress in reducing Medicare fraud, with a whopping $10.7 billion recovered, including $4.1 billion in 2011, which is a record. Prosecutions of con artists have nearly doubled since President Obama took office. This has all taken place despite Republican attempts to slash funding for fraud-busting efforts.

Making modest revisions that strengthen safety-net programs, while taking measures to increase efficiency by curbing fraud, will go a long way toward ensuring that these benefits are available if and when our children need them. If we can accomplish this, our generation would not be the one that dismantles the legacies of Presidents Roosevelt and Johnson. Rather, we have the opportunity to honor them, as well as our ancestors, by showing that we understand America's greatness is defined not purely by its power but also by its generosity.

THREE

Health Care:
A Right Worth Fighting For

As far back as I can remember, my father told me, "If you don't have your health, you don't have anything." But this was such an abstract notion, I couldn't comprehend it completely—not until 2008, when a disease put my health in jeopardy.

It actually began in December 2007, about six weeks after my first mammogram came back clean. I was doing a self-exam in the shower and felt a lump. I hoped it was just a cyst, but I scheduled a doctor's appointment to make sure. My doctors and oncologist debated whether it was necessary to perform a biopsy. Being just forty-one years old, the odds were that it wasn't cancer. I was given three choices: I could do nothing, except monitor the lump. I could have a fine needle aspiration, which if it was cancer carried the risk of spreading the cells elsewhere in my body. Or I could go through with the biopsy.

Later, I learned that many doctors tell women of my age that they're probably too young for cancer, and dismiss them without a more thorough check and a discussion of their options. After close consultation with my medical team, I chose the biopsy. I remember coming out of surgery and being in the recovery room. The doctors had just done the frozen section, and they reported that I was okay. But a few days later when the results of the pathology report came back, there was a different conclusion. The doctors told me I had breast cancer.

It was like getting hit with an anvil—this huge weight that crashes down on you. My children were so young. The twins, Rebecca and Jake, were just eight, while Shelby was four. I couldn't help thinking of the milestones in their lives I might miss. I couldn't help wondering how many more anniversaries I would have with my husband, Steve. Breast cancer strikes at our very identity as women, affecting how others perceive us, how we perceive ourselves. I had been vigilant about breast cancer, educating myself about the importance of self-exams and knowing how my breasts normally felt, but still breast cancer had always been something that happened to other women. And now it was happening to me.

The news came during the heat of the primary battle between Senators Obama and Hillary Rodham Clinton. At the time, I was a national campaign cochair for Senator Clinton, making media appearances as a surrogate, in addition to my role as a Democratic Party fundraiser for competitive congressional races. My job as a member of Congress was very demanding, as was the job of being a mother to three children. While I was determined to continue these responsibilities, cancer doesn't wait for anyone, and I was resolved to beat it.

I had an excellent team of doctors on my side. They told me the cure rate for a tumor the size of mine, less than a half-centimeter, was over 90 percent. I had a lumpectomy and prepared for radiation. But first my health-care team recommended a genetic test. The doctors had learned that I was an Ashkenazi Jew, meaning my ancestors came from Eastern Europe. They explained that Ashkenazi Jews are more likely to have a BRCA1 or BRCA2 gene mutation that dictates an increased chance of recurrence, along with a high risk of ovarian and other cancers. Despite having worked with breast cancer advocates for years, I was totally unaware of this link. The test was performed, and it came back positive for the BRCA2 gene mutation. I had no family history of breast cancer, but had I been aware earlier about this gene mutation, I would have known that I had up to an 85 percent chance of getting the disease at some point in my life. Finding this mutation made it easier to determine a course of treatment, since recurrence was more likely.

In another way, it presented me with a difficult choice. I could have a lumpectomy and radiation, but with the gene mutation, the cancer had a high likelihood of returning. Or I could have a mastectomy, which would mean no radiation but the loss of my breast. Additionally, since I was diagnosed with cancer in one breast, and especially with the presence of the gene mutation, the likelihood of cancer occurring in my other breast and in my ovaries was significantly elevated. I talked with my doctors. I talked with my husband. And I made the choice that was right for me: a double mastectomy, and later, removal of my ovaries to reduce the chance that I would get breast or ovarian cancer in the future. Before proceeding down that path, I recalled another admonition of my father's, to always seek a second opinion before making a significant health-care decision. I asked my doctors about the reliability and accuracy of the BRCA genetic test and if I could get a second opinion test so I could have the peace of mind that I was making the right choice. I had been diagnosed with very early stage breast cancer and as mentioned previously, the initial recommended course of treatment was a lumpectomy and radiation. Faced with removing both breasts and my ovaries, which would mean immediate menopause at forty-one years old, was a step I did not want to make without the confidence that the genetic diagnosis was accurate. I was assured that the reliability of the test result was 100 percent but then my doctors informed me that it was not possible for me to get a second opinion test because the company that made the test, Myriad Genetics had a patent on the BRCA genes and the test itself. They had the exclusive right to all testing for BRCA gene mutations. I could not believe that a company could have a patent on my biological material and worse, that I was forced to make life-altering decisions based on the results of one test. Thankfully though, in June of 2013, the Supreme Court handed down a decision in *Association for Molecular Pathology v. Myriad Genetics* that declared that patents cannot be held on naturally occurring genes. This was a victory for everyone who believes that a company cannot patent parts of our body. So, never again will a woman be faced with the decision I faced, without the benefit of a second opinion. It took a year, but by March 2009 doctors determined that I was cancer free. Only then did I tell my kids, the majority of my congressional staff, and my colleagues about what I had gone through.

When you have a life-threatening illness, it monopolizes you. You are suspended in an awful state of vulnerability. As a member of Congress, I was fortunate to be able to choose a very reliable health-care plan. That gave me the ability to be timely about my annual well-woman visit; when I turned forty, I was able to get my first (and what turned out to be my last) mammogram. I knew from regular doctor visits, and from being an advocate in the fight against breast cancer as a legislator, the importance of self-exams; and when I felt the lump I didn't hesitate to consult a physician. That may have saved my life.

It's hard for me to imagine what would have happened if in 2008 I was one of the tens of millions of Americans who was uninsured or underinsured. How long would it have taken for me to discover the lump? How big would the tumor have grown and how much would the cancer have spread before I decided it was worth the expense of a doctor's visit? Would I have paid the several thousands of dollars it cost to be tested for the BRCA1 and BRCA2 gene mutations? And how would I have afforded the crippling cost of care without insurance? Too many women face those impossible decisions every day.

No American should have to make a choice between paying the rent and seeing a doctor. And no American should face bankruptcy simply because they get sick. Health care should be a right in this country, not a privilege. I have always believed that, but breast cancer underscored the importance of having comprehensive coverage.

Debating health-care reform as I shared my own experience with breast cancer made me more resolved than ever to do my part in helping Congress make comprehensive health-care reform the law of the land. I want my children and the children of the families I represent to have the chance to see a doctor without a moment's hesitation. I know from personal experience that access to quality health care leads to early detection when unexpected illness strikes. Early detection is the key to survival.

◆ ◆ ◆

This same goal has proved elusive for generations that have come before. I was reminded of this every time I would encounter venerable Massachusetts Senator Ted Kennedy on Capitol Hill. Of course, comprehensive health-care reform was the cause that most galvanized Kennedy. When Nixon proposed a health-care plan in 1974, however, it was Kennedy who helped defeat it, because in his view the plan didn't go far enough. This was one of Kennedy's most profound regrets.

It took nearly twenty years before Washington tackled the issue again. The Clinton administration's bid for universal coverage, led by then First Lady Hillary Clinton in 1993, met fierce opposition from the health-care industry and from traditional conservative forces like the Heritage Foundation, which criticized the plan for being too bureaucratic. Democrats in Congress did little to move the Clinton administration's plan forward, offering only tepid support, not nearly enough to counter the momentum against reform. Any opportunity to build consensus for a modified version of the Clinton plan dissolved with the sweeping 1994 Republican congressional election victories, which vaulted Newt Gingrich into the House Speaker's role. Another fifteen years would pass, with more and more Americans unable to afford health-care coverage joining the ranks of the uninsured.

Against this historical backdrop, there's no question that the Affordable Care Act of 2010 was the most hard-fought legislative victory of the modern political era. A true breakthrough, its passage paved the way for roughly thirty-one million uninsured Americans to finally receive health-care coverage. It contained a slew of consumer protections and efficiency measures that would help rein in runaway costs. I only wish that Senator Kennedy had lived another six months, so that he could have celebrated this milestone with us.

I remember vividly the resolve and determination we had as a caucus when we left our caucus meeting to go and debate the Affordable Care Act before the vote was to be called. That Saturday we met together in the Cannon House Office Building, which is located across the street from the Capitol. Rather than take a tunnel under the street that links the buildings as we often do, we decided to link arms and walk out across the street past protesters shouting things I can't even repeat in this book and even spitting on members of the Congressional Black Caucus. All of this anger, all of this vitriol, in exchange for our campaign to ensure that every American would be able to see a doctor. At town hall forums around the country members of Congress, including myself, were shouted down by the Tea Party activists as we tried to talk to our constituents about how the legislation would affect them. Those same activists came to Washington to display signs that compared the President to Hitler and Stalin, that accused him of being a Muslim terrorist. They even trafficked in conspiracy theories about a grand plan to destroy America's capitalist economy. It was the most hysterical reaction in American politics since Sen. Joseph McCarthy's paranoid campaign against so-called communist spies.

For a party that for decades has been foiling efforts to bring comprehensive health care to Americans, that's to be expected. But you'll notice that the GOP's attacks are almost exclusively distortions, lies, and mischaracterizations about health-care reform, including the oft-repeated lie that it was a government takeover of health care. These party members conveniently ignore the fundamental changes the Affordable Care Act brought to the nation's health-care system while leaving the private market health care and health insurance system intact.

The partisan battles over health-care reform carried over to the 2012 election, not even stopping when the conservative-leaning Supreme Court ruled the law to be constitutional. During the Republican primary, presidential candidates practically fell over one another promising to repeal "Obamacare," originally a derisive term the President eventually embraced. As he said, "Obama does care."

Even some Democrats have asked me whether these reforms made it harder for us to win elections in 2010 and 2012. There are voices within the party who say we should not have made health-care reform our top legislative priority in 2009, that it wasn't worth it. This is a fair question. I think this triumph was absolutely worth the political sacrifices we made.

To take the true measure of this program, it's necessary to look back just a few years at the way the American health-care system was working just before the inception of Obamacare. The Deloitte Center for Health Solutions conducts annual surveys of American health-care consumers. Their 2011 survey was essentially a final snapshot of consumer behavior pre-Obamacare. It wasn't pretty.

Perhaps the most basic standard for evaluating a nation's health-care system is whether citizens feel they can seek medical care when they get sick or injured. The Deloitte survey found that in 2011, roughly half the consumers avoided seeing a doctor because the cost was too high, including some who had insurance but didn't want to use it. Among the uninsured, 83 percent said their refusal to seek care was due to the exorbitant cost.

Given that the nation's health-care expenditures are over $8,000 per capita, an astronomical 18 percent of GDP, it should be no surprise that roughly three in five Americans told surveyors that their monthly health-care expenses made it hard for them to afford other life essentials like food, housing, education, and fuel.

Americans were mired in a system where there were huge inequities in health care based on income. While we constantly heard the refrain that America had the best health-care system in the world, the research and statistics told a different story. According to an Organisation for Economic Co-operation and Development analysis from 2007, U.S. citizens have a lower life expectancy and a higher rate of death from illness than citizens of other Western nations studied, despite the fact that Americans spend more on care than any other country. Research shows it is traditionally harder in the United States to get same-day doctor care when sick and that we have the highest incidence of obesity, cancer, and AIDS, suggesting our health-care culture does a poor job of discouraging behavior that creates health risks.

Facing a severe economic downturn as he was sworn into office, President Obama recognized that the economy and our health-care system were inextricably intertwined. Fixing health care was an important component of fixing our economy.

With a Democratic President and a Democratic Congress in 2009 and 2010, the time had come for elected officials to put politics aside and do what was right for the country, electoral consequences be damned. I am proud of the President for having that courage and fortitude. And I am proud of all of the Democratic members in the House who knew voting for health-care reform would put their political career at risk, but did so anyway. That is the kind of leadership that serves this country best. Many of my Democratic colleagues in the 111th Congress lost in 2010 at least in part because of their vote for Obamacare. To this day, I've not been able to find one of them who regrets their decision.

In the introduction, I shared with you that before I began my career as a legislator I was encouraged to sit down and list the policies that matter most to me. Near the top was making health care affordable. In this sense, voting for Obamacare was the fulfillment of my most deeply held beliefs about the role of government in being a force for positive change in people's lives.

Before Congress passed the Medicare Part D prescription drug benefit in 2003, traditional Medicare did not provide coverage for prescription drugs. Many seniors faced a difficult choice between medicine and meals. When Congress passed Part D, the Republican majority at the time left a gap in coverage known as the "donut hole." When a senior on Medicare spends approximately $2,600 on prescription medication, they fall into the donut hole coverage gap and have to pay for their drugs 100 percent out of pocket until they reach approximately $5,600 in prescription drug spending. Some seniors never reach that top amount in a calendar year, so they pay for 100 percent of their prescriptions for the rest of the year, until the next year. Of course, many seniors living on fixed incomes can't afford to pay their way through that gap in coverage. The Affordable Care Act phases out the donut hole, closing it for good in 2020, saving seniors up to $3,000 a year in drug costs.

About a year after President Obama signed the Affordable Care Act into law, I spoke at the West Broward Democratic Club, one of the largest Democratic clubs in Florida, whose membership is largely made up of senior citizens who live in my congressional district. When I finished and began taking questions, a woman I'd known for twenty-three years— who I'd never thought of as struggling to make ends meet—rose to make a statement. She said, "Debbie, thanks to Obamacare, I don't have to ask the pharmacist to score my pills anymore. I used to do that so they would last me longer, but because the donut hole is closing, I can afford my prescriptions now." It was an eye-opening moment for me because I had used that story generally, as an example in arguing for the Affordable Care Act's passage. I had even stood in line behind seniors at the pharmacy who couldn't afford to pay for all their presciptions, so they had to decide which to fill and which to leave. But here was a woman I knew well who directly benefited from the closure of the Medicare prescription drug coverage gap. It was more clear to me than ever before that Obamacare and safety-net programs like Medicare are essential to maintaining a minimum quality of life for our seniors.

Of course, the reforms have improved the lives of Americans of all ages. I have friends and constituents who worried about health-care coverage for their young adult sons and daughters, who after graduation sometimes find it hard to find a job with benefits. In years past, insurance companies were free to end coverage for dependent children who were enrolled in their parents' plan at the age of nineteen. Thanks to Obamacare, insurance companies must allow those young people to remain on their parents' insurance plan up to the age of twenty-six.

But the most significant provision of the health-care reform law is how it protects Americans with a preexisting health condition. That starts with children, who were protected from denial of coverage as of September 23, 2010. For adults, that same protection takes effect in January 2014, because that is when the individual mandate takes effect. The addition of those newly enrolled healthier beneficiaries' payments will balance the cost of covering the higher-needs patients who had been excluded on the basis of preexisting conditions.

Under the old system, even being female was treated by insurers as a preexisting condition, meaning that women were charged higher premiums simply because of gender. This was a reprehensible practice—and since my bout with breast cancer I have had a double whammy. After I shared my experience, I heard so many stories from women diagnosed with breast cancer at a time they didn't have health insurance. They needed both radiation treatment and chemotherapy, but under the old system they had to choose only one of those two treatments because they couldn't afford the copay and deductible for both. I can't imagine how terrifying it must be to make that choice.

In October 2009, during the American Cancer Society Cancer Action Network lobbying day, I met a Florida woman who had a devastating story to tell about her encounter with breast cancer. She described how she learned of her diagnosis shortly after she'd gotten divorced and lost her job, and with it her health-care coverage. The woman, who was undergoing chemotherapy at the time we met, even had to deal with the grief of her dog dying. After she'd told her story, there wasn't a dry eye in the room. This woman needed to put her energy into fighting cancer, yet she had to deal with her life's losses and fight for health coverage on top of it. As a three-time cancer survivor, her preexisting conditions prevented her from securing reasonable health insurance, and she was not going to be able to secure coverage until she found employment with comprehensive insurance. She told me that her doctors recommended she go through chemotherapy and radiation, but without health insurance, she wasn't sure she could afford either and would most likely be forced to choose one or the other. This is a grievous injustice, and it underscores why we so desperately needed health-care reform.

So on a personal level, I'm very much looking forward to the end of this cruel era in American health care. I feel confident that millions of women feel the same way.

With so many provisions of Obamacare yet to take effect, it's important that fair-minded Americans stick to the facts of this legislation and resist the misinformation that has been spread by opponents.

Those who have been happy with their medical coverage will hardly be affected by the reform. Roughly 60 percent of consumers receive their health insurance through their employers, and they have been free to keep those plans perfectly intact. But if they should lose their job, or if they should learn of a preexisting condition, they have the comfort of knowing that they will still be insured, thanks to health-care reform.

Obamacare is not some radical "socialist" enterprise, as opponents of the legislation have suggested. In fact, credit for the original idea belongs to the Heritage Foundation, the same ultraconservative think tank that played a leading role in the defeat of the Clinton administration's effort at health-care reform in 1994. The foundation conceived a formula whereby all consumers would not only get health-care coverage, they'd be obligated to get it, such that young and healthy consumers are brought into the system, providing balance against the high-risk patients who may have preexisting conditions. To offset the proportionally high cost to low-income consumers, the system would provide subsidies.

For real-world evidence of how it works, just look to the state of Massachusetts, where in 2006 Governor Mitt Romney signed a similar plan into law. That system has delivered higher quality care for less than it costs in the traditional American health-care system while extending health-care coverage to some 98 percent of Massachusetts residents. So President Obama took a conservative idea, which was first put into action by the man Republicans chose to be their presidential nominee. Indeed, I and many other Democrats, including President Obama, wanted the health-reform legislation to go further and include a public option, but you can't let the perfect be the enemy of the good. This government-sponsored public option would have been one of the choices in the health exchange, keeping private plans honest and competitive. Like the President, I don't care if an idea comes from a Republican or a Democrat; if it solves a problem and works for the American people, it's good enough for me! And Obamacare solves big problems: helping millions of Americans who didn't have health insurance and putting reins on runaway health-care costs.

Much has been made of the costs of Obamacare, but many of the accusations are false. For starters, it is not "the largest tax increase in the history of the world," as the bombastic Rush Limbaugh told his listeners after the Supreme Court upheld the legislation in June 2012. In fact,

Republican Presidents Ronald Reagan and George H. W. Bush both passed tax hikes that generated more revenue in proportion to the national GDP, which is the appropriate way to judge the size of tax increases.

These distortions have even appeared in the mainstream media. In an August 2012 *Newsweek* cover story entitled "Hit the Road, Barack," the conservative academic Niall Ferguson implied that Obama had betrayed his pledge to achieve health-care reform without adding to the federal deficit. As evidence Ferguson quoted the July 2012 CBO and Joint Committee on Taxation report on the Affordable Care Act, which said that the legislation's insurance provisions would have a net cost of $1.2 trillion from 2012 to 2022. Ferguson conveniently avoided mentioning the next line in that same document, wherein analysts point out that Obamacare contains other provisions that more than pay off that $1.2 trillion, such that the reforms will actually reduce the deficit by $84 billion.

I admit, it seems counterintuitive: Broadening health-care coverage in America can actually cost less than a system where there were so many uninsured? Yes, because the fact is that the uninsured still receive medical attention under the traditional system—it's just that their bills are typically paid through a variety of government programs, especially Medicare and Medicaid, and also through emergency room care. This shifts costs from those without insurance onto those with insurance and results in higher taxes. Yes, many opponents of universal coverage may be surprised to learn that for as long as they've been paying taxes, they've been paying for uncompensated care given to the uninsured. Have you ever wondered when looking at a medical bill why a hospital gown or Tylenol cost so much? The answer is cost-shifting. Additionally, the average American family pays $1,017 per year in higher premiums to cover the cost of medical care provided to the uninsured.

Obamacare, however, contains a number of provisions to increase efficiency in providing health care to previously uninsured patients, and that's part of the reason it can bring down the costs. For instance, everyone will have free access to preventive care, meaning that when a previously uninsured individual is sick or injured, he or she won't let a mild or curable condition worsen into a full-blown emergency, with all the additional expenses that come with it—expenses borne by taxpayers and by those with insurance.

The Deloitte survey also showed that roughly half of uninsured Americans did not have a primary care physician, with the majority of those citing cost as the reason. Regular access to a primary care physician is a proven way to provide lower-cost preventive care in the hope of avoiding high-cost emergency care. To address that need, health-care reform contains a provision for every American to have at least one annual wellness checkup, without a copay or deductible, helping doctors and nurse practitioners to catch worrisome medical conditions before they require more aggressive, costly treatment.

As we discussed in chapter 2, Obamacare puts in place more effective measures for identifying fraud and abuse. This will trim over $7 billion in the next decade, according to CBO projections. Additionally, more than $100 billion will be saved by eliminating wasteful subsidies that are part of the Medicare Advantage plans. Obamacare also addresses the efficiency of care for those who are insured. As former Office of Management and Budget director Peter Orszag pointed out in *The New England Journal of Medicine*, the expenses of the American health-care system are unevenly distributed: 10 percent of the patients are responsible for a whopping 64 percent of the costs. There are imbalances in any system, but we can reduce this imbalance by coordinating care for that 10 percent of costly patients. Obamacare invests $26 billion in health information technology to do exactly that, reducing medical errors and paperwork for all Americans while dramatically increasing the quality of care. As this system is put into place, expensive mistakes such as patients being readmitted to a hospital for the same condition will be much less likely to occur. By 2015, nearly all U.S. hospitals will be linked by this modern information-sharing system. These and other cost savings are then invested in other health programs, like Medicare, which is part of the reason Obamacare is projected to add years to the life of the Medicare trust fund, which will be paying full benefits at least through 2024.

So the argument that America can't afford to pay for health-care reform is woefully misguided. We still have work to do in terms of bringing down medical costs, but Obamacare is the first and most important step in that direction. From a financial perspective of managing our nation's budget and from a moral perspective of providing coverage to millions of uninsured Americans, this was legislation we couldn't afford *not* to pass.

Still, the hardest part of health-care reform is likely ahead of us. As of October 1, 2013, Americans whose employers don't already offer insurance have been able to shop for, and enroll in, a health insurance plan through the Health Insurance Marketplace, also known as exchanges. These health insurance plans go into effect on January 1, 2014.

The law was designed to allow each state to create a health exchange that is geared toward its own specific needs. But many states whose governors or state legislatures disagreed with the law either chose to "slow-walk" its implementation, or refused to set it up altogether.

This means we're at a critical juncture of the implementation of Obamacare. If people find the exchanges too cumbersome or confusing, enrollment will suffer, as will public perception of the law. Democrats have made a political investment in reform, but we must not treat every minute provision in the law as sacred. Rather, we should be open to suggestions for improving the law and move quickly to implement needed changes as they arise. That engagement certainly should include past critics of the law who come forward with ways to enhance coverage within their states.

We all know the adage about how sometimes you have to take one step back before you can take two steps forward. The Republicans have talked about taking that one big step back, by repealing Obamacare. Through mid-2013, they voted more than 40 times to take that step back. But they have said almost nothing about how to take two steps forward. And they have never voted on an alternative to Obamacare. If they have a better plan for addressing the horrible inequities that characterize the status quo of American health care, why are they keeping it a secret?

Because that plan doesn't exist. The health-care problem is incredibly complex and there is no perfect solution. Rather, it comes down to making incremental improvements, borrowing the best ideas from state governments and foreign nations, researching the cause and effect of existing policies, analyzing trends, and planning for contingencies. In short, it's wonky, requiring intensive study and critical thinking rather than simple sound bites from the campaign stump.

I understand that politics is a contact sport, and I probably give as much as I get. But with an issue like comprehensive health care, the stakes are too high to engage in fear mongering. If Republicans think this health-care reform law doesn't trim enough from future deficits, by all means let's talk about ways we can make it even more efficient—but as part of that conversation, we have to at least agree that every American is entitled to quality affordable health-care coverage. If we can't agree on that, then it won't be possible to have a constructive discussion about moving forward.

The American people have the right to demand more from their leaders on an issue so far-reaching. They should be skeptical of a politician who conjures fear in the audience without offering a specific alternative. We're all susceptible to emotionally charged arguments, especially if we're told that the money we've earned is going toward those who don't deserve it, which is the overarching theme of anti-tax, anti-government diatribes on the right. But in that moment of frustration and resentment, are we really our best selves?

This is not a battle between those with health care and those without. We are all connected, young and old, rich and poor. We all have a stake in the future, and good health is what ensures that future. This is not a fiscal issue; we have always been able to afford comprehensive health care. It is a moral issue.

Finally, it is a personal issue, for each in his or her own way, because none of us knows what health scares may be around the corner. After I went public with my treatment for breast cancer, my daughter Rebecca came to me, her eyes wide as saucers. She wanted to make sure I was okay, but then she asked something else: "Mommy, am I going to get cancer?"

That's a question for which no mother is ever fully ready. I couldn't tell her "No, you won't." I told her the truth: that it wasn't something she had to worry about for a long time, but that, as she grows, I'll help her to be as healthy as she can. In every way possible, I will do that. And I will fight for a health-care system in America that will enable me to keep that promise.

FOUR

———◇———

A Superpower for Peace

I learned about the death of Osama bin Laden the same way most Americans did—a breaking news bulletin on television. When I saw CNN interrupt its broadcast at 9:00 P.M. on Sunday in May 2011 to say that President Obama was going to make an announcement at 10:30, I racked my brain for what it could mean. I called my Chief of Staff, Tracie Pough, and gave her my prediction: "I think we got Osama bin Laden."

The news soon leaked out, and I remember feeling overwhelmed by relief for the families who had lost loved ones in the 9/11 attacks and all of us who felt more vulnerable just knowing that Osama bin Laden was alive, somewhere. We could rest somewhat easier with the knowledge that the world's most fearsome terrorist was gone. A surge of patriotism flowed through me as well, and this became stronger as I learned more details of the operation. It was extremely complex. So much could have gone wrong in that mission, not just on the ground in Pakistan where bin Laden was hiding but at home for President Obama. If the mission failed, or if bin Laden wasn't actually in the compound, the President would have been buried by an avalanche of criticism. He was willing to take that risk because as long as bin Laden was alive, more Americans' lives were at risk.

It is important to remember that the sense of relief was not limited to America's borders. Many other countries, recognizing both the horror of 9/11 and the scourge of terrorism in general, celebrated this victory over Al Qaeda as well.

I remember, back in the 1990s, attending ceremonies for Veterans Day and Memorial Day as a member of the state legislature, telling veterans who fought in World War II, Korea, and Vietnam how grateful I was to them, how their sacrifices made it possible for another generation to avoid going to war. The Cold War had ended several years before, and it seemed then that the members of our Armed Forces would be called on only for short skirmishes and humanitarian interventions, such as occurred in the first Iraq War and in the Balkans. Of course, that changed on 9/11. There was no question the attacks on the World Trade Center made it necessary to go after the Al Qaeda terrorists being harbored by the government in Afghanistan. We did so with the full backing of our allies from NATO. Within weeks, the Taliban had fallen and Al Qaeda leaders were on the run, having to live in fear for the rest of their lives, their network scattered and their ranks dramatically thinned. If we had kept our focus in that first year, we might have delivered a coup de grace to the terrorist elements of that country.

But in the months that followed 9/11, the Bush administration's jingoistic rhetoric made it clear that they envisioned a broader military campaign. Specifically, they were building a case for the invasion of Iraq based on later discredited intelligence that linked Saddam Hussein to weapons of mass destruction. There was virtually no evidence that the Iraqi dictator had ties to Al Qaeda terrorists, but the administration insisted that possibility posed another threat to American security. When some of our NATO allies like France and Germany tried to talk us out of it, the Bush administration charged ahead, backed by a hesitant Congress but one that gave the President bipartisan support based on what we now know to be trumped-up and faulty intelligence reports that were presented about the scale of Iraq's threat. Of course, by the time we figured out that there were no weapons of mass destruction and no ties between Saddam Hussein and Al Qaeda, it was too late.

This was a dark period in American foreign policy, but it can teach us so much about how to respond to dynamic international events that lie in our future. It's our obligation to pass these lessons down to our children, so that the next generation of leaders will not make the same mistakes.

For starters, the Iraq War should teach us to be careful to fully examine intelligence reports and information to reduce the likelihood of what the Bush administration did: cherry-pick reports to support their agenda and their preconceived notions of a security threat. The flaw in this approach is that it puts more stock in the data that support one's hypothesis than in the data that contradict it, thus manipulating the predicted outcome.

Second, when our country is moving toward military action, a lack of support by primary allies may be a signal for us to pause and reevaluate our position. That doesn't mean the United States should never act unilaterally; it just means that when we're acting alone, both the President and Congress should hold the country to a higher standard for justifying the use of force. It shows our allies that we value their counsel, which strengthens our relationships. It demonstrates to our military personnel that we perform our due diligence before putting them in harm's way. And it shows the world that we are responsive to the international community, giving us more legitimacy in negotiations, when we're asking other countries to do the same.

The decision to invade another nation, however righteous the cause, should not be taken lightly and should relate to the security interests of the United States. While we cannot police the world, we owe American taxpayers a comprehensive plan for how we can help another nation complete a peaceful transition to a new government. In other words, we need to have a plan to clean up after ourselves. We should offer our citizens and soldiers something more solid than Dick Cheney promising that we'll be "greeted as liberators" in Iraq. I hope future leaders have a better grasp of the realities on the ground and use intelligence to make strategic and tactical decisions rather than deciding on the outcome they want and fitting the intelligence to support the desired decision.

It's also important to make informed decisions prior to launching military strikes because the reality is, war is hellish. As someone given the responsibility by my constituents to nominate prospective candidates to our nation's military academies and vote on resolutions to commit the American military, I strive to comprehend war's consequences. As part of this, I pay visits to the wounded soldiers recovering in Washington, D.C. I distinctly remember a young man I visited at Walter Reed Army Medical Center who had recently graduated from the U.S. Military Academy at West Point. He told me about the day in Iraq when his convoy came up alongside a red Opel hatchback. It had been packed with explosives, and somewhere an insurgent waiting for the right moment triggered the bomb. In the seconds after the blast, the young man realized he had survived and hastened to help his gunnery sergeant, who had been severely burned. The young man didn't realize until he reached down that his leg had been blown off.

He did not feel sorry for himself, to be maimed at such a young age. Rather, his most bitter regret was not being able to return to the soldiers in his unit.

That memorable conversation instilled in me a profound, lasting admiration for the depth of courage and patriotism of the young people who serve our country in battle. But it also reminded me that our government owes them a clarity of purpose.

In late November 2009, President Obama made the difficult decision to order a surge in Afghanistan—thirty thousand troops in roughly six months to vanquish the last remaining Taliban forces, once and for all. But he made that decision only after a trip to the Arlington National Cemetery, because he wanted to be mindful of the sacrifice he was asking soldiers to make on the nation's behalf. I remember when the vote came up in the House of Representatives. Just as I voted in favor of President Bush's surge during the Iraq War, I voted to fund President Obama's surge in Afghanistan. I did so in both cases, even though very likely many of my constituents were against the war, because we needed to give our commander in chief and our military leaders the opportunity to see their strategy implemented and the time to be effective. I also believed that when our troops are fighting a war in another country, they should have the resources they need to support the campaign. It was then my responsibility to go home and talk to my constituents about my decision to continue funding the war and why I felt it was the right one. Thoughtful rather than knee-jerk decisions that take in the full impact of the consequences of sending our troops into battle must be our approach.

This, I believe, is a model of how American commanders in chief should use the world's most powerful military force: judiciously. They should demand solid intelligence, and once they decide to strike, should do everything possible to limit or eliminate civilian casualties and those to our soldiers. Finally, I think we've learned the folly of thoughtlessly unfurling a "Mission Accomplished" banner. We should show the world that we can be humble in victory. More important, we shouldn't spike the ball before the clock runs out.

We have had enough "shock and awe." In the future, our foreign policy should be characterized by nuance, with a premium placed on diplomacy, all the while making it very clear that any threat to our national security will be met with serious consequences. Each country is its own case, requiring its own strategy, with a healthy dose of informed analysis and a clear purpose.

President Obama and then Secretary of State Hillary Clinton understood this, showing great adaptability in their response to the Arab Spring in the Middle East and North Africa. Here was a dynamic foreign policy challenge. Demonstrators all had a similar goal—deposing a dictator. But each country had a unique political complexion. For instance, Tunisia was a case where the dedication of demonstrators for democracy was enough to send the President into exile, and it happened so quickly that American intervention wasn't a serious consideration. As other Arab nations followed Tunisia's lead, it got much more complicated.

There are some who believe the United States should have come to the defense of Egyptian ruler Hosni Mubarak, since he was an ally in confronting global terrorism and maintaining regional stability. But from the American point of view the overarching principle was to heed the call for democracy made by millions of Egyptians. That call struck a chord with our nation's values and history. The scale of the protests was so widespread it is debatable whether or not Mubarak's government could have sustained itself. Regardless, propping up Mubarak would have enraged a large segment of the Egyptian population. An opportunistic group could have exploited that anti-American sentiment, using it as a recruiting tool for terrorist acts against the United States and our allies. Instead, by siding with the democratic aspirations of the Egyptian people, we sent a powerful message to similar regimes: If you mistreat your own people, we won't protect you from a revolution. Only time will tell whether Egypt's fledgling democracy will succeed, but I'm proud of the way Obama and Clinton clearly communicated to Mubarak that he should step down from power and yield to the will of the Egyptian people.

As Mubarak's regime collapsed in February 2011, the anti-Gadhafi protesters swarmed Libyan cities. That explosive situation called for its own approach. International condemnation over the situation in Libya allowed the Obama administration to work with NATO partners, dispatching American stealth bombers to destroy Libyan air defenses so that European and American warplanes could provide air support to Libyan rebels. The strikes were even supported by the Arab League, an organization of states in the Middle East and North Africa that hasn't exactly been thrilled with prior U.S. military ventures in the region. For the League to join the United States in support of military action against one of its own member countries shows how far this administration has come in repairing the damage done under President Bush.

The international community hasn't been as united on the question of how to resolve the civil war in Syria. In the United Nations, China and Russia have opposed the U.S. approach to that conflict, and members of the Arab League have also been divided. Syria, with its considerable army, stockpile of chemical weapons, and its status as a proxy nation for Iran, is a much more complex case for intervention. President Obama consistently called for the president of Syria, Bashar al-Assad, to cease the brutal slaughter of his own people, to step down, and to allow democratic reforms to take hold. As this book went to press, the administration had begun to supply nonlethal aid—food rations and medical supplies—to the Free Syrian Army. As of June 2013, those humanitarian efforts have amounted to an $815 million commitment, making the U.S. the world's most generous donor. Still, that same month, as intelligence reports made it evident that the Assad regime had used the nerve agent sarin against the Syrian people, it became necessary to expand our assistance. As the President made clear in his remarks, the use of chemical weapons is a "red line" that warrants a strong response, which is why I supported the administration's move to provide direct support to Syria's Supreme Military Council. There have been too many occasions in the past when regimes were killing their own people and the U.S. was too cautious to act. President Obama recognizes the seriousness of the situation in Syria and is responding in a measured but proportionate manner so we protect American lives and American interests, while addressing an increasingly dire humanitarian situation.

To be sure, the uncertainty posed by the Arab Spring presents significant challenges to our national interests. But while we cannot expect to control the outcome of democracy in the region, we can and must be vigilant in holding these new, emerging democracies accountable for fully implementing democratic reform and adhering to past agreements, like Israel's peace treaty with Egypt.

The ethnic tension and bloodshed in the Middle East may seem far away to some. But instability in any region is a threat to innocent Americans.

Daniel C. Wultz was a sixteen-year-old boy who lived in my congressional district, in my hometown of Weston, Florida. In 2006, he was visiting Israel for Passover. He was seated at an outdoor café in Tel Aviv with his father when a suicide bomber, standing two feet from their table, detonated forty pounds of explosives strapped to his body. The blast left them both with severe injuries. Daniel's father, Tuly, survived. Daniel did not. He was among the ten people killed in the attack.

It was a heartbreaking funeral, especially hearing Daniel's father describe how much he wishes he could have protected his son that fateful day, when in fact it was his son's body that took the brunt of the blast, saving the father's life.

When I returned from the funeral, my kids asked me about Daniel and how he died. Trying to explain something like this to my children, I realized I had no words that could make sense of brutality that was, truly, senseless. It is unfathomable that for decades innocent people like Daniel Wultz have been killed as part of the conflict between the Israelis and Palestinians. But we cannot allow terrorists and extremists to dictate the outcome for this region. As Americans and for the sake of all of our children and our children's children, we must continue to try to bring the two sides together for direct, bilateral negotiations in pursuit of a sustainable peace. Having seen the heartbreak in the eyes of Daniel's mother and father up close, I know we cannot throw up our hands in defeat even when our efforts at Middle East peace seem fruitless. We owe our best, sustained effort to generations of Israeli and Palestinian children, who deserve to live life free of violence and fear.

If I were to single out one aspect of President Obama's foreign policy record that has provoked unwarranted criticism, especially among Republicans, it's been his supposed mistreatment of our strongest ally in the region, Israel. As the first Jewish woman to represent Florida in Congress, I often say that I bring my love of Israel to work with me every day. I've made numerous trips to Israel over the years, meeting with Prime Ministers Ariel Sharon, Shimon Peres, Ehud Olmert, and Benjamin Netanyahu as well as other powerful figures in the government, and I would like to emphasize: Our alliance with Israel is as strong as ever.

As an expression of that bond, our nations' diplomatic, military, and intelligence agencies have worked in close cooperation toward the goal of isolating the Islamic Republic of Iran, which in my mind presents one of the biggest national security threats to Western democracy and global stability. Under no circumstances will we allow Iran to have access to nuclear weapons. Obama and Netanyahu agree that to prevent such a scenario, all options are on the table. President Obama has consistently said that we do not have a policy of containment. Allowing Iran to obtain nuclear weapons capability is unacceptable.

Under President Obama's leadership, and with bipartisan support from Congress, the United States has levied the most severe economic sanctions in our nation's history. In a diplomatic maneuver that would have been inconceivable just a few years before, the United States brought Russia and China to the table to enact sweeping multinational sanctions on Iran. In Congress, I cosponsored and supported multiple pieces of legislation aimed at isolating Iran. For example, House Resolution 2194 penalized those who invest in Iran's development of petroleum resources. In the summer of 2012, the House and Senate agreed on a new round of sanctions targeting Iran's energy sector, financial institutions, shipping companies, and insurers. Iran needs to be made aware that if its leaders continue their quest for nuclear weapons, eventually their time will run out. As President Obama said in his September 2012 address to the UN General Assembly, "America wants to resolve this issue through diplomacy and we believe there is still time and space to do so, but that time is not unlimited."

In July 2012, President Obama signed the United States–Israel Enhanced Security Cooperation Act of 2012, a continuation of our countries' tradition for sharing military technology that will keep Israel safe from attacks. That legislation included increased funding for the "Iron Dome" missile defense shield, an innovation first deployed with foreign aid funding from the United States that is already protecting southern Israel against the rockets and mortar rounds fired by Hamas and Hezbollah against civilians. President Obama saw firsthand the impact of these rocket attacks when he traveled to Israel and went to the southern city of Sderot, where he met with families and stood among the rubble of their homes. This encounter informed his decision as President to push through the initial $205 million in funding for Iron Dome and the subsequent increase in funding so that additional Iron Dome batteries could be deployed around Israel's perimeter.

Recently, the Palestinian West Bank government led by Fatah and the Palestinian Gaza government led by Hamas reached an agreement to govern together. From a U.S. point of view, this arrangement is highly problematic, given that it occurred without Hamas agreeing to the Quartet Principles, most specifically that Hamas renounce its terrorist charter, forswear violence, and fully recognize Israel's right to exist as a Jewish and democratic state. By rejecting these principles, and by holding fast to a charter that still calls for the destruction of Israel, Hamas has left no doubt that it will continue to be a terrorist threat. (To date, there has not been much evidence of significant collaboration between Fatah and Hamas.)

In 2011, with the peace process stalled, the Palestinian Authority began moving aggressively toward a unilateral declaration of statehood in the United Nations Security Council. It was almost assuredly an expression of the Palestinian Authority's desire to proceed to the United Nations General Assembly, where it was estimated they had at least 130 countries supporting their effort.

In some cases, that support would be an outgrowth of UN members' history of being critical of Israel and voting against its interests. The United States and our closest allies are frequently the only votes in support of Israel in the General Assembly and UN constituent organizations. The United States regularly exercises its Security Council veto to protect Israel against harmful actions.

In the summer of 2011, President Obama worked aggressively to persuade many of our European allies, such as France and Germany, to oppose a Palestinian unilateral declaration of statehood and subsequent application for membership in the UN. That diplomatic effort came to a head in September of 2011, when President Obama addressed the UN General Assembly and threw down the proverbial gauntlet. He made it very clear that the only path for the Palestinian Authority to achieve status as a state was through direct, bilateral negotiations in pursuit of a two-state solution. Two states, living side by side in peace: Israel, as a Jewish and democratic state, with the right to expect security from its neighbors and recognition of the right to exist; and a viable Palestinian state.

President Obama didn't stop with a speech, however. Words are helpful, but actions bring results. During the annual meeting of the UN General Assembly, the President, Secretary of State Hillary Clinton, and U.S. Ambassador to the United Nations Susan Rice deployed the full strength of American diplomacy and made it very clear that the United States would veto any such bid in the Security Council. The U.S. delegation made it known that if the Palestinians pressed for a vote in the General Assembly, there would be real consequences. The vote was never called.

I remember being in the heat of this debate during most of 2011. At the beginning of that year, most pro-Israel, American activists could not have imagined U.S. diplomatic efforts would succeed in preventing a vote from ever taking place in the General Assembly on Palestinian statehood. President Obama's judicious and effective use of diplomacy, and his clarity of purpose, resulted in a positive outcome.

The Palestinian Authority was registered as a UN observer until the fall of 2012, when it was granted an upgrade in its status to "non-member observer state." The United States opposed this move because it circumvented the peace process and bypassed direct bilateral negotiations.

In March of 2013, President Obama traveled to Israel and Jordan as the first foreign trip of his second term. I had the privilege of traveling with him as part of the American delegation. During the trip, the President stood in Yad Vashem, Israel's Holocaust Museum, and paid tribute to the memory of the six million who perished in the Holocaust, saying, "Here, on your ancient land, let it be said for all the world to hear: The State of Israel does not exist because of the Holocaust. But with the survival of a strong Jewish State of Israel, such a Holocaust will never happen again."

Over decades of diplomatic, military, and economic cooperation, the United States has stood by Israel's side, to ensure a strong, secure Jewish state. But the hearts and minds of Israelis were won when President Obama addressed one thousand young Israelis in a public speech at the Jerusalem Convention Center, saying in Hebrew, "*Atem lo lavad . . .* you are not alone."

In listening to that speech and joining the President of the United States in a foreign country, my heart was bursting with pride as an American, as I witnessed the response of Israelis to our President. As a Jew, I was so proud to be in Israel, to hear our President speak with feeling about the historic, unbreakable ties between our two countries. These ties date to the moment President Truman became the first leader to officially recognize Israel, only minutes after independence, to the close of President Obama's visit when he facilitated the reestablishment of diplomatic ties between Turkey and Israel, which had been in tatters for several years. What struck me about the trip was the President's desire, through the shaping of his itinerary, to stress the ancient connection of the Jewish people to the land, to look towards a hopeful future, and to highlight the historic security and intelligence cooperation between our two nations.

Like so many generations of Jewish mothers before me, I fiercely hope for peace between the Israelis and Palestinians so that mothers and fathers like my constituents, Sheryl and Tuly Wultz, are attending the "mitzvahs" in their children's lives rather than their funerals. Secretary of State John Kerry has made several trips to the Middle East since the President's trip. He testified before the House Appropriations Subcommittee on State, Foreign Operations (on which I sit as a member) that he believes there is a chance to make progress between the Israelis and the Palestinians and bring both sides back to the negotiating table. The United States must continue to serve as a catalyst toward peace. I'm proud we have a President who believes in that important role.

Just as the United States monitors global hot spots like the Middle East, it should look within itself to gauge how this nation's values are projected to the world. The Internet and other forms of modern media have made it possible to share American culture in an unprecedented way. People in less

open societies see the freedoms we enjoy in terms of speech and assembly—
and it makes them long for those same freedoms and privileges, to which
any human being should be entitled. It may even rouse them to demonstrate
against their leaders.

Residing in South Florida, representing Cuban American families in
my district and serving with Cuban American colleagues as a state legislator and member of Congress, I couldn't help but wonder how the Castro
regime reacted to the sight of dictatorships collapsing around the Middle
East and North Africa. Even more, I wondered what the Cuban people
would have thought of these events, had they been allowed to see them
unfold on the news and the Internet. In Cuba repression and limited access to information are the norm and only news approved by the Castro
government is allowed.

Even for leaders as entrenched as the Castros, however, it is no longer
possible to entirely control the media message, in which the United States
is cast as the villain. We have made efforts to get information to Cubans
suffering under the Castro regime through the funding of Radio Martí
and Televisión Martí in Miami, as well as through legitimate educational
outreach exchanges and funding of civil society programs.

Americans have continued to debate whether the United States should
lift or continue the economic embargo we've had in place for more than
fifty years. The U.S. embargo alone has not been effective in bringing
about the desired result of toppling the Castro brothers from power and
bringing about democratic reforms like those we've seen in the Middle
East and North Africa. But that certainly doesn't mean that lifting the
sanctions completely will achieve this objective, as some argue. That
notion is based on a misperception of what U.S. sanctions are designed
to do.

In short, we need a carrot-and-stick approach. Foreign nations must
earn the right to have a relationship with America, and at a minimum,
those nations should be respectful of their people's civil rights. When
you throw critics of the government in jail, as occurs in Cuba, you as a
nation fail that test. President Obama, while supporting the embargo, eased
sanctions in the hope of the Castro regime reaching back across the

Florida Straits to begin, even slowly, to take steps toward democratic and economic reform. Instead, the Castro regime responded by cracking down on family members of Cuban dissidents who had the courage to publicly demonstrate for Cubans' rights. An American, Alan Gross, was arrested, imprisoned, and sentenced to fifteen years simply for working in Cuba's tiny Jewish community, distributing cell phones and laptops. He remains in a Cuban prison today, in spite of his deteriorating health and illness in his family.

If the United States acted to normalize economic relations with Cuba, without negotiating reform in exchange, the result would be the status quo on steroids, with the Castro regime enriching itself and prohibiting its citizens from enjoying the bounty that comes with free trade. This would further entrench the Castro regime, ensuring that it outlives both Fidel and Raúl.

With the embargo intact, coupled with continued funding of civil society groups organizing dissident activism, the demand for change will continue to grow in Cuba, until it finally becomes impossible for that regime to deny its people the freedom to which they are entitled.

The goal of American policy should be to bring about democratic and economic reform and restoration of basic human rights in Cuba, as we do around the world. As a general principle, investments we make in diplomacy today will result in less spending on military interventions in the decades to come, leaving more money to spend domestically. Our aim should be, as President Obama has said, "to focus on nation building here at home." In this fashion, the true source of America's superpower status would be its ability to inspire admiration from other countries, rather than fear. America must continue to be a superpower for peace.

This sentiment was most eloquently expressed by President John F. Kennedy, speaking at the 1963 ceremony honoring the poet Robert Frost. He said,

> I look forward to a great future for America, a future in which our country will match its military strength with our moral restraint, its wealth with our wisdom, its power with our

purpose.... And I look forward to an America which commands respect throughout the world not only for its strength but for its civilization as well.

Our children will grow up and live in a more globally connected world than ever before. Their ability to instantly communicate, at little to no cost, with anyone, anywhere in the world, will dramatically alter long-standing international relationships. With this increased exposure to foreign cultures, there is reason to hope that future generations will have a more nuanced understanding of global security matters, of our economy's role in the world, and of how our environmental policies affect other nations.

The promise of tomorrow, however, depends upon whether we can get through today. That's why when it comes to dealing with foreign policy matters, especially those with the potential to lead to wars and human suffering, I think it's helpful to imagine our children bearing witness, as they undoubtedly will in a high school history class, sooner or later. Imagine, too, how these pivotal votes and diplomatic meetings will be portrayed by the historians of other countries.

Let us never forget that our foreign policy decisions can lead to parents marching off to war and the impact a parent's death or injuries may have on the sons and daughters at home. To those who would take such a risk on our behalf, gratitude for their service is the least of our debt. We owe these brave men and women the guarantee that we will only ask them to go into battle when we are certain that it is the only way to protect our sovereign land from those who would do us harm.

The United States must be a force for good around the world, promoting democracy, speaking out against human-rights abuses, and acting as an honest broker between nations in disputes that could escalate into war. As a truly "exceptional" nation we must lead by example, treating others with the humility and respect which we expect in return.

———◇———

FIVE

We Know the Drill:
It's Time to Explore Alternatives

C hildren tend to think of the world in very simple terms. They have not lived long enough to understand what causes the environment to deteriorate, nor what geopolitical factors increase the price of gas and how that ripples through a national economy. They certainly can't comprehend the fierce resistance with which Big Oil lobbyists oppose environmental reforms. These considerations are not easy to grasp even to the most conscientious adults.

But children can distinguish between having resources and lacking them. They also know that one day they will be adults, and that the same earth that sustains their parents will have to sustain them and their children.

I was in sixth grade when I first developed my own consciousness about the politics of energy. It was 1978, and President Jimmy Carter had embarked on a public awareness campaign, beseeching Americans to be mindful of their fuel and energy usage. This was the domestic front of an international crisis, spurred by the cartel behavior of the Organization of the Petroleum Exporting Countries (OPEC), which had increased petroleum prices from $1.80 per barrel in 1971 to $13.54 in 1978. During the second oil crisis in 1979, triggered by the Islamic revolution in Iran, the price topped $40.00.

President Carter sought to instill in Americans the sense that they could each do their part to oppose the tyranny of OPEC by reducing the need for—and the waste of—energy from oil. My family did their part: I remember during that oil crisis sitting in sweltering heat in long lines for gas in my parents' car—a big Buick that probably got ten miles per gallon on a good day. We did our best to respond to the President, using that Buick as little as possible. We lived on Long Island in the town of Lido Beach and my father took the train every day into Manhattan, where he worked as the chief financial officer for a girls' clothing manufacturer, but my mom worked part-time at a local plant store. We needed the car as badly as any other suburban family.

At my school, Magnolia Open Elementary School in Long Beach, the teachers implemented an energy-savings program, which included lessons and classroom activities. Stickers were placed on all the light switches to remind people to turn them off. "Don't you know there's an energy crisis?" was the admonishment to anyone caught wasting gasoline or electricity. Frugality with energy was an expression of patriotism. In keeping with the spirit of the times, President Carter even had thirty-two solar panels installed on the White House roof so that they could be used for heating water, a gesture that he hoped would provide momentum toward his administration's goal of deriving 20 percent of America's energy needs from renewable sources.

Sadly, that commitment was not renewed by the next administration. President Ronald Reagan ripped those solar panels off the White House and slashed the Department of Energy's budget for developing sustainable energy. Recent estimates by the agency show that the United States gets only 7 percent of its energy supply from renewables. We didn't come close to President Carter's goal. The lack of urgency was also evident in automobile fuel standards, which were allowed to remain virtually stagnant for the thirty years after Carter left the White House. Recently though, the Obama administration has helped refocus the nation on fuel efficiency, establishing standards that would require U.S. cars to average 54.5 miles per gallon by 2025. But in the time it has taken for those standards to rise, carbon emissions have done incalculable damage to the atmosphere.

We have not come far enough in our pursuit of more sustainable energy sources. Consider the scale of our current petroleum habit. According to the U.S. Energy Information Administration, in 2011 we consumed 18.9 million barrels a day. That's nearly 25 percent of the world's consumption. We also use more electricity than any other nation: 4,105 billion kilowatt-hours of electricity a year. Coal and gas remain the primary methods for power plants to generate electricity, usage that inflicts a heavy toll on the environment and on our supply of fossil fuels.

As we deplete those natural resources, the energy crisis grows. The recent discovery of significant oil reserves in North America has done nothing to change the fact that the supply of fossil fuels will eventually be exhausted. It does not change the harmful effects that consuming those fuels has on our environment. Historically, economic growth has coincided with an increasing demand for fossil fuels. As those fossil fuels become more scarce the shortages will significantly inhibit economic growth, unless we prepare now by investing in alternatives.

I recognize the relationship between the availability of energy and economic growth—that if you don't have one, you can't have the other. But this is why it is so important to develop energy sources that are truly sustainable. By fully committing to this agenda, alternative energy can be the next great American industry, the source of innovation that will lead to scores of new jobs. In fact, thanks to the emphasis on sustainable energy in the American Recovery and Reinvestment Act, we're already headed in that direction.

Still, if we are to have any hope of following through on our intention to preserve the land, sea, and air for the next generation, we cannot lose momentum. We need to be united in our dedication to the environment, not just in support of responsible policies but in being conscious of how our individual energy habits affect the planet as a whole. As President Obama said during his January 2013 Inaugural Speech, "We will respond to the threat of climate change, knowing that the failure to do so would betray our children and future generations."

◆ ◆ ◆

I suppose that for all of us, the word "environment" brings up a distinct image, whether it's a lush forest, the foamy rapids of a river, or snow-capped mountains. When I think of the environment, I think of the Everglades, which lie just beyond the western border of my congressional district. On my many flights home, I'm reminded of their awesome expanse. From the sky, the "River of Grass" resembles a sea, with saw grass marsh lining the horizon in all four directions. The only marks of human civilization are a set of power lines and Alligator Alley, the long, lonely freeway that bisects these sprawling wetlands, connecting the cities in southeast and southwest Florida. As huge as this wetland mass is, it is also delicate. The plants and animals, whether rare or profuse, come together and exist in a unique world: orchids, cranes, spoonbills, wood storks, crocodiles and alligators (the only place in the world they coexist), and the symbol of the Everglades, the Florida panther. Among those animals that depend on the Everglades are millions of Florida residents, for whom the wetlands are the primary source of drinking water.

Over the past century, the Everglades have had to fend off wave after wave of human encroachment. The River of Grass has been drained, channeled, drilled, and developed. The most recent threat came in 2008, when rising gas prices inspired Republicans to craft a three-word solution: "Drill, baby, drill." Every inch of U.S. soil was in play for prospectors, including the Everglades.

Fred Thompson, the former Republican senator from Tennessee, was one of the first to endorse the idea of allowing heavy industry into this fragile ecosystem. Unfortunately, the notion did not perish with Thompson's 2008 presidential bid. It was revived by another ill-fated candidate, Representative Michele Bachmann, in advance of the 2012 election cycle. "The United States needs to be less dependent on foreign sources of energy and more dependent on American resourcefulness [sic]," said my arch-conservative congressional colleague from Minnesota. "Whether that is in the Everglades, or whether that is in the eastern Gulf region or whether that's in North Dakota, we need to go where the energy is." This crowd would rather chase the last drop of oil than think about a long-term energy strategy.

It's almost understandable that Bachmann would be cavalier about drilling in the Everglades, since she's not a Floridian. But to hear the same sentiment come from the Governor of Florida is almost too much. In the month following Bachmann's remarks, Rick Scott told a business group he was also open to the idea of drilling in the Everglades. That caused a public outcry and Scott tried to recant. I am proud of those who reacted to this threat. Still, that the Governor of Florida—who has a home in Naples, on the western border of the Everglades—would consider such a thing shows the difficulty we face in finding allies among the GOP. The "Drill, baby, drill" crowd also lusts for the oil reserves off the coast of my home state. This proposition presents more risks for Florida, considering our sun-worshipped beaches are a primary draw for our $65 billion tourism industry. An oil spill off our coast could result in billions of lost revenue, not to mention the damage it would inflict on Florida's ecosystem.

The British Petroleum oil rig explosion in April 2010 illustrated that point, causing 4.9 million barrels of oil (205.8 million gallons) to spill in the Gulf of Mexico. This spill was nineteen times larger than the *Exxon Valdez* spill in 1989 that was a flash point for many in my generation. The Deepwater Horizon spill coated the coastlines of Louisiana, Mississippi, and Alabama, while Florida was partially spared only thanks to weather conditions and tidal patterns.

Besides, if my home state were to expand offshore drilling, it would be feeding a fossil fuel habit that is responsible for the carbon emissions that have led to global warming and the ensuing rise in sea levels, which is eating away at our land. The Army Corps of Engineers released a report in 2009 that predicted sea-level rise in southeastern Florida of three to seven inches by 2030 and two feet by 2060. One study, written by analysts at Tufts University, concluded the following:

> In Florida, the area vulnerable to 27 inches of sea-level rise, which would be reached soon after 2060 in the business

as-usual case, covers 9 percent of the state's land area, with a
current population of 1.5 million. In addition to residential prop-
erties worth $130 billion, Florida's 27-inch vulnerable zone
includes: 2 nuclear reactors; 3 prisons; 37 nursing homes; 68
hospitals; 74 airports; 82 low-income housing complexes.

Although I've never been to the Arctic National Wildlife Refuge, I
oppose drilling there for the same reason I oppose it near Florida. The
Arctic Refuge covers nineteen million acres in northeastern Alaska and
is home to hundreds of species, ranging from polar bears to lemmings to
terns. Two Native American tribes make their home there, the Inupiat
Eskimos near the coast and the Gwich'in Athabaskan Indians inland.
Drilling would have a destructive impact on an untouched natural environment, bringing with it industrial settlements and, of course, a pipeline. To produce oil there and then transport it back to refineries in the
contiguous states would disrupt the Arctic Refuge's wildlife. Moreover,
no one can guarantee that there would not be an oil spill. That would be
a true catastrophe, perhaps one with no return for the ecosystem.

That public officials are serious about exposing this exquisite, un-
trammeled terrain to the risk of oil spills suggests our desperation for fuel
is obscuring our obligation to preserve this nation's environmental trea-
sures. We should not threaten our most sensitive and precious natural
wonders in a chase after every last scrap of fossil fuels. As a mother, I feel
a duty to my three children and their peers to do all I can to ensure that
the Everglades, the Arctic National Wildlife Refuge, and other pristine
lands are off the table when it comes to oil and gas exploration.

To be clear: That doesn't mean we have to forsake America's energy
needs. We have the energy, waiting to be tapped. We must identify and
develop alternative sources of energy instead of investing in drills and
trampling over pristine environments. It's outrageous that from 2002 to
2008, when the scale of our environmental crisis was widely known, the
federal government gave $72 billion in subsidies to fossil fuel companies,

when only $29 billion in subsidies went toward propelling discovery of sustainable fuel sources. That imbalance suggests that lobbyists for Big Oil have succeeded in putting their interests before those of forward-thinking Americans. I have voted to cut subsidies to Big Oil and to scale back their tax breaks. We must continue to scale back subsidies to dirty fuel producers to show that we are serious about modernizing our energy policy. Our message must be crystal clear: Those companies that develop clean energy will be rewarded and those that insist on dirty energy will be left behind. Fortunately, the Obama administration is leading us in that direction. Between the federal stimulus package and other legislation with environmental impact, we will have spent over $150 billion on green initiatives in the five-year span from 2009 to 2014.

These struggles with energy have been with America for decades, changing very little from one generation to the next. Let's end that by passing on to our children a nation that has put the worst of its energy problems behind it, embarking on a new era where we can power our economy without jeopardizing the environment.

Even if we didn't face the specter of exhausting our supply of fossil fuels, it would still be necessary to wean ourselves off them, if only because we know that the use of carbon-laden fossil fuels is the major cause of pollution that contributes to global warming. It is silly, if not reckless, to treat global warming as a mere "theory" when over a stretch of more than thirty years, weather measurements have indicated an increase in global temperatures. Since the dawn of the industrial age, which brought about the burning of fossil fuels for energy, the volume of carbon dioxide in the atmosphere has increased by an astounding 40 percent. That pollution, along with dramatic increases in other gases associated with human activity, has altered the way that sunlight is absorbed in the atmosphere. All four federal agencies that study the earth's atmosphere agree that the earth is warming. At the same time, the scientific community agrees that there have been no significant changes in the sun's heat, nor in the reflectivity of the earth, leaving greenhouse gases as the only possible suspect.

The scurrilous campaign to deny global warming has slowed the

momentum needed to forge policies that will reduce our nation's depen-
dence on the fossil fuels that destroy the ozone and raise temperatures.
In Congress, the campaign of global warming denial is led by James Inhofe, Republican senator from Oklahoma. In 2003, Inhofe was quoted
saying, "The claim that global warming is caused by man-made emissions
is simply untrue and not based on sound science." As recently as 2010,
Inhofe countered global warming claims by asserting that the earth is
"going into a cooling period." His intent, I suspect, was to insulate the oil
industry from blame and from the financial losses that would come from
energy policy reform.

Whatever Inhofe's motives, the effect has been to cloud the minds of
voters. More than a third of adults, most of them self-described conservatives, think global warming can be ignored. Before we can hope to make
meaningful reforms, we must overcome this attitude of willful denial.

There is cause for optimism. Following the devastation of Superstorm Sandy, polls showed an overwhelming majority of Americans believed that climate change played a role in that and other extreme weather
events. Those findings marked a significant change since 2009, suggesting
that Republicans and independents are beginning to accept the reality of
global warming. Let's hope that this growing recognition can provide a
foundation for broader environmental reforms. Year by year, inch by
inch, we are losing the land we love. It may lack the spectacle of an armed
invasion, but the effect of our surrender is the same.

To have a chance of outpacing our current energy crisis, our nation must
have the same collective sense of purpose we had during other moments
of national crisis, from the energy crunch of the 1970s to the attacks on
the World Trade Center on 9/11. That may sound like a high-minded
goal, but I have unshakable faith in the will of the American people to
effect change on an issue that vexes them—and we get awfully irritated
by gas prices.

I remember talking with constituents at one of my town hall meetings
when gas prices were skyrocketing in 2008. Some would stand up and

share with me that the $60–$80 it was costing them to fill their gas tank meant they couldn't afford to drive to work. I remember one young mom telling me that the spike in gas prices meant that she couldn't afford the cost of her daughter's day care and thus couldn't go to work—she had no one to care for her child. Another constituent, who owned a small business that depended on driving its trucks to service customers, shared with me his frustration over having to lay off employees, despite expanding demand for his services.

So we're mad as hell, and we're not going to take it anymore. But we should channel that frustration toward the most practical goal: developing a balanced approach to meeting our energy needs, one where solar power, wind turbines, hydroelectric plants, and other alternative sources will provide a larger and larger share of our energy diet compared to oil and gas. For instance, consider the proposal to open new portions of the eastern Gulf of Mexico to oil drilling, which would potentially increase domestic production of oil by less than 5 percent. For an average family, the effect on the price of gas would be negligible, and we would have the burden of all the additional pollution that comes with burning that oil. On the other hand, if that same family responded to the rise of gas prices by prioritizing fuel efficiency in its next car, the family could save thousands of dollars over the lifetime of that car, while creating fewer carbon emissions.

These are the kinds of calculations that working families will be making in the years to come, and I have faith that they will choose the sensible route. As attitudes change across America, it will be necessary for those attitudes to change in Washington, as well.

As frustrated as I get with the lack of political will for green energy and reducing our environmental footprint, there are moments that give me hope that a culture change is within the grasp of this generation of lawmakers. In August of 2011, I traveled to Ames, Iowa, on behalf of the Democratic National Committee (DNC). The Republicans were staging a well-publicized straw poll, the first major political event of the presidential election cycle, and my job, as chair of the DNC, was to make sure that our side of the story would be written and talked about in the media. As I walked around the grounds of the convention center on the Iowa State University campus that was the site of the straw poll, I noticed a huge wind turbine set up in between the Republican candidates' tents in the parking lot. It had signatures all over it, freshly written in felt-tip pen. Standing on some steps leading up to the turbine, I noticed a Republican colleague of mine, Rep. Steve King (R-IA).

If you had to choose a Republican member of Congress more opposite from me on every major issue, Steve King would be the one. We actually have a very cordial relationship—at least until we talk in detail about issues. Many times on the House floor, I have heard Steve push for drilling with the same gusto as the most conservative members of his party. So as I approached the turbine, imagine my surprise when I saw that Steve was extolling the virtues of wind energy! Once I was close to the steps, Steve saw me in the crowd that had gathered and pulled me up on the platform with him. We had a good-natured laugh and together we put our signatures on the turbine. To see Steve in Washington, surrounded by lobbyists and fellow conservatives, you'd never know that his home state was the nation's number-one producer of wind energy. But when Steve is in Iowa, surrounded by the wind turbines that provide such an economic boost to his region, he's a forceful proponent of this alternative energy and the wind energy production tax credit that has added nearly seven thousand wind jobs, boosting Iowa's economy. As I traveled around Iowa that weekend, I noticed a great many farms with wind turbines stretching across their cornfields, and I remembered that age-old mantra from a former Speaker of the House, Tip O'Neill (D-MA): "All politics is local."

Politics is also the art of the possible. If Representative King, a rock-ribbed Republican, believes that wind energy is a viable alternative to our almost exclusive reliance on fossil fuels, then consensus really is possible. It's up to Democrats with a sincere interest in improving the environment to reach out to members of Congress like Steve King to build a coalition of the willing. When we do that, we'll truly have the wind at our backs!

I suspect that Democrats would have more luck recruiting Republicans if it weren't for the insidious influence of Big Oil lobbyists, who pour millions of dollars into GOP coffers and super PACs every election cycle.

The biggest petroleum company (and the most profitable corporation in the world), ExxonMobil, gives 90 percent of their campaign contributions to Republicans. For Chevron, it's 88 percent. The GOP gets 98 percent of the millions of dollars contributed by Koch Industries and the Koch brothers, whose conglomerate is largely devoted to petroleum refining.

I'm not so naïve as to believe that Republicans would walk away from these donations. Rather, my hope is that Republicans would recognize that continuing with our overdependence on fossil fuels is not in the long-term interests of the U.S. and join Democrats in pushing back on Big Oil so we can promote an all-of-the-above energy strategy that is more balanced between fossil fuel and renewable energy. Far from being "hostile" to business, as GOP critics claim, this presents spectacular opportunity for established energy providers to transition from dirty power to clean. Florida Power & Light (FPL) certainly took advantage of the trend, using the lure of its photovoltaic solar facility in DeSoto County, Florida, to land $200 million in Recovery Act funds to assemble a cleaner and more efficient energy grid. According to FPL figures, the DeSoto Next Generation Solar Energy Center produces enough power for 3,000 homes, avoiding some 575,000 tons of greenhouse gas emissions.

These are achievements that both parties should cheer. But we Democrats should have learned by now that it takes a great deal of finesse to bring Republicans aboard for environmental reforms. Certainly, we can't afford to repeat the mistake of failing to pass the American Clean Energy and Security Act of 2009. The legislation was a bold step in trying to reduce carbon emissions. If passed, it would have created millions of new, clean-energy jobs here in America; saved consumers hundreds of billions of dollars in energy costs; and enhanced America's energy independence, cutting foreign oil imports by five million barrels a day by 2030. All of which would have slowed the pollution associated with global warming. I supported it, as I would any responsible effort to shift America to self-reliance in meeting our energy needs.

The legislation called for "emissions trading," also known as "cap and trade"—a concept that was embraced and put forward by President George H. W. Bush in 1989 but is now anathema to most Republicans.

These measures were contained within the 1990 Clean Air Act, which passed the House 401–25 and the Senate 89–10, a show of bipartisan support that seems unimaginable in today's fiercely partisan climate. The legislation sought to reduce sulphur dioxide and nitrogen oxides, the pollutants associated with acid rain. For decades, those chemicals were belched from factories and power stations, producing acid rain that polluted waterways and caused health problems.

The Clean Air Act put a cap on the amount of pollutants that industrial facilities could expel. Factories were each granted the "right" to emit a certain quantity of pollution. Those rights could be used or they could be sold to industrial firms seeking to expand production. This cap-and-trade process yielded a 99 percent compliance rate, giving new life to damaged lakes and streams. Most significant, the reduction saved lives—in monetary terms, $70 billion in annual health-care costs.

Given that this was a proven way of addressing industrial-based pollution, it made sense to include cap-and-trade legislation in the 2009 bill to scale back carbon emissions. But like most regulations—even those that are motivated by a desire to preserve a public good like clean air—the bill offended conservatives' sensibilities about government involvement in the private sector. Despite a strong coalition of many large businesses, utilities, and environmental groups supporting the legislation, Republicans derided it as "anti-business," comprised of restrictions that would allegedly hurt profits during a difficult economic period.

Even though we managed to pass the bill in the House, there was an even bigger roadblock in the Senate, where Inhofe led the resistance. The Oklahoma senator dismissed the urgency of global warming—"alarmism," he called it. He suggested China go first in limiting emissions. Can you imagine? An elected official suggesting that America should follow rather than lead! The Senate didn't even hear the bill, largely because cap-and-trade legislation was considered toxic. It was a victory for the fossil fuel companies—the oil, natural gas, and coal industries—but not for Americans in general and certainly not for the next generation of Americans who will inherit our dwindling fossil fuel supply and earth's environment. It was also a disappointment for Speaker Pelosi who had hoped to make the legislation a signature issue of her tenure.

Still, it's a good thing that the American Recovery and Reinvestment Act (the stimulus bill) passed in February 2009, included a number of mechanisms for improving energy efficiency and developing alternative sources, as well as creating a large number of new, green-energy jobs. For example, the legislation paid for long-overdue improvements to an electric grid which would allow us to collect, possibly store, and distribute power from disparate sources. It made it possible for energy to be easily traded among a variety of suppliers, and the build-out would mean good jobs for construction workers, specialized electricians, physicists, and engineers. And the legislation provided $2.3 billion in tax credits for businesses and individuals that invested in energy-efficient technologies.

There is still much to be done. There is so much renewable energy available to America that isn't being fully utilized. In terms of the energy generated for electricity, 42 percent comes from power plants burning coal and 25 percent from plants burning natural gas—both are fossil fuels; 19 percent of our electricity is generated in nuclear power plants. Just 13 percent comes from the renewable forms of energy that need to be our emphasis, starting now. According to estimates by the U.S. Department of Energy, by 2030 wind alone could supply up to 20 percent of America's electricity needs with the installation of some 500,000 turbines.

Among other renewables, hydroelectric power can be harnessed efficiently; the concern is that it involves returning slightly warmer water to its original source, which can cause harm to fish, and the dams themselves can interfere with fish migration patterns. The lesson here is that all energy sources have some impact on the ecosystem—for each, we must go in with our eyes wide open and look for ways to mitigate the damage as much as possible. Bird migration paths are a consideration in the siting of wind farms, while solar farms must be located with an awareness for sensitive desert ecosystems.

There is no single source that will allow us to achieve sustainable energy independence. Rather, we must extract the most potential from a variety of sources. Wave and tidal energy have yet to be fully explored, and these have the benefit of being consistent and predictable. Solar power, in both photovoltaic and concentrated solar power forms, has yet to reach a fraction of its potential. Rapid advances in technology, combined with government/business collaborations like President Obama's SunShot Initiative, aim to make the cost of generating solar electricity on par with that of nonrenewable energy sources such as coal. If we were to meet that target, we would see solar generation of electricity move from .05 percent of the current electricity supply to roughly 14 percent by 2030 and 27 percent by 2050.

These are all examples of cleaner, job-creating alternatives to oil. If we really commit to these renewable sources of American energy, we will create thousands and thousands of new jobs. We could employ Americans in the fields of engineering, construction, installation, and maintenance— jobs that can't be outsourced to other countries. Just imagine a future where solar panels to power your entire home are as inexpensive and as easy to buy as a refrigerator or washing machine. It would be so profoundly satisfying if in thirty years we could look back and say that we recast the world for our children, that we made it cleaner and, in terms of energy, more sustainable. We could know that we freed ourselves from the moral complications that come with buying energy from countries who have a less than stellar record of protecting human rights. To take these worries off the table would be a great favor to our children.

For all this talk of renewable energy, even Democrats like myself realize that we're many years away from replacing fossil fuels as our leading source of energy. We cannot become a renewable energy–based nation overnight. While we should invest in the technologies to make this conversion as quickly as possible, until the technologies are mature and cost-competitive with traditional nonrenewable energy sources, we will need to move toward the all-of-the-above energy strategy, called for by President Obama.

Unfortunately, the more delay there is in the implementation of clean energy, the more rapacious the proponents of fossil fuels become. Our mission today is to liberate the next generation from the burden of an energy-versus-environment contest. The problems we talk about now ought to be solved by the time the children of today are adults. If we succeed, today's children will still have some of the most stunning places on earth to hand down to their own children.

Weaning this country off oil will take decisions that people thought were too tough to make when I was a child in the 1970s and 1980s. Energy independence could be our next space-age challenge. I know that we can make the necessary decisions, but we need members of Congress to be willing to put politics aside and support policies that push innovation, efficiency, and sustainability. We need fossil fuel industry executives to be willing to make some hard choices to curb their industries' impact. These executives need to be willing to evolve. Most important, we need everyday Americans to make a commitment to energy efficiency in their homes and businesses, which will increase the demand for production of alternative energy products. Making this shift will ensure that Americans don't face a crisis when—inevitably—our fossil fuel supplies run dry, leaving our children to face an energy and environmental crisis that was entirely avoidable.

The United States is full of citizens who care: intelligent men and women who are dedicated to finding a sustainable solution to our energy needs. This is our chance to create a new energy lifestyle for the twenty-first century, to start putting oil and other finite fossil fuels in our rearview mirror, where they belong.

SIX

Infrastructure Powers
Economic Growth

Virtually every job in the American economy depends on our nation's infrastructure. That infrastructure takes many forms: It's the electric grid that delivers power to homes and businesses as well as the fiber-optic connections that provide high-speed Internet service, connecting cyber-commuters to their coworkers and clients. It's the clean water that comes into your home, as well as the sewers that whisk away your wastewater. We rely on roads and shipping ports to bring consumer goods to market and as a way for our goods to reach buyers. In short, infrastructure is the very foundation of our economy—and it's crumbling before our eyes.

That's because in recent years we have failed to maintain and modernize the existing components of that infrastructure. Unfortunately, we don't recognize the importance of our infrastructure until the moment it fails. This is that moment.

If we don't appreciate the need to modernize our infrastructure already, then we can expect reminders that are increasingly dramatic in nature. Cars will hit potholes and get snagged in traffic. Planes will be stuck on runways or circling interminably for clearance to land. Bridges will weaken, then collapse. Levees will be breached. Underground gas lines will explode. These calamities are avoidable, but only if we stop procrastinating and take action.

We can all relate, on some level, to the irritations that come from an overwhelmed infrastructure. For example, on days when I'm in my congressional district, I may be in Miami at the end of the day, making it necessary to brave the I-95 rush-hour commute north to my family's suburban home in Weston. The odds of being able to make that thirty-five-mile drive in less than ninety minutes are slim to none, because we have failed to make investments in our transportation infrastructure. As a result, that time is lost to me, just as it's lost to the millions of other American workers who are less productive and waste natural resources due to the necessity of commuting. Of course, the most frustrating aspect of that gridlock is that it's time I can't spend with my husband and children. It means I miss something with them or my time with them is truncated, whether it's dinner, helping with homework, or even making it home before they go to sleep. I suspect that every American has stories like this from his or her own life. In a subtle way, the shortcomings of infrastructure detract from the American quality of life, which may have a deleterious effect on how productive we are when we work.

It doesn't have to be that way for the next generation of American workers. The investments we make in infrastructure today will have a multiplying effect in the future, allowing for more jobs and productivity, which is necessary for competing in the twenty-first-century marketplace. In the course of making those improvements, we will guarantee our children will be safer when they travel and that they're less vulnerable to the flooding, power outages, and other unnatural disasters that occur when infrastructure fails. To be sure, these long-overdue improvements will be costly; but those costs must be considered next to the priceless value they create for the country.

Infrastructure has always played a pivotal role in American growth. In the first half of America's nineteenth century, the construction of the

Erie Canal in New York State hastened the Western expansion of the nation. That course was made complete in 1869 when the final spike was driven home in the transcontinental railroad. In the 1930s, the construction of the Hoover Dam recast the Southwest as the home of agriculture and big cities. One of the boldest public works projects in world history remains the Dwight D. Eisenhower System of Interstate and Defense Highways, which commenced in 1956. In the decades since, our country has invested in an increasingly sophisticated array of communications technology, from fiber-optic networks to radio wave technology and satellites.

This infrastructure forms the backbone of the American economy, allowing for efficiencies without which commerce would slow to a crawl. Our children's future will depend in large part on whether that infrastructure fosters innovation. We may not always know what's around the bend, but we can safely predict that in twenty years American jobs will be more closely connected to international markets. Our nation will be increasingly in competion with other nations, and capital will flow in the direction of the country that has a more positive environment for job creation.

Our generation's responsibility has been to maintain that infrastructure and to make technological improvements that will ensure economic growth in the future. Yet we are not doing a very good job: The evidence is everywhere. There are bottlenecks on federal highways that force commuters to inch back and forth to and from work. Urban intersections turn into parking lots in all four directions. Rolling blackouts will be more common as we put off modernizing our electric grid, while the failure of sewer systems has the potential to spread illnesses like hepatitis and cholera.

The American Society of Civil Engineers (ASCE) acts as a monitor in this respect, grading the state of U.S. infrastructure across fifteen categories: aviation, bridges, dams, drinking water, energy, hazardous waste, inland waterways, levees, public parks, rail and trains, roads, schools, solid waste, transit, and wastewater. The engineering analysts gave our country's infrastructure a D as in "deteriorating."

If I had received a D in my school days, I would have been answering to my parents. They would have asked me: Did you do your best work? Maybe that's the question we should ask ourselves.

We can agree that bridges are vital to our transportation needs. In California, 13 percent of the total 24,557 bridges have been deemed "structurally deficient" by the Department of Transportation. Another 16 percent are "functionally obsolete" (past their intended longevity or carrying traffic loads for which they weren't designed). The tally in Pennsylvania is even worse. Fully 26 percent of the state's 22,359 bridges are structurally deficient. Another 16.5 percent are obsolete. Nationwide, 11.5 percent of all bridges are structurally deficient and 13 percent are functionally obsolete.

Crossing a bridge shouldn't be a risky venture. One bridge rated as "structurally deficient" on the Department of Transportation's list carried traffic on Interstate I-35W in Minneapolis. That bridge collapsed in August 2007, killing 13 people and injuring more than 140. While the annual list was being compiled, the Schoharie Creek Bridge on the New York State Thruway collapsed. All of the 9 people whose cars flew off the broken roadway died.

Engineers who designed levees, buildings, and power plants in the twentieth century could not have anticipated the force of weather systems made more intense by climate changes. Hence the widespread devastation that followed Hurricane Katrina, and more recently Superstorm Sandy.

Flying has also become more dangerous with each passing year that we fail to modernize the air traffic control systems in our nation's airports. With air traffic controllers overworked and using antiquated technology, it is only a matter of time before a spectacular tragedy. This trend is reflected in the Federal Aviation Administration (FAA) statistics of "runway incursions," defined as any incident where an aircraft, vehicle, person, or object on the ground creates the risk of a collision. In fiscal year 2012, the FAA tracked 1,032 such incidents, a nearly 10 percent increase since 2011. That's a new record.

"As much as 60 percent of the productivity slump in the United States can be attributed to neglect of our core infrastructure," according to the late David Aschauer, former senior economist of the Federal Reserve Bank of Chicago, who studied the slide in U.S. worker productivity in the last part of the twentieth century. "New highways allow faster transportation of goods from factory to market," he explained.

To pay for the repairs and expansion of those highways, there is a fuel tax of 18.4 percent per gallon—this is the Highway Trust Fund. But the rising costs of fuel have caused Americans to drive less, meaning they're purchasing less gas. As fuel economy standards for American cars rise in years to come, tax revenue for the Highway Trust Fund will be reduced. Going forward, we will have to identify new funding for this critical resource.

Commerce depends not just on highways but on ports, and with two major ports in or adjacent to my congressional district, I'm particularly concerned about deteriorating conditions. Currently, we have earmarked only about half of what is necessary to pay for repairs to these aging structures. Given the trillions of dollars flowing through ports each year, these arteries must not be clogged, or else there will be dire economic consequences. As ports slow down, the costs of shipping will increase and so will the prices of consumer goods. Most critical, perhaps, U.S. products will struggle to compete in a global market with nations who have invested in infrastructure.

The annual Global Enabling Trade Report analyzes the capacity of nations around the world to smoothly facilitate trade across borders. In just two years between reports, from 2010 to 2012, the United States slipped from number nineteen in the report's Enabling Trade Index to number twenty-three, a "downward trend" that the report's authors attributed to America's "deteriorating infrastructure."

America must also be on the vanguard of commercial spaceports. Companies around the world will pay handsomely for the chance to launch satellites, and thanks to NASA, the United States has a wealth of experienced workers and infrastructure. But if we don't move fast, we'll lose ground to international competition. The state of Florida, for instance, is seeking to develop shuttle launch pads and a shuttle runway on land owned by NASA, just north of the Kennedy Space Center's launch pads in Cape Canaveral. If space is truly "the final frontier," then we have a head start, but other nations are making up ground fast—in 2010, Russia invested $800 million in a commercial spaceport in the nation's far eastern region. The Baikonur Cosmodrome, a launch facility in Kazakhstan leased by Russia, is already performing commercial missions. With ten of those launches in 2011, Russia captured 56 percent of the commercial market worldwide, according to an FAA report. European nations lanched four commercial missions, while China had two. All four of the commercial launches planned in the United States that year were delayed. In 2012, Russia had seven commercial launches while Europe had six and America had just two.

The scale of the infrastructure challenges can be daunting. The way I look at it, we should approach our infrastructure needs the way a family might sit down at the kitchen table to discuss a big but necessary expense. Let's figure out what it will cost, then how we're going to find money for it.

In the fall of 2009, a group of eighty transportation experts gathered at the University of Virginia with these very questions in mind. Based on their analysis, the United States ought to spend around $262 billion annually to improve roads, railways, and air travel infrastructure through 2035.

For the time being, however, there is a large gap between what we need to spend and the political will to spend it. When the President submits his budget he knows that it must go before a Republican-controlled House, where House Budget Committee chairman Paul Ryan and his Tea Party allies want to cut—not raise—spending on infrastructure. In fact, scaling back improvements to our nation's transportation infrastructure accounts for roughly 25 percent of the $2.2 trillion in spending cuts Ryan envisions over the decade to come. That is completely irresponsible. The ASCE estimates that the failure to improve our transportation and communication networks would cause the loss of 870,000 jobs by 2020 and a forfeiting of $3.1 trillion in infrastructure-dependent economic growth. In other words, spending billions today will reap trillions tomorrow.

I'm simply mystified that my Republican colleagues fail to realize that their lack of investment in America's infrastructure jeopardizes the future of the American economy. They say that spending on highway projects and other assorted infrastructure needs is "wasteful," but that analysis ignores the job creation that comes with the spending, not to mention the efficiencies that businesses enjoy from a well-functioning infrastructure that can get our economy in the fast lane. If they think these costs can be borne by state and local governments, they're mistaken. I'm reminded of a particularly outrageous example that occurred in Florida, where the federal government had offered through the Recovery Act to provide $2.4 billion in funding for a high-speed rail line, first between Orlando and Tampa and eventually to Miami.

Considering that tourism is the state's number-one industry, a high-speed train would take visitors to regions all over the state. Today, someone who comes to Florida primarily to visit Walt Disney World wouldn't necessarily get in the car and drive three and a half hours to Sawgrass Mills mall in Sunrise, a leading destination that happens to be in my congressional district. But if Sawgrass Mills was at the other end of a 170-miles-per-hour trip on high-speed rail, suddenly that becomes a more attractive option. And the increase in economic activity would bring more jobs.

This is a decision that has ramifications for decades to come. Super-fast trains would not only boost job creation now and in the future, they would reduce pollution from cars and improve quality of life for residents who make frequent trips between the state's major metropolitan areas. According to the projections of independent firms that studied the project, the project would have generated roughly $30 million in profits by its tenth year of operation. In government we constantly look for win-win propositions. They don't come along often. High-speed rail in Florida was not only that, it was a win-win-win-win.

Only one thing kept it from becoming a reality: Florida Governor Rick Scott, who was conscious of appeasing his Tea Party supporters and prioritizing a "my way or the highway" approach to governing. Governor Scott rejected the funding for high-speed rail, effectively destroying the ambitious plan. The public explanation he offered was that the cost and ridership projections were not reliable, and he predicted that Florida taxpayers would be on the hook for any cost overruns. Scott rejected the plan even after the private sector and municipalities committed to cover overruns, if there were any. Not even the House Transportation and Infrastructure Committee chairman John Mica (R-FL) could convince Scott that he was making a colossal mistake. Later, it was revealed that the information on which the Governor supposedly based his decision was faulty. He rejected the high-speed rail funding for two reasons: because it was offered by President Obama and because he could.

Due to Scott's shortsightedness, my state will be left behind as others develop a nationwide network of high-speed rail lines. In Texas, rails would take riders from San Antonio through Austin to Dallas and on to Oklahoma City and Tulsa. Five lines would lead into Chicago, the nation's historical railroad hub. The passengers who take those trains will relieve overcrowding at the nation's airports and highways. Florida is considering privately funded ventures for a commuter train between Orlando and Miami, but concerns remain about whether those trains can deliver reliable service and whether the train horns will make it necessary to construct "quiet zones"—expenses that could fall to taxpayers.

Infrastructure needs are too important to be treated with corner-cutting political maneuvering. As we postpone these improvements, we make it harder for farmers and other businesses to get their products to market. Our workforce gets mired in traffic jams and potholes. Bridges will be closed due to structural instability, with no replacements in the pipeline.

That's not the America I want my children to inherit. The people of this country must rally to the cause of these important investments. That ground-swell will give me and my fellow Democrats the political momentum we need to address these long-term threats to our nation's economic vitality.

Despite this admittedly bleak portrait of our country's current infrastructure, I'm hopeful because I know America has pride in its role as the world's leading innovator. We will not lose that status without a fight.

It was Americans, for instance, who conceived of a train that would use magnets to actually levitate above the rail, then move at speeds in excess of 300 mph. Those Americans campaigned tirelessly to install this technology in an American city, but there were no takers. Japan was the first to implement maglev, which can now be found in Shanghai as well.

It goes to show that when we're presented with an opportunity to make a technological improvement that will bring jobs and increase workers' productivity, we have to jump on it.

The NextGen system of airplane route and traffic control is one such opportunity. It is a sophisticated network that would link airports around the country, allowing air traffic controllers and jet pilots the ability to orient themselves according to satellite technology. Currently, most airplanes use World War II–era radio technology, flying over radar towers as a way to ensure constant communication with air traffic controllers. Since these often require planes to take indirect routes between destinations, time and fuel are wasted. NextGen is a superior way of directing air traffic on the ground, too, meaning that air travelers will get to the gate faster, and they'll be safer while taxiing.

This may seem like a high-tech luxury we can ill afford during difficult economic times, but implementation would be an important step in broadening the economic base. According to FAA projections, NextGen's full installation will make it possible for there to be 60,000 flights per day by 2030, up from 43,000 per day in 2010. Flights that are shorter in terms of time and distance will deliver a projected $123 billion in savings by 2030. There are so many businesses that require workers to fly, it follows that the more of those business people we can get in the air, the more the firms can hire. Infrastructure-minded Democrats like myself were frustrated in April 2012 when House Republicans made $4 billion in cuts to the FAA, which will slow the implementation of NextGen significantly. But we will continue to fight for this long-overdue upgrade in air travel technology. As my colleague Rep. Alcee Hastings (D-FL) remarked at a meeting with air traffic controllers we both attended, the name of the system should be WhenGen, as in the only relevant question is, when will we get it?

President Obama's American Jobs Act of 2011 included an investment in infrastructure that would have added funds for repairing bridges and roads, improvements that would have meant good-paying jobs for thousands of unemployed construction workers. It also included a provision for railroad improvement, for both freight and passenger trains—rails being another example of an infrastructure investment that directly helps business. Unfortunately, the Republicans refused to even take it up in the House. Hopefully, we will make another bid in the 2013 congressional session, but more Republican resistance is likely.

There is, however, some hope for a bipartisan commitment to infrastructure improvements. In July 2012, Republicans worked with congressional Democrats and the President on House Resolution 4348, which reauthorized some $105 billion in funds for highway improvement, among other infrastructure needs. To their credit, some GOP members recognized that the highways of this country connect our businesses to one another, and the better condition they're in the more smoothly commerce can flow. My cynical opinion is that if it were not an election year, this legislation likely would not have gotten done. The Republican Conference in the House has too many Tea Party–affiliated members who have a belief that we should dramatically—and I think dangerously—cut spending.

To ensure that water flows in and out of U.S. homes, Democrats will also make a concerted effort to upgrade water management and treatment facilities across the country. The ASCE report found that it will take $11 billion annually to replace facilities that provide drinking water. Sewer systems that have suffered from neglect discharge billions of gallons of untreated wastewater into U.S. surface water every year, meaning our lakes and rivers will continue to get more polluted and less safe for swimmers until we repair and replace the sewers.

As with so many aspects of the nation's infrastructure, there are components that have a huge impact on American lives but which are practically invisible to those who have the most to lose. For instance, towns and cities that border rivers are protected by thousands of dams, quietly doing their job far upstream from residents. ASCE engineers found 1,819 dams present a "high hazard" for failure. To ship material around inland waterways, barges must move through a locks system to avoid waterfalls and rapids. Incredibly, we are still using thirty locks that were built during the 1800s, and they're in desperate need of an upgrade.

So much of America's identity is found in the rural communities and sparsely populated countryside. These families may enjoy a more rustic way of life, but they at least need to have the opportunity to participate in basic modern technology like high-speed Internet and cell phone connections. Otherwise, those villages will continue to lose residents, and conversely, our major cities will grow even more crowded.

For folks who live year-round in rural areas, it can be hard to coordinate a meeting with a business owner whose main point of contact is a cell phone. Rural residents often wait hours for service calls from businesses unable to reach their technicians for an update on their whereabouts and timing because cell phone service is so spotty. It's also a potentially dangerous situation in an emergency.

The American Recovery and Reinvestment Act contained a $7.2 billion investment for expanding access to broadband service in locations where it didn't yet exist, but more connectivity will be needed.

That effort will bring broadband Internet access to remote locations like the Navajo Nation, in the American Southwest, where some 60 percent of residents lack telephone service. In upstate New York, Recovery funds are paying for the construction of a 1,500-mile fiber network that will serve 70 rural communities and deliver reliable access to 38,000 businesses. Thanks to these investments, children in these areas can enroll in distance learning programs—a rapidly growing field that will only become more prominent in a twenty-first-century economy.

As President Obama said during his January 2011 State of the Union address, "This isn't about faster Internet or fewer dropped calls. It's about connecting every part of America to the digital age."

In that same speech, the President talked about a "Sputnik moment." Of course, it's a reference to the 1957 launch of the Soviet orbiter that suggested the United States was falling behind in science and technology. That event was a challenge to American pride and added new urgency to the task of educating our youth, engineering scientific discovery, and exploring our solar system. That urgency is lacking today, and Obama exhorted us to recover it so that once again we could "out-educate, out-innovate, and out-build the rest of the world."

Before long, there will be a Sputnik moment in infrastructure. I hope that moment comes by virtue of greater awareness—Americans who are fed up by the inconveniences that come with an overwhelmed transportation system and an incomplete communication network.

But I fear that it will take a catastrophe of epic proportions. The levees that failed during Hurricane Katrina in 2005 nearly destroyed the city of New Orleans and left hundreds of thousands of residents homeless. But that disaster did not create urgency for improvements across other infrastructure fields. In 2007, the collapse of the I-35W bridge in Minneapolis was not dramatic enough to make highway funding a top priority in 2008 congressional races. Nor did the September 2010 explosion of a natural gas pipeline in San Bruno, California, create urgency to invest in making our fuel delivery systems safer.

It's really very simple. We pay a modest amount now for infrastructure improvements, or we pay a massive amount later. And if we wait till later, we may also be paying in lives lost.

Let's be a more forward-thinking society. It's no fun to pay taxes and we need to be careful not to spend more than we take in, but like that family sitting at their kitchen table, we need to plan for our needs. In doing so, we should be mindful that in exchange we will be safer, enjoying more economic security and a better quality of life.

SEVEN

Kids Learn Best
When Parents Teach First

To the parents of school-age children, it probably seems like government is constantly tinkering with education—how to fund it, how to structure the curriculum, how to measure achievement, how to structure the right framework for accountability. And they're right. As an elected official who has a say in national education policies, and who happens to have three school-age kids of her own in public school, as well as representing tens of thousands of families with children, I am deeply concerned about our ability to, in the words of President Obama, "out-educate, out-innovate, and out-compete" the rest of the world. Today's schools still struggle to generate involvement from parents, wrestle over how to measure teacher performance, produce test scores that reveal knowledge gaps, and fail to equip their pupils with the skills they need to excel in college or their chosen path in life.

But the solution may be closer than we realize. There are so many inspirational stories of programs that individually have managed to overcome the same obstacles that seem to cause failure in schools collectively.

It gives me hope to hear about Breakthrough Saint Paul, for instance, where low-income students, many of whom come from single-parent households, are literally leaping out of their beds in the morning, looking forward to that day's classes, focused from the age of twelve on earning a scholarship for college so they can get a degree in a field of study that fascinates them.

A similar group of kids from mostly low-income families with single parents is thriving in Greenville, South Carolina, thanks to a summer program called Bridges to a Brighter Future. Every enrolled student has graduated high school and 92 percent have gone to college. A student named Desiree came from a family that was homeless, living from the money they made picking tomatoes at a farm. Thanks to the confidence and study habits she says she learned at Bridges, Desiree was accepted at Winthrop University, where she planned to pursue a teaching degree. Those programs got results with hundreds of kids; Education is Freedom achieves success for thousands of kids every year in the Dallas Independent School District, where 87 percent of the students are low-income. Of those 2,400 kids who voluntarily joined the program and graduated in 2011, 93 percent were accepted into college, and together they raised $7.7 million in scholarships to pay their tuition.

These were three of the programs selected for closer inspection by the Educational Policy Institute, which was seeking a "blueprint" for effective education practices that could be replicated at other schools. In the institute's report, released in April 2012, it found that a key to the programs' results was their "intrusive" approach to keeping in close contact not only with the enrolled students but with their parents, ensuring that the family sincerely believed in the child's ability to succeed and that the school was an extension of the family.

Unfortunately, not every parent can enroll their child in one of these exciting programs. And many parents are balancing work schedules, but they need to take it upon themselves to be intrusive: Talk to the teachers about how you can help with homework. Volunteer at school activities. If your child is struggling, request a parent-teacher conference, no matter what grade your child is in. And seek out elected officials, including members of the school board, to make sure they share your commitment to improving education. Finally, take every opportunity to learn more about the educational agenda of your school district's superintendent, as well as the principal of your children's school.

Parents have every right to demand more from an education system that, too often, treats children as if they're faceless products on the assembly line of some giant factory, which is the grim legacy of No Child Left Behind. Rather, we should strive to tailor the education system, as well as a child's education, so that it fits the individual student.

No matter how wrongheaded some of today's education policies may be, I have no doubt that informed parents can be agents of change, compelling policymakers to establish a more coherent agenda that more fully maximizes the potential of American children, giving them enrichment at every level of their education until the moment they accept a diploma and join this nation's modern workforce.

Before we consider the finer points of that agenda for change, let's look into how the U.S. education system came into its current state. Mostly, today's public schools are the product of education reformers who believed standardized test scores were the best way to measure a school's success and who doubted that public schools with unionized teachers could ever measure up. Little consideration was given to parents. In essence, teachers were the quarterbacks, students were the players, and parents could do little more than watch from the stands, hoping their kids put big numbers on the scoreboard.

I was still in the Florida Legislature in the mid-1990s when charter schools were considered the best hope for closing the achievement gap between poorer, disadvantaged students and those in the middle class. The architects of the charter school idea believed that public school districts were a tangled bureaucracy obsessed with self-preservation and hostile to the boldest innovations in teaching. A key component of most charter schools was the hiring of non-union teachers, which made it possible for school administrators to avoid hiring teachers who were supposedly being protected by the union. Whereas traditional schools were administered by the district, charter schools could be run by nonprofit organizations and for-profit companies that received funding from the state, with discretion for how those funds should be spent. Because parents were given the right to pursue charter school enrollment for their children, reformers hoped to compel the traditional public schools to make improvements necessary for keeping pace with the quality education available at the charters.

Although I am not opposed to charter schools as a method of giving parents more choices, the original argument made for their necessity was specious. For one thing, teacher unions were not the major obstacle to innovation and reform. Their ranks have always been filled with talented, self-sacrificing individuals who do their best to educate children under less-than-ideal circumstances. The argument made by charter school advocates around the country has been that removing curriculum, wage, and hour requirements in a charter school would allow innovations that would improve student test scores. But changing the method of teaching, restructuring the curriculum, or reducing the wages of the teaching staff doesn't change the circumstances the child has at home. The school environment might be even worse at charter schools, considering the staff often doesn't have the same job protection as at traditional public schools. At traditional schools, tax dollars are invested in school services. It follows that companies who seek to wring profits from charter schools would have to earn them by withholding services. There is nothing to ensure a minimum level of quality or consistency. In those instances where charter schools do succeed in recruiting the best and brightest kids from the traditional school, there is the danger that the exodus will cause the traditional school's test scores to get worse as a result. This might then lead to more parents pulling out their kids, just as depositors rush a failing bank. It takes the school in the wrong direction. A struggling school should get intensive assistance in addition to accountability measures to help the school improve. A carrot-and-stick approach is always better than just the stick.

Too often, charter schools create only an illusion of success. They have largely failed to attract more talented teachers or to make good on their goals for improving efficiency in education. For example, based on the most recent National Assessment of Educational Progress (NAEP) test, also known as the Nation's Report Card, charter school students on average scored lower than their peers in traditional public schools. In Chicago, where the struggles of inner-city schools are well chronicled, there wasn't a single charter that ranked among the top forty elementary schools in Illinois Standard Achievement Test scores in 2011, despite charters having adopted test scores as the measuring stick for their success. To be sure, there are excellent charter schools, but those are no more common than excellent traditional schools.

In my home state of Florida, education has long been a tug of war between Democrats, who want to strengthen public schools by giving them a larger portion of the state budget, and Republicans, who would effectively starve the public schools through funding cuts and by giving parents vouchers they can spend on private schools, where low-income students would retain the same set of complex challenges they've traditionally faced in a public school setting.

The modern era of this rivalry began in 2001 with President George W. Bush's burdensome education reform, the No Child Left Behind Act. This legislation had a promising name, and perhaps a noble goal, but it was based on a fundamental misunderstanding about how to achieve success and measure educational progress.

Under the pretext of what President Bush called "accountability," students in public schools were compelled to take standardized tests, like the Florida Comprehensive Assessment Test (FCAT). Based on those students' performances, schools were assigned letter grades, which were then made public. Schools that failed to demonstrate "adequate yearly progress" were punished in a variety of ways, including the possible termination of the principal and teachers, and even closure.

With so much riding on one exam, school administrators had every reason to demand that teachers abandon more creative lesson plans in favor of drills proven to boost test scores, no matter how stultifying those drills might be for all involved. Desperate schools channeled their resources away from any subject that didn't directly impact students' scores on standardized tests. The casualties were courses like physical education and electives like art and music in grade school. In high schools, drama, business, and foreign language classes perished. Within the course of a school day that may seem long to antsy schoolchildren and adolescents, those elective courses offered variety, as well as the opportunity to identify unknown talents that might help students decide on their future career. Those elective classes are often the only thing holding a student's interest to prevent them from dropping out.

Undoubtedly, President Bush was influenced by his brother Jeb Bush, the Florida governor who touted the so-called "A+ Plan for Education." It was an unimaginative mix of standardized testing, vouchers, and "merit pay" for teachers whose students achieved higher test scores. The private school voucher program in the A+ Plan was a stick-only approach to school improvement, which is why I vehemently opposed it during my time in the state legislature. After a school received a failing grade for three years in any four-year period, the parents of students in the school could receive a voucher for the full-time equivalent (FTE) funding for their child and use it to pay the tuition at any private school. There were no standards required, no testing or follow-up to see if the private school was serving the student any better than their public school. No prohibition on utilizing the voucher for religious instruction and no requirement that the private school accept the voucher as full tuition payment. The pitfalls to this approach were massive and ultimately, after a major constitutional legal battle, the Florida Supreme Court declared the Jeb Bush voucher program unconstitutional because it violated the Florida Constitution's prohibition on spending public dollars on religious education.

As vouchers were being debated in Florida, Republican governors and legislatures were continually cutting education funding. This, plus Florida's massive population growth, made it necessary for schools to increase class size.

Around the same time, my husband and I were agonizing over the decision of where to send our children. On one hand, we wanted to express faith in our community's public education system. (We were both products of the public school system, including college and graduate school.) However, I was also extremely concerned about what these growing class sizes meant for the student-to-teacher ratio. Inevitably, the teacher could spend less time with individual students. Steve and I ultimately decided that, while we'd have to cut back on spending elsewhere, we would tighten our belts so we could send our kids to a local private school with a lower student-to-teacher ratio, allowing them to get more individualized attention.

We know that we were fortunate that as parents we could afford that option, but we also realize this is not an option for many parents. As a state legislator, I took what I'd learned from studying local options for our children and then I fought hard alongside former Congressman Kendrick Meek (D-FL) who was gathering signatures to qualify a constitutional amendment that would mandate public school classes adhere to strict limits per grade level. In 2002, Florida voters passed that amendment, over Jeb Bush's strenuous opposition. As a result, every family's children would have the benefit of a smaller class size.

Our decision on where to send our children to school changed as they got older and as our public schools began offering more academic and extracurricular opportunities. Our three children now attend public school. They are thriving and doing well, but every parent has to be engaged enough in their own child's education to know what is best for each child.

The adoption of the class-size amendment coincided with an improvement in a variety of important educational indicators, like the fourth-grade NAEP reading test. But other smart education policies, such as a state reading initiative and another state constitutional amendment creating universal pre-Kindergarten instruction for all four-year-olds surely also played a significant role.

In more recent years, parents have organized to oppose Bush-era education policies that are still being pushed by Republican legislatures like the one in Florida. I have been amazed by the impact of the Orlando-area moms who founded Fund Education Now in 2009, a response to spending cuts that made Florida schools plummet to fiftieth in per-pupil funding. Founders of this group went to Tallahassee in 2012 to lobby against the "parent trigger" bill that would enable parents with children at schools with low test scores to vote for the restructuring of those schools, including privatization. In effect, it would have given private charter school organizations incentive to launch smear campaigns against public schools, undermining them in the minds of parents. Thanks in large part to the efforts of Fund Education Now, the bill failed to win the last vote it needed to pass the Florida Senate, despite the lobbying of Jeb Bush himself. In fact, much of Jeb Bush's education legacy has been dismantled and discredited, with policies that had been adopted but later defeated in court. The parent trigger bill—now called Parent Empowerment in Education—was again passed by the Florida House in April 2013, but despite predictions of its passage into law, the bill was defeated once again in a 20–20 tie vote in the Florida Senate.

This proves that active, galvanized parents can make a significant difference when they intervene on behalf of their children's education. Currently, Fund Education Now is a plaintiff in a lawsuit that charges the Florida Legislature with failing to honor its constitutional commitment to provide a high-quality education to the state's families. I hope the courts agree with me that they have a persuasive case.

Momentum is now on the side of a new generation of reformers. Progress has been slow, but government has been learning from its mistakes—and it tends to learn extra fast when parents organize to bring an issue to politicians' attention.

It's great to see parents go on the attack against bad policy, but it's just as important for them to be aggressive in promoting policy that works. As a parent with her own personal stake in the way the government spends education dollars, it's my belief that we need to start children with a quality education in pre-Kindergarten and use incentives to encourage parents to have a larger role in the education system.

For this reason, I have long admired the work that occurs within Head Start programs serving impoverished neighborhoods of American inner cities. Paid for with $8 billion in annual federal funds, Head Start ensures access to early childhood education for families who qualify based on their low-income status. It's an opportunity for three- and four-year-old kids to adapt to a learning environment, interacting with trained teachers as well as children their own age. Just as important, it gets low-income parents in the habit of bonding with their children through education. Given what studies have told us about how early childhood education boosts children's cognitive and social development, it's essential that we protect Head Start's funding, as well as the Child Care and Development Block Grant, which provides a safe and nurturing environment for young children whose low-income working parents may not be readily available to participate in every aspect of their child's early learning.

I'm aware of the study released in 2011 by the Department of Health and Human Services examining the impact of Head Start. It found that, at the end of first grade, kids who had been enrolled in Head Start at age three showed only slightly better vocabulary than their peers. The analysts concluded that the program has a negligible effect on children's academic, socio-emotional, and health status.

Still, this only underscores the challenge that low-income students present to educators, and as long as programs like Head Start and the Community Development Block Grant make it possible for children to be among teachers and peers, we have the chance to improve the program so that it makes a bigger difference in their lives. There is no disputing the positive impact of early childhood learning on children from middle-class and wealthy families. Children from poor families deserve the same opportunity.

Another excellent program is the Home Instruction Program for Preschool Youngsters (HIPPY), which is a national program for training parents how to be their child's first teacher. HIPPY USA is a parent-involvement, school-readiness program that helps parents prepare their three-, four-, and five-year-old children for success in school and beyond. The parent is provided with a carefully developed curriculum—a set of books and materials designed to strengthen their children's cognitive, early literacy, socio-emotional, and physical development skills. As its Web site explains,

HIPPY helps parents empower themselves as their children's first teacher by giving them the tools, skills and confidence they need to work with their children in the home. The program was designed to bring families, organizations and communities together and remove any barriers to participation that may include limited financial resources or lack of education.

Working with their children at home, parents learn creative ways of establishing a culture of learning, bonding with their children, and making it more natural for the child to learn when they reach Kindergarten.

Once a child is enrolled in school, parents have every right to worry about whether the teachers are fully committed to their job shaping the minds of children. But parents must be careful not to be so antagonistic or confrontational that they chase away talented educators. For parents who were upset to learn that their child attended a "failing school," as defined by No Child Left Behind policies, it's worth asking whether it's fair to judge a teacher purely on the basis of how his or her students perform on a single high-stakes exam. You just can't compare the task of teaching students at a public school in an affluent suburb with teaching students at a low-income inner-city school. Poverty presents challenges such as hunger, inadequate housing, higher crime rates, and the need to work while in school. Some students may have to grapple with domestic violence, or with parents who work three part-time jobs. This kind of environment is distracting for children who need to come to school ready to learn.

According to the No Child Left Behind law, the teacher in that poor neighborhood would be denied "merit pay" based on those students' performance—which is sure to discourage talented teachers from taking a job at such a troubled school in the first place. Additionally, the school earns a lower overall grade or doesn't make "adequate yearly progress," which affects the school's funding and future. A lower school grade also has an effect beyond the school doors, often lowering property values nearby, as potential homebuyers want their children to attend successful schools.

In my own experience with the education system, I have seen the consequences of relying on high-stakes exams. My son, Jake, was sick on the day in seventh grade when he was to take the reading portion of the FCAT, and we didn't think it was possible to take it another day. As a result, he did poorly on the test, despite having earned As and Bs in language arts classes in the gifted student program in school. Certainly, Jake's performance wasn't his teachers' fault. It was a one-shot chance for him on that day and as a result of the lower score, we discovered the next school year that the state legislature had passed a law requiring, with no exceptions, every student with a below-average FCAT score to take a remedial reading class. Jake clearly did not need remedial reading, but the one-size-fits-all, no exceptions approach that No Child Left Behind and state education accountability programs take don't allow a student's individual needs to be considered. As an involved parent, I did some homework and was able to enroll Jake in our school district's online high school to fulfill his reading course requirement. This was an enrichment, rather than a remedial course. But I discovered this doing my own research. If I had just accepted what I was told by the school, Jake would have missed the chance to take an elective course at his school and wasted a period for an entire school year in a course he did not need, to say nothing of the potential stigma he would have endured walking into a class every day that wasn't necessary. Jake was healthy on the day of the reading FCAT in 2013 and earned the highest achievable score, underscoring that the one-size-fits-all reading requirement was pointless.

It is not an easy job, but most teachers have such a strong belief in the value of education that they are willing to devote their working lives to it. I admire programs like Teach for America, which recruits highly skilled people from a variety of backgrounds, often right out of college, then asks them to make a two-year commitment to teach in a disadvantaged area. This is a way to attract instructors who have pride in their work and who enjoy a challenge.

I'd like to see us find more ways for communities—both in low- and middle-income neighborhoods—to reward their teachers, elevating the perception of the profession and making it more attractive to excellent students. Those teachers' successes will also give parents faith that their kids are receiving a quality education in a public school.

If we strive to understand the challenges that teachers face and empower them to improve flawed policy, we will get so much more from our investment in their salaries. Forcing teachers to compete against one another for better scores on a standardized test is not the way to improve education, nor is busting the union that ensures teachers have a living wage and decent work conditions. Treating our nation's teachers in the same way we treat our doctors, lawyers, and other professionals is essential to upgrading the quality performance of a profession critical for America's future in the development of the next generation.

We should encourage teachers to collaborate with their colleagues. Finland, which has a world-class education system and a strong union presence, cites the spirit of teamwork that pervades their public schools, making instructors more passionate about their work and giving prestige to the teaching profession, which in turn attracts talented individuals.

Emulating Finland's schools might lead to hysterical conservatives decrying a "socialist" agenda. But we can stay on this side of the Atlantic to copy American models, like those in Montgomery County, Maryland, and Toledo, Ohio, where teachers have a rigorous system of peer evaluation and review. After all, the teacher who stands to inherit a class of students from the grade below has every reason to make sure the previous grade's teacher is doing a good job. If merit pay is an important principle, then let every teacher share equally in the success of their school. This way, teachers would have even more reason to swap secrets of their trade in the faculty lounge, as well as weed out the worst teachers among them.

President Obama and Education Secretary Arne Duncan recognize that too many aspects of No Child Left Behind are discouraging to teachers, as well as to schoolchildren. In the President's view, educators are more responsive to rewards than they are to threats. This was the framework behind his administration's Race to the Top program, which promised additional funding to states that crafted targeted, sensible improvements to their education systems. States that applied for funding through the program could be granted waivers that offer flexibility from the mandates contained in the No Child Left Behind Act.

In February 2012, when President Obama announced that Florida would receive a waiver, he pointed out that it paved the way for reforms that were at least five years overdue. As someone who has long bemoaned Jeb Bush's education policies in Florida, I would say that's a conservative figure.

For example, one of the most frustrating aspects of No Child Left Behind is that most states had their own assessment exams, like Florida's FCAT, meaning that it was hard for different states to compare educational outcomes in an apples-to-apples way. Without being able to do so, it was more difficult for would-be reformers in one state to adopt education policies that worked in another state. Race to the Top encouraged states to work with one another in developing common academic standards and to measure student achievement with the same comprehensive exam. Thanks to the federal waiver, Florida is now phasing out the FCAT and will soon be among the 22 states that administer to students the Partnership for Assessment of Readiness for College and Careers, often referred to by its acronym, PARCC. Depending on how one state's students perform relative to those in other states, education officials can make changes in curriculum that stand an excellent chance of improving the depth of student learning.

I still have concerns about the way some states have tied test scores to teacher and principal evaluations, but Race to the Top—an enhancement, not a replacement, of No Child Left Behind—encourages states to use a broader variety of standards for evaluating their performance and contains rewards for those teachers who achieve strictly defined goals. Having talked to plenty of teachers myself, I know that the carrot works better than the stick.

A similar incentive program is hoping to compel states to commit resources to education fields associated with technology. In recent years, U.S. schools have fallen behind other nations in math and science. Students from those fields are attractive to technology companies, but due to the lack of available candidates in the United States, such firms have found it necessary to pursue international candidates. Mindful of this trend, Race to the Top gave incentives to states to commit to reinvigorating their approach to teaching math and science. As these improvements take effect, we can expect to see more of our American sons and daughters landing the high-pay, high-skilled jobs at tech companies. This process is already under way in Florida, where state education officials received a Race to the Top grant that will fund analysis that compares Florida students' achievement in science, technology, engineering, and mathematics with that of international students.

We have to be more efficient with education dollars, in part because we simply have no other choice. Despite the positive direction of programs like Race to the Top, the modern era of American education can be characterized by the central challenge of trying to do more with less. Consider that in 2010, public school systems received $593 billion in funding, an increase of just a half percentage point over 2009, meaning that spending increases have failed to keep pace with inflation.

The primary culprits are state legislatures that reacted to the diminished revenue that came with the Great Recession by cutting a range of programs, including education, in order to balance their budgets. Had it not been for the $53.6 billion in stabilization funds that came from the 2009 American Recovery and Reinvestment Act, thousands of teachers might have been laid off. In total, the stimulus package contributed $79 billion to K–12 schooling.

Nevertheless, in 2013 federal education spending will fail to reach the funding "baseline" established by the U.S. Department of Education, determined by enrollment figures for American schools. In the years to come, budget projections show that we will continue to drift farther beneath that baseline, as our spending fails to keep up with inflation and the resource demands that come with additional students.

Without more funds available to educators, it will take longer to reestablish the elective courses like art and music that were the first to perish in the wake of No Child Left Behind. It will be difficult to pay teachers and principals the salaries they deserve. Textbooks will become tattered and outdated. Classrooms will become larger. I know this from firsthand experience when Shelby's elementary school was forced to lay off the media specialist and cut media completely as a "special." This meant that the students had almost no time in the school library, which is simply unacceptable in the twenty-first century. This year, media was restored at her school, but many other schools cut music, art, and in some cases, science, which are critical components to our children's educational curriculum. They should not be considered "extras" or "luxuries."

It may not be a coincidence that spending on education has been relatively stagnant at the same time that America's middle class has been shrinking. A 2011 study by the Center for American Progress Action Fund compared education spending in a variety of nations, alongside measures of those nations' middle class. Analysts concluded:

> Societies with a strong middle class make greater investments in public goods such as education, which helps fuel their future economic success. Because paying for private school imposes a much greater, sometimes impossible, hardship on middle-class families than it does on the wealthy, middle-class families have a strong incentive to make public schools work. The middle class invests its time and energy in public schools and supports higher levels of spending on education—and especially the taxes necessary to pay for it—than do the rich.

U.S. Census data shows that for decades the income earned by those in the middle 60 percent of households has been on the decline. If the average American's wages had kept pace with the economic growth this country has experienced since the 1970s, most Americans would be making about $92,000 per year, as opposed to the $50,000 that was the median American household income in 2009. Instead, the nation's top 1 percent has seen a wildly disproportionate share of recent economic growth, a trend that has had a major impact on all social institutions, especially education.

Without increasing investment in education, in the future it will be increasingly difficult for low-income Americans to work their way into the middle class, just as it will be harder for students from middle-class families to transform their education into a career that vaults them into the ranks of the wealthy. Put more simply, we are making it less likely that the next generation is better off than the one before, a hallmark of American progress.

Still, I am hopeful that as President Obama puts into effect policies that strengthen the middle class, it will be easier both politically and economically to replenish our schools' share of tax dollars. During the 2012 campaign, the President stressed the need to invest in education and innovation, while addressing our need for deficit reduction in a balanced way with responsible spending cuts and more revenue from those who can afford to pay a little bit more. Americans' decision to reelect President Obama suggests this is the path they prefer.

This is not to say that American schools haven't done more with less—they have. They deserve praise for having weathered a very difficult period in their history. If not for the effort of such committed educators, both parents and teachers, our education system might be in even worse shape. School boards across the country deserve special mention, because so often they're made up of professionals who have plenty of other chores to juggle. Those board members have a role in shaping the district's curriculum, in defining the boundaries and bussing designations. They have oversight of spending and help choose programs to be administered within a district. Ideally, these public servants are assisted by the input they receive at board meetings and from friends and neighbors who share their concern about the state of local education.

Amid all the doom and gloom that tends to surround modern education statistics, I would point out that schools have managed to improve on perhaps the most crucial measure of success: the graduation rate. Between 2002 and 2009, that rate rose from 72 percent to 75 percent. Still, there are many states where the graduation rate remains stubbornly low. We would all like that number to be even higher, but in this challenging educational climate we should cheer any kind of progress, however modest, and work diligently toward improvement across the country.

None of the previously mentioned programs, by themselves, will deliver miracles in education. Rather, the catalyst for progress is attitude. To help children get the most from their education, parents, teachers, and society at large must adopt a frame of mind that contains genuine hope and confidence, combined with a commitment for improving achievement.

Hope is especially scarce within the nation's most troubled schools, which tend to be populated by students from low-income, disadvantaged families. I worry that too often our society takes the attitude that those schools are ensnared by a "culture of poverty" that makes improvement virtually impossible. It suggests that low-income parents are lazy and that they are simply not interested in taking an active role in their child's education, which is why those children do poorly in school.

This is a destructive myth that must be confronted.

According to the National Center for Children in Poverty's analysis from 2010, 47 percent of the kids who belong to low-income families live with a parent who is working full-time, year-round. These adults averaged an income of just $25,000 in 2006, based on research by the Urban Institute. Many others work multiple part-time jobs as a way to put food on their family's table. Whether employed full-time or part-time, the working poor rarely claim unionized jobs, according to the Bureau of Labor Statistics, meaning that most of these parents have little to no method for bargaining for health coverage and other benefits. This reflects a shortage of living wage jobs, especially for parents who do not have post-secondary education—a shortage that plays a significant role in the number of poor parents who do not work.

The inescapable conclusion is that the vast majority of parents sending their children to schools in low-income neighborhoods are poor either despite the fact that they do work or because it is difficult for them to find work. These parents are often blocked from higher-paying jobs by their own lack of college education or vocational training, and it is difficult and often impossible for them to be involved in their children's education.

Past generations of Americans may have lacked a more formal education as well, but they could still get union jobs in factories, among other facets of the nation's industry-based economy. With a structured forty-hour work week, plus benefits like paid leave and wages that relieved them from the all-consuming stress of living in poverty, it was much easier for those parents to participate in their children's education. This explains how the factory worker of one generation could produce sons and daughters who become employed in a professional trade, a higher-pay status they earned thanks to an education that was superior to their parents'. Truly, education is the mechanism that powers the grand American tradition of social mobility.

But that tradition is suffering. In a modern American economy moving from an industrial economy to one based on technology and services, there is a lack of unskilled labor jobs that pay a living wage. As such, today's less-educated working Americans do not have the same capacity to involve themselves in their children's schooling, a huge factor in providing for their children's upward social mobility. Researchers who have taken the time to interview these parents find that they understand the importance of being active in helping their kids with homework and attending school functions, and they profoundly regret their inability to do so. From a systemic level, we must help pull these families out of poverty with a living wage that allows parents to be more active in their child's education. The minimum wage in this country has simply not kept up with what is needed to keep these families out of poverty. In short, we need a new call to arms for a "living wage." I certainly support the idea of a $9 minimum wage as the President suggested in his State of the Union remarks, just as I supported the 2004 constitutional amendment in Florida that required that the minimum wage be adjusted each year to keep pace with inflation.

Contrary to notions of a "culture of poverty," a more accurate portrait of the families connected to schools in poor neighborhoods is one in which they are striving to succeed themselves and to improve their children's lives, but understandably are frustrated by a formidable set of obstacles. There is profound dignity in their efforts, as well as those of students who may be enrolled in so-called "failing schools." All of us must recognize that dignity, treating them with respect, not with condescension or derision.

If we can accomplish this attitude change, we can approach educational reform with a clearer focus. We will be able to more plainly see the curse of low expectations created by placing students on a low academic track or in special education courses. Teachers who are more fully aware of the challenges faced by low-income families may be more patient in seeking a consultation with those parents, increasing the odds that the meeting will ultimately take place. The perspective might even help us shape the content of lessons—children who come from a poor neighborhood ought to learn in history class about how great Americans like Andrew Carnegie rose out of poverty by sheer force of will. They should learn about contemporary rags-to-riches stories, like that of Ursula Burns, raised in a poor, crime-ridden neighborhood, only to earn a college diploma then become the first African American woman to run a Fortune 500 company. Perhaps those children will realize school's capacity to amaze and inspire. For this to happen, textbook publishers and school districts must work with state textbook adoption committees to be sure that the content will reach all students, not just those from fortunate circumstances.

We also can ask teachers to make more of an effort to accommodate parents who have multiple jobs and difficult domestic situations. Schools should be flexible and creative in reaching out to parents, particularly when the neighborhoods that feed the school are low-income and disadvantaged. What works in a wealthy, upper-income suburb may not work in a low-income neighborhood with high unemployment and parents working multiple jobs. The schools that succeed at reaching and engaging parents are the ones whose students' grades soar. Yes, teaching is a demanding profession, with more and more paper-pushing and administrative requirements. But too often, the rigidity of teachers' schedules result in the same one-size-fits-all approach that the hated No Child Left Behind requirements produced. Although many, many teachers do all they can, the fact is, too many teachers don't go beyond their comfort zone; worse, some expect parents to work around the teacher's rigid, inflexible, school-hours-only schedule, putting up hurdles for working parents to jump over to be able to engage in their child's progress.

We must work at every level to create a vision for better school programming. For example, the Council of the Great City Schools, which is an umbrella organization of many of the nation's urban school districts, including my home district of Broward County, is working on action plans to change the dynamic in urban schools with a vision that recognizes that these schools are often asked to educate the nation's most diverse student bodies, while creating programs that will "prepare them to contribute to our democracy and the global community."

Last, parents themselves must care enough to find a way to be involved in their child's education. Learn about the many programs available to parents interested in pitching in at your child's school. Make time every day to ask your children about their homework and upcoming exams and projects. Encourage your kids to identify talents and activities that stir their interest, that could some day lead to a career. Most of all, project both to your child and to the outside world a sense of purpose in your work and faith that society will reward your efforts. Parents are the adults that children trust most, and this optimistic outlook is sure to rub off.

The children may be the ones who are going to class, but we parents have "homework" of our own. Beyond helping our kids with their lessons, it means performing our own research to make sure they're being well-served by their schools. Then parents have to accept a level of responsibility in terms of helping teachers succeed.

During one school year, when I received a note from my son's teacher expressing concern over his "organizational" difficulties, I requested parent-teacher conferences with his teachers and we hammered out a strategy for helping him improve. They knew I was paying attention, and as a result they noticeably paid more attention to my son. Teachers are human and they respond like anyone would. "The squeaky wheel gets the grease" is the expression that comes to mind. My son may not be crazy about that extra attention now, but I have a feeling he'll thank me later!

The bottom line is, a child's success in school is a team effort that requires cooperation, involvement, and commitment from the parents, the students, their teachers, and the school.

✦ ✦ ✦

As parents, we must take the long view on our children's educational goals. I have no doubt that many parents recognize that a diploma will take their child farther than a test score will. Just listen to Catonya, an Iraq War veteran who moved to Saint Paul, Minnesota, following her military service. There, she met a lot of families where the parents had failed to graduate from high school or college and whose children were not going to graduate, either. "That's the trend that I see, but that's not the trend I'm setting for my children," she says. "There will be a graduate coming out of my house." Catonya is the guardian of her niece, who enrolled in the Breakthrough Saint Paul program for helping low-income students develop the skills and knowledge they need to excel in college.

There's simply no overstating the advantages that come from a young person graduating with an education that prepares him or her for a post-secondary education and then professional career. During the Great Recession, which bottomed out around January 2010, workers with a college degree still managed to gain 187,000 jobs. Compare that to those who had an associate's degree or some college education, who lost 1.75 million jobs during that same period. But the recession proved most catastrophic for those who had only a high school education or less. This group lost 5.6 million jobs during the recession, and their unemployment levels have been more stubbornly resistant to improvement through the recovery period.

So it is clearly not enough to get our kids through high school; we must do everything we can to assist them in earning a post-secondary education, whether that is on a college or vocational track.

In the United Kingdom, the government largely subsidizes the tuition costs for citizens who want to attend a university, and given the economic benefits of educating young people, I believe that's a concept that's worth giving serious consideration in the United States. Of course, an argument could be made that this system breeds complacency among British students, who may not have the same incentive to earn excellent grades so as to qualify for scholarships, the way American high schoolers do. There is also the danger that these students would take their university lessons for granted, leading to an academic environment that is less collegial and less competitive.

But American universities could still rely on an an admissions process to select students, meaning that high school students would have extra incentive to earn the grades they would need to get accepted by their favored university. As for the effect on the collegial culture, it appears to be thriving at universities like Cambridge and Oxford, which rank among the elite institutes of higher learning in the world. The American difference could be to remove cost and affordability as an obstacle, but keep the rigor of the application and acceptance process. In the U.S., more than a hundred years ago we adopted free universal access to public education, because education was deemed essential for a successful adult life. In the twenty-first century I would argue that we have reached the point where a post-secondary education is essential as well.

At the very least, the United States needs to make post-secondary education more affordable and bring it within reach for millions more young people. Millions of American families fall between the cracks that separate high school from higher education. Often, that's because the family income may be too high to qualify a student for aid, but without enough savings to be able to pay the student's tuition without severe hardship.

Tuition costs have been rising at a spectacular rate—8.3 percent from 2010 to 2011 alone. The spike in tuition for public two-year schools was even more pronounced over that same period, rising by 8.7 percent. In the 2010–2011 school year, the average cost of attending a four-year institution, including room and board, was $20,100 at public universities and nearly $40,000 at private universities, according to the National Center for Education Statistics.

Even for those who qualified, student aid wasn't nearly enough to cover the full cost of attending a college or university, meaning that many young people had to take out loans to pay for the balance of their education costs. Twentysomethings who are entering the workforce at this uncertain time already have enough to worry about; it's a shame that making college loan payments is one of those worries. Spending a large portion of an American adult's life paying off student loans hampers American college graduates' ability to hit the ground running on the path to the middle class and beyond.

If that isn't outrageous enough, consider that the banks that make those loans to students had for years enjoyed generous government subsidies. One of the little-known amendments to the Affordable Care Act (Obamacare) was legislation called the Student Aid and Fiscal Responsibility Act, introduced in the House by Democratic Congressman George Miller. This legislation ended these government subsidies to the banks and moved that $60 billion into the direct student loan program. Removing the middleman put more money directly into the hands of college students and made the loans more affordable and more easily available. Another helpful step taken by President Obama was his We Can't Wait initiative, which allowed new graduates to decrease monthly payments to no more than 10 percent of their monthly income, so they don't suffer sticker shock when they finish school, while their income may not be where they need it to be to make substantial loan payments.

I can safely speak for all Democrats when I say that we are doing our best to slow down the runaway costs of post-secondary education, but it's not easy. When the President signed the Affordable Care Act with the student loan program reforms attached in March 2010, $40 billion was made available to those who apply for a Pell Grant, the federal student aid that can be worth up to $5,500 per year for students at the lowest income levels. The same bill contained provisions to lower costs for community colleges and to help graduates reduce the amount of loan payments.

These efforts are already paying dividends. Between 2000 and 2010, college enrollment in America increased 37 percent from the previous decade, from 15.3 million to 21 million, according to the National Center for Education Statistics. This is an indication that the next generation of American workers recognize the need for a post-secondary degree in the modern economy and that despite the exorbitant costs, they're going to find a way to pay for it. That kind of dedication deserves to be rewarded. Government must continue to help these students graduate with manageable debt so that they have a measure of financial stability as they begin their careers.

✦ ✦ ✦

Enrolling in college isn't enough, however. We want our college students to graduate, and that is the final stumbling block: According to a 2011 Harvard study, only 56 percent of students who enroll in a bachelor's degree program graduate within six years. Among those seeking an associate's degree, only 29 percent get their diploma. A recent survey by the Pew Research Center suggested that the cost of tuition was the leading factor.

Congress and the President can certainly do our part to make postsecondary education more affordable to more Americans; but it will be difficult to corral those costs quickly. Taking steps like enrollment in a 529 college tuition savings plan at the earliest stage of a child's life, when it is more affordable, is important, because these plans often lock in today's tuition rates. When financially possible to make these monthly payments, this saves money in the long run. My husband and I purchased Florida Prepaid College Plans for all three of our children, which locked in 1999, 2000, and 2003 tuition levels for our family when our three kids go to college. According to the Southern Regional Education Board, the 1999 median annual tuition and required fees for full-time, Florida in-state students was $2,196. The same annual tuition was $19,682 in 2010, a 796 percent increase. This will save us at least $17,486 annually for just one of our children in college. Clearly a tuition savings plan like this makes sense, even if it is a financial reach. All the more reason we need to create an environment allowing more American families to join the middle class.

We are all in this together: kids, parents, teachers, and everyone in the nation. Quality education creates universal good and national strength. Applying concerted individual, governmental, and community effort will ensure that we are on the brink of a new era in American education characterized by excellence—through not only the tax dollars we invest but with the hours we spend helping our children learn, excel, and thrive.

EIGHT

Keeping Kids Healthy
and Safe

I magine trying to feed your child when you can only afford $1 per meal. I don't have to imagine it; I know that it's nearly impossible. Anti-poverty groups encourage members of Congress to take the Food Stamp Challenge as a way of empathizing with low-income families who rely on food stamps, and in 2011, I participated. The average benefit is $3 per day, per person. The four days I participated, I was able to purchase two cans of Hormel chili, two boxes of macaroni and cheese, one box of granola bars, one bag of potatoes, three bananas, three apples, a loaf of white bread, a package of white tortillas, and four cans of tuna. This was all I had to eat for four days. Not exactly healthy or satisfying, to say the least.

Forget about finding nutritious food that tastes delicious. When you have so little to spend, the real challenge is rounding up enough calories—especially those from protein—to keep your stomach from growling. It's hard to concentrate on work, you become irritable, and the craving for food is a constant source of stress. The academic term for this condition of poverty is "food insecurity." The U.S. Department of Agriculture estimates that in 2011, about 18 percent of American households were food insecure. Roughly 16.7 million children live in these households, meaning they're spending their youth in a state of hunger, without consistent access to food. For me, the Food Stamp Challenge was a brief and incomplete glimpse of this hardship. For so many families, it's a way of life.

That's hardly the only health dilemma faced by the nation's children. For those who have enough food, there's still the issue of whether they're getting nutritional value from it. Often they're not, which is why childhood obesity has exploded into a national epidemic. In addition, many low-income parents are caught between the lack of access to quality, affordable health care and qualifying for Medicaid. As a result, they often can't get treatment for children who get sick, which could make a minor ailment become major. Fortunately, the passage of the Affordable Care Act confers nearly universal coverage for children beginning in 2014, meaning that this problem will essentially be eliminated.

But even conscientious parents who are able to feed their kids healthy food and rush them to the doctor at the first sign of illness must guard against the potential threats: There are too many consumer goods that haven't been sufficiently child-proofed. For this reason, kids are hurt in accidents that were entirely preventable.

Finally, the single most horrific hazard is a child being made the victim of a crime of exploitation. The scars inflicted by abuse can last a lifetime. I'm very proud that a bill I coauthored, the Child Protection Act of 2012, will give law-enforcement officials more resources to track and prosecute the increasing numbers of child sex predators who lure victims online. But as with any crime that relies on technology, we will need to continue to adapt our methods for keeping criminals away from kids.

Along with education policies, the legislative decisions we make within these health and safety issues will do much to determine what kind of adults today's children will become. Because children are too young to know all the complexities of the real world, they are totally dependent on adults. Children are also hugely dependent on government. Since they can't vote, they aren't truly a constituency, meaning that the two political parties share the duty of serving them. Today, we don't seem to be sharing that responsibility very well.

As ever, kids' first line of defense is their parents. But the sad fact is that a responsible adult isn't always there to protect and guide them. There are some who would exhort those children to "pull yourselves up by your own bootstraps," but this is not realistic, especially for the very young children who have grown-up problems. For a child who endures significant economic obstacles that block access to stable housing in a safe neighborhood, well-balanced meals, and sound health care, getting a good education presents a daunting challenge. At a minimum, we must educate parents about how to keep their children safe, especially from preventable harm.

For those without responsible parents, however, laws must be in place that can protect those kids. For the gaps in care that remain, the community at large must sew a safety net that no child can slip through. As part of that mission, we adults must make children's issues a top priority on the day we go to the polls. Ideally, we will all make the welfare of children a daily consideration, educating ourselves on the issues that have an impact on the development of kids, then forming opinions on policy with that in mind.

Considering the full scale of challenges faced by our nation's children can be overwhelming. But I hope that it is not unmanageable. Kids' lives will be improved as we strive to enact legislation that has the most broad-based impact. Economic policies that strengthen the middle class, for instance, will have a seemingly miraculous effect on reducing child hunger caused by poverty, at the same time as it transforms the quality of education in inner-city neighborhoods.

It would be unwise, however, to focus exclusively on such top-down strategies for resolving the health and safety issues of today's kids; they should not have to wait for a piece of legislation to inch its way through congressional committees. We need to put resources and efforts into what we can control. If there's a crisis in our community, we need to take action.

The childhood obesity epidemic is one example. It has outstripped all our efforts to contain it. And its effects are even more visible in low-income neighborhoods, which are so often the site of failing schools.

Research suggests that obesity contributes to children's poor performance in schools. The Healthier Options for Public Schoolchildren Study enrolled elementary school students from Osceola County, Florida, in a holistic obesity prevention program, consisting of a healthy diet and lessons on exercise and nutrition, among other wellness projects. Over a two-year period, the children not only improved their body mass index (the standard method for tracking obesity), they also performed better in school. This trend was particularly strong among high-risk populations who traditionally are the hardest for reformers to reach, like African American and Hispanic children, nearly 40 percent of whom are obese.

Another study, released in a February 2011 edition of the *Journal of Epidemiology and Community Health*, tracked the diet of children along with their IQ scores as they grew. Researchers found that children with a diet high in sugar and fat tended to lose IQ points while children with a nutrient-rich diet tended to gain them. Given what science has told us about the interaction between food and the functioning of the brain, it makes sense that diet and nutrition affect children's ability to concentrate.

Too often, American children, for one reason or another, don't eat breakfast. A number of published studies have shown that students who started the day by fortifying themselves with a nutritious meal were more attentive in their lessons. Some schools have introduced a program for providing universally free breakfast to their students. Teachers in those schools have reported improvements in their pupils' behavior and academic performance.

Unless we intervene, overweight children will become overweight adults. Schools are the ideal setting for that intervention. Whatever the cost of providing free breakfast in public schools, or other services to address childhood obesity, it cannot be compared with the billions paid by the Social Security Administration to Americans whose obesity and associated poor health qualifies them for disability benefits. Nor can it compare to the billions in Medicare and Medicaid billings to treat diseases linked to obesity, including diabetes, heart disease, and some forms of cancer.

Fortunately, those of us who are passionate about children's health have an ally in a prominent place in the White House. First Lady Michelle Obama's Let's Move! initiative promotes physical activity and nutrition among young people. She has led the fight against unhealthy, processed food traditionally served in school cafeterias. Her husband deserves credit, too, for teaming up with Congress to pass the Affordable Care Act of 2010, which included the important provision that restaurants list the caloric content of the food on their menus. When we're shopping for bargains at the mall, don't we look at the price tag to see if we can afford a piece of merchandise? The same budget mentality goes for vending machines when we're shopping for a snack; we should inspect the calories to make sure it suits our children's diet.

Besides a nutritious diet, the most sure-fire way to keep America's children healthy is to see that they get their daily dose of physical exercise. When I was in high school, there were two classes you had to take every semester of every year: English and Physical Education (PE). The implicit message was that language and exercise are absolutely essential elements of childhood. English remains a constant. But what has happened to PE?

Having read the previous chapter, you can probably guess the answer: Over the past decade since No Child Left Behind, school budgets have been reshuffled and too often, physical education was one area many administrators chose to cut. In June 2012, high school students surveyed by the Centers for Disease Control and Prevention (CDC) reported that they had no physical education classes in an average week. That's unacceptable, given the rates of obesity among American schoolchildren and the obvious role that exercise plays in good health. In my home state of Florida, former Governor Charlie Crist recognized that physical education classes were key to a child's healthy future and he pushed successfully to require PE in the public school curriculum. There is flexibility for students who play after-school sports to waive the requirement, but the point is to ensure physical activity from an early age.

Getting rid of gym class may save money in the short term, but the consequences of unhealthy children will end up costing the country much more in the long run. It goes without saying that parents should encourage their children to be active, but there's only so much that society can do to compel those parents. By making PE a regular feature of their students' schedule, we can at least be assured that the child is getting one hour of exercise per day. That's better than nothing, and maybe the child will enjoy the sports in PE so much that he or she will try out for a team, leading to even more exercise.

Team sports have a special place in my heart, offering not just the universal benefits of exercise but all the social good that comes from belonging to a team. As a girl growing up in New York on Long Island, I spent Sunday afternoons in the bleachers with my brother, watching our father play softball. After the game was over, he would practice with the two of us. In elementary school, I was the only girl on my Little League baseball team, and I still recall how in the beginning I was standing in the outfield, praying that the ball didn't come to me.

Even though I wasn't the most naturally talented player, I loved the game and practiced a great deal. I was focused on getting better. In the seventh grade, I tried out for the girls' softball team and made it. In ninth grade I made the team again, but I struggled to break into the lineup. I kept at it, and eventually, by the time I was a junior in high school, I was the starter at second base on the varsity team. When I look back on it now, I realize I was able to stay dedicated to the game because it brought me closer to my family and because my teammates became my friends—I wanted us to succeed together. So at the same time that I was getting exercise, I was learning values about community that still serve me today. Equally as important was the lesson it taught me: I wanted to be good at this game and nothing was going to stop me. I was very competitive and determined to succeed at an activity I loved. This lesson has carried through my entire life and served me well in school as well as during my professional life. Through competitive sports, I learned leadership skills, participating in the Girls Leaders Athletic Club and lettering in softball all through high school. Team sports teaches life lessons that you just never forget. A group of researchers at West Virginia University, curious about the social effects of being on a team, interviewed middle school boys and girls, comparing the attitudes of those who participated in team sports with those who did not. Kids who exercised on a sports team were happier than their less active peers, and researchers even found that team-playing kids showed superior cognitive abilities.

There's no doubt that experience gave me a sense of pride. As Michelle Obama points out, the healthy body that comes with nutrition and an active lifestyle will spare children from the low self-esteem that is a characteristic of obesity. It will help them cope better with stress as they enter adolescence and then adulthood. These healthy students will be on track to have the energy and willpower to make meaningful contributions to society, passing on their good habits to their own kids.

The government must be an ally to activists who care about children's eating habits—and the reforms don't all have to take place in schools. Community centers are a great way to promote exercise and get kids involved in athletics when they're not in school. Ideally, children can move from one physical activity to the next without any of the downtime that tends to result in sedentary diversions like Web surfing, video games, and television. Maybe we can get back to the days when children "playing" meant running, jumping, and swimming.

While our children are enjoying those exercise-rich activities, however, it's important that we adults ensure they don't hurt themselves. When I was a child, our school assemblies were filled with safety drills. We learned to never ride two on a bicycle and to avoid talking to strangers. Children may believe "it won't happen to me," but parents should know that it can and it does. Safety starts with the parents educating themselves, whether it's through attending an evening school program about Internet safety or learning how to keep young children safe around water through the YMCA or the local Red Cross.

It is easy to imagine one's self in Nancy Baker's position, a mother of five daughters. Her eldest, Rosemary, was celebrating a high school graduation in June 2002 with a pool party at a neighbor's McLean, Virginia, home. Nancy Baker's other four daughters, including seven-year-old twins Jackie and Virginia Graeme Baker, were all enjoying the fun, leaping into the pool while their mother and older sisters mingled with friends.

The girls were all accomplished swimmers—Graeme had even won a medal for diving—and the pool was surrounded by adults. So Nancy Baker had little reason to fear for her twins' safety, until suddenly Jackie came running up. "Her eyes were like saucers," Nancy recalled.

"Mommy, Mommy, Graeme's in the hot tub," said the seven-year-old.

Nancy raced to the hot tub, which was bubbling with dark water but seemed otherwise empty. "I couldn't see anything," she recalled. "I kept saying, 'What? Where?'" Nancy dove to the bottom of the hot tub. She found seven-year-old Graeme on the bottom, her hair and arms wafting with the current of the water.

With all her adrenaline-fueled strength, Nancy tried to pull her little girl to the surface. She couldn't. Graeme was somehow attached to the bottom. Nancy tugged more desperately, coming up for air several times, screaming before she dove back down for another try. Two men jumped in the tub and struggled, too. They finally pulled her free but to do so, they had to break an eight-inch metal grate that covered the hot tub's intake hole.

Graeme was immediately rushed to the hospital. Nancy, still soaking wet, was sitting on the floor of the emergency room, waiting for word about her daughter. But the doctors delivered the news Nancy dreaded: Graeme had died from drowning. She had been submerged too long, trapped by the suction of the intake hole that drew water into the hot tub's filtering system.

It is especially heartbreaking to know that this accident was preventable. Graeme was not the first child to die due to entrapment, and many more have suffered terrible injuries. Hot tub manufacturers should have taken steps to correct known safety issues with their product. Since they failed to do so, the government should have ensured that regulations were in place for the safety of young children.

Too often, it takes a tragedy like Graeme Baker's to remind us of the importance of safety standards. I am not willing to swallow the self-serving argument of industry lobbyists who say that this is a problem exclusively related to parental responsibility. The swimming pool industry fights pool safety standards each time they are proposed. They have consistently been an obstacle to establishing laws and local ordinances that protect children in those moments when there's a brief lapse in supervision. With thousands of pounds of suction coming from swimming pool drains, we had to ensure there were drain covers that protected children and other swimmers from becoming trapped like Graeme Baker was. This is one of those instances where our children needed the law to protect them.

Coming from a state with so many beaches and backyard pools, water safety has always been at the forefront of my mind. Drowning is a leading cause of accidental death for toddlers four years and younger, and for every fatality there are ten more children who are treated at the emergency room for a submersion injury. This is the reason that drowning prevention has been a priority for me since my time in the Florida Legislature. In 2000, I authored the Preston de Ibern/McKenzie Merriam Residential Swimming Pool Safety Act, which required safety barriers around residential pools to guard against accidental drowning.

The U.S. House of Representatives was designed by our Founding Fathers to be a representative body with individuals from different walks of life. One of the reasons this diversity of experience is so important is to enable issues affecting a wide variety of Americans to be addressed. As a mother with young children, from a state with a significant child-drowning problem, I knew that, nationally, drowning in residential swimming pools was the number-two killer through accidental death of children younger than fourteen. With this in mind, I authored the Virginia Graeme Baker Pool and Spa Safety Act, modeled after the legislation I passed in Florida, to provide a range of federal safety standards that would prevent drownings like Graeme Baker's. The bill authorized $29 million over five years to incentivize pool safety laws in states, with an additional $25 million for educational outreach for swimming pool owners and those who work in the pool and spa industry.

A modest price tag, given the priceless nature of a child's life—hundreds die every year in drowning incidents. Yet Senator Tom Coburn, a Republican from Oklahoma, placed a "hold" on this legislation, meaning it couldn't reach the floor to be voted on. I swung into action, reaching out to Republicans and Democrats for help in passing the bill. We had a powerful ally in Graeme's grandfather, former Secretary of State James Baker. Protecting children is not a partisan issue, and I asked Secretary Baker, who had been helping push the legislation named for his granddaughter, to contact Senate Majority Leader Harry Reid and ask him for help. A few days later, I received a call from the Majority Leader who let me know he would go around Senator Coburn's hold and fold the VGB Act into a massive energy bill that was soon to pass the Senate. In this fashion, the bill cleared its last hurdle and, I'm very pleased to say, is now the law of the land. Since the law's passage, according to the Consumer Product Safety Commission, there has not been a single suction drain entrapment death in the U.S.

That drowning prevention legislation narrowly survived, and it illustrates just how difficult it is to pass laws even when they cost little and are capable of saving the lives of children. To really drive home the point about how political gamesmanship can make elected officials lose their priorities, consider the resistance I encountered in fighting for the PROTECT Our Children Act of 2008.

I sponsored this bill, which would create the largest law-enforcement effort ever assembled for going after sexual predators, especially the ones who swap child pornography and lure victims via the Internet.

According to estimates, less than 2 percent of these crimes were being investigated, and even less than that resulted in jail time. This was in spite of the fact that the statistics showed that when investigated, an arrest was made in 30 percent of the cases. We know that child pornography is not typical pornography. They are crime scene photos that depict the deliberate sexual exploitation of young children. Child pornography is an insatiable beast that leads its perpetrators to go out and find more children to exploit and photograph in order to generate more material for this gigantic network of purveyors.

The low rate of investigation was partly due to a lack of coordination between law-enforcement agencies, and the PROTECT Act would address that by requiring a national plan to be written by a high-level official created in the Department of Justice. No longer would various agencies be working in silos; they'd be coordinating their efforts. It also provided badly needed funds to pay for more officers to be assigned to an Internet Crimes Against Children (ICAC) Task Force Program devoted exclusively to stopping cyber-crimes against children. The bill was championed by the Surviving Parents Coalition, led by Ed Smart, the father of Elizabeth Smart, who had been abducted and held captive as a sex slave for nine months, until she was rescued. They approached me to sponsor the bill in the House, while targeting an influential Democrat in the Senate, Joe Biden (before he joined the Obama ticket). The bill was bolstered by the cosponsorship of Rep. Joe Barton, a Republican from Texas, and Sen. Orrin Hatch, who has long been one of the most powerful members of the GOP.

If there was any doubt about the urgency of this legislation, it should have been annihilated by the testimony given at the House Judiciary Committee meeting by nineteen-year-old Alicia Kozakiewicz. Showing phenomenal poise, Alicia told the committee how she had been lured by a child sex predator she met online when she was just thirteen years old. Living in Pittsburgh at the time, she was driven to Virginia, then kept chained in a basement, where she was raped and tortured by a sadistic monster who filmed his deeds for an equally depraved online audience. Alicia might never have been rescued, if not for the fact that Pittsburgh happened to have one of the nation's first cyber-crime task forces, while Virginia had an effective ICAC Task Force in place. These investigators fielded a tip from one of the child rapist's online acquaintances, then tracked his location using the IP address connected to his e-mail account. Said Alicia: "They are my angels."

But as with the pool safety bill, the PROTECT Act encountered political turbulence. The would-be spoiler was, again, Senator Tom Coburn.

He balked at the cost of the PROTECT Act. Clearly, the scourge of child sex abuse was spreading rapidly with the emergence of online technology, and that threat required dedicated resources, but more important, coordination between the myriad agencies who were duplicating efforts. I am not a believer that more money solves every problem, but the reality of fighting crime requires more officers, more resources for investigations. Here was another example of a senator who was not just penny-wise and pound-foolish, but was willing to keep children at grave risk in spite of evidence that more investigations would directly save childrens' lives. I remember thinking, "What if this was his child he could save?"

Senator Harry Reid swooped in again, combining PROTECT with thirty-six of Coburn's other notorious holds into one omnibus bill, termed the Tomnibus. Most of the bills were similarly humanitarian in nature. When Coburn's fellow Republicans rallied in support, blocking the Tomnibus, a new champion, Oprah Winfrey, was inspired to use her fame to inform her viewers of the PROTECT Act. As Oprah's legions complained to their representatives in Congress, the tide slowly shifted and the bill was finally passed. Yet another worthy, commonsense reform that shouldn't have needed a miracle.

Having overcome that obstacle, we are now gaining momentum. In early 2012, I introduced the Child Protection Act in the House, where I was joined by Rep. Lamar Smith (R-TX). The bill proposed to increase the penalties for child pornography, while offering more protection for victims as well as witnesses who provide evidence that leads to the apprehension and conviction of a child sex predator. Specifically, the legislation would make it possible for judges to issue protective orders that would guard victims or witnesses from being intimidated. With the assistance of Senators John Cornyn (R-TX) and Richard Blumenthal (D-CT), this truly bipartisan bill made it to President Obama's desk, and in December 2012 it was signed into law. For that Oval Office ceremony I joined Congressman Smith and Senator Blumenthal. There will always be partisan rivalry in Washington, but as the Tea Party hysteria fades into the past, I have fresh hope that issues like protecting kids will transcend political gamesmanship.

* * *

All the health risks and safety dangers that we've discussed in this chapter can be minimized for kids who have the benefit of conscientious parents. So imagine how much more perilous life is for children who are born to parents who aren't responsible. In many cases, those parents not only fail to protect their children, they become the single biggest threat to that child's well-being, abusing that child physically or emotionally.

In these tragic instances, we must depend on the nation's child welfare system. Yet at the present time, that system is stretched too thin to adequately protect children who have suffered abuse in the home. A recent report by the Child Welfare League of America cited statistics from 2010 that indicated 3.3 million reports of abuse or neglect in the United States. Of those cases where the complaint had been substantiated, only 61 percent of children received follow-up services from a child welfare agency. That means that for abused or neglected kids, the chances of a meaningful intervention offered only slightly better odds than a coin toss!

Mind you, this is not the fault of social workers, many of whom have caseloads that were twice the size of the recommended limit. The demands of that job lead to high turnover, and it takes time and money to find other committed, qualified professionals who will step in to take the place of the departed. The reality is that more caseworkers need to be recruited and hired to reduce the caseload. There are simply too many horror stories of abused children who end up dead because overloaded caseworkers could not monitor them more closely.

By giving these agencies more funding, we could hire more social workers and pay them a salary commensurate with the stress they endure as an advocate for children. In addition, we could afford to invest in technologies that would increase efficiency, making it possible for those social workers to more easily handle their swollen caseloads.

Ignoring problems like this doesn't make them go away, and more recent analysis shows that the abused kids are still getting approximately the same woefully inconsistent rate of follow-up from their over-extended caseworkers.

The real-world impact is devastating. Among a group of young people who had been in foster care and were tracked by researchers at the University of Chicago, one-third had a "high level" of involvement with the criminal justice system. A 2008 survey of California prison inmates found that 14 percent had been in foster care at some point in their youth. In that state, the flow of young people from foster care to jail was so pronounced that in 2012 California enacted legislation allowing foster kids to stay with their families through the age of twenty-one.

In Florida, we have programs like PACEWorks!, the Pace Centers for Girls, which provides a range of transition services to girls and young women in counties across Florida, giving them the knowledge and skills to achieve financial independence. At Ohel Children's Home and Family Services in Aventura, Florida, a variety of ingenious methods are used to help at-risk young people. These programs boost kids' self-esteem while teaching them how to resolve conflict peacefully and build meaningful relationships. A similar program in Washington, D.C., called ARISE, helps develop critical thinking skills in kids who have been in the juvenile justice system, helping them to recognize that joining gangs and dealing drugs is a destructive path. As a member of Congress, I made appropriation requests to secure funding on behalf of all these worthwhile endeavors.

Giving more of our tax dollars to child welfare agencies may sound like one of those "big government" ideas, but this is a case where an ounce of prevention is worth a pound of cure. Failing to help an abused child may lead that same child to feel alienated from society, and thus more likely to commit antisocial acts, like crime. A young person who is convicted of a felony will likely be housed in a prison at taxpayer expense; with a record, he or she will have great difficulty finding a steady job following release, increasing the likelihood that the person will live in poverty, far more likely to be dependent on government programs to survive.

As with so many other issues covered in this book, the most moral policy is also the most practical. We must break the cycle of violence, crime, and poverty that inflicts such profound damage to society and do more to get the best out of our children.

* * *

We're accustomed to setting goals for our children, then giving them a report card to tell them how they performed relative to those goals. But every now and then, we ought to step back and look critically at our adult selves: What grade do we deserve for our performance in keeping the best interest of kids in the forefront of our minds?

I would like to see American towns and cities create a "Community Report Card for Children," containing assessments of their young population's education, health, and safety. They should convene workshops and plenary sessions to analyze the report card and recommend solutions that are the product of consensus among a wide range of stakeholders. The group should devise an action and advocacy plan with a clear vision for how to execute the recommendations. Communities engage in assessments like this for a great many other issues—why not children's well-being? After all, so much of the community's future relies on those young people.

Government cannot guarantee that all consumer products will be safe, just as it will never deliver perfect schools or completely eradicate childhood obesity. It can merely be an agent for positive change. But that starts with adults. Let's demand more from those who represent children in government. And let's demand more of ourselves as the adults whom children emulate and whose empathy they depend on. Because as long as we keep their interests in mind, this country's best days will continue to be ahead of it. We cannot be so selfish as to only live in the right now. We owe it to our country and to ourselves to think about how our decisions today affect our children now and when they come of age.

NINE

Putting the Fight Back in Women's Rights

Being in Washington, I hear a lot of politicians invoke the Founding Fathers in reverent tones. You don't hear nearly as much about the women who played a role in forging America's identity as a democratic republic. The woman whose story made the most profound impact on me as a child was Abigail Adams.

When I was in sixth grade, my school staged the play *1776*, a musical that dramatizes the events surrounding the Declaration of Independence. I was given the part of Abigail Adams, who was not just the wife of John Adams but one of the future President's closest political advisers. From reading the couple's correspondence, it is clear that Abigail was a keen political observer and that her analysis did much to inform the perspective that John brought to the Continental Congress.

"I long to hear that you have declared an independency," wrote Abigail Adams to her husband in Philadelphia in March 1776. She continued,

> And, by the way, in the new code of laws which I suppose it will
> be necessary for you to make, I desire you would remember

the ladies and be more generous and favorable to them than
your ancestors.

Unfortunately, Abigail couldn't influence John in that regard and
progress for women would be painfully slow in the centuries to come.
The progress has not been linear. There have been moments where the
rights and freedoms of women have expanded, only to bring an even more
powerful backlash by a sexist status quo.

Since the early days of American settlers, women had been treated like
property, which is why women's rights activists forged a natural alliance with
slaves and abolitionists. This coalition gained strength in the 1850s, with
Harriet Tubman and Sojourner Truth champions of both causes. But after
the Civil War sent the institution of slavery into retreat, the male patriarchy
persisted. Women's rights activists like Susan B. Anthony were so frustrated about being left behind that they lined up with racist whites in the
South who were willing to let women vote if only they'd cast ballots against
the Fifteenth Amendment, which would give African Americans the right
to vote. Fortunately, that awkward, regrettable alliance did not last long.

The movie *Lincoln*, released in 2012 and based on Doris Kearns Good-
win's book *A Team of Rivals*, illustrated just how ingrained American male
opposition was to giving women the franchise. A gripping scene depicting debate in the House of Representatives over the Thirteenth Amendment to the U.S. Constitution, which prohibited slavery, shows the
opposition arguing that prohibiting slavery could lead to granting blacks
the franchise, but what brought overwhelming roars of opposition from
Democrats and Republicans in 1865, was the suggestion that this could
lead to women being granted the franchise as well!

The campaign to let women vote stalled for another generation, until in
the twentieth century Elizabeth Cady Stanton modified the message, pressing for civil rights not because women were "equal" to men, as previous suf-
fragists maintained, but because American elections could profit from
women's maternal sensibilities. Idealism had given way to pragmatism. Still,
it took until 1920 before the Nineteenth Amendment to the Constitution
was ratified.

We should not, however, assume the advancements that have taken place over a few decades are a permanent fixture in American society. That progress can be reversed. Every woman must realize this: Our reproductive rights, privacy, and personal freedoms are all much more fragile than it may seem. As we saw during the 112th Congress and during the 2012 election cycle, Republicans have been waging a "war on women." This is a party that claims to want small government—but wants it big enough so they can tell women exactly what to do with their bodies.

Any woman who is content with the status quo in gender politics hasn't looked closely enough. Men are still paid more than women for the same job—that fact alone should turn every woman into an activist. Because women often remain the primary caregivers of children, we have more incentive to fight for reforms that would make it easier to balance the demands of parenting with the demands of a professional career. It is unacceptable for a woman to be placed on the "mommy track," deprived of a promotion because company management is worried that she'll be too distracted by her parenting job to excel in her profession. It is time for women to speak with one voice to insist that we deserve nothing less than the full measure of the civil rights enjoyed by men and to show that we have the political will to fight for issues that matter to us most.

Pay equity should be one of our top priorities. If women are to stand on the same political and social ground as men, then equal pay for equal work is an urgent, long-overdue economic reform.

Every woman has a stake in this campaign, and any woman can make history for the rest of us. I first encountered Lilly Ledbetter when she testified before the House Judiciary Committee in June 2007. She told us she had been working as an area manager at Goodyear Tire & Rubber for nearly twenty years when she learned of a long-standing pay discrepancy between her and her male colleagues who performed the same job. Ledbetter earned $3,727 per month, while the lowest-paid male area manager earned $4,286; those with seniority similar to hers earned even more. Immediately upon learning this, Lilly took her case to court. She won.

But her employers appealed the ruling and the lower court decision was reversed, citing law that required discrimination suits to be filed within 180 days of the most recent act of discrimination. Ledbetter's attorneys had argued that she met that standard, since each paycheck she received that was less than her male colleagues represented a new act of discrimination.

Having lost at the appeals court level, Ledbetter petitioned to the Supreme Court. Justices elected not to follow long-standing precedent that each new unfair paycheck represents a new cause of action, and her claim was dismissed. Incredibly, they ruled that she needed to have filed a suit within six months of the first unfair paycheck, even though she had no way of knowing about the disparity at that point. In fact, the only way she learned about the disparity between her pay and that of her male co-workers was that someone had anonymously slipped payroll records into her mailbox.

Fortunately, the division of powers in America's government made it possible for Congress and the President to right this wrong. Legislation was crafted that would clarify that an employee is discriminated against anew with each unfair paycheck. The Lilly Ledbetter Fair Pay Act of 2009 was the very first piece of legislation that President Obama signed into law.

It was a milestone. It was progress. But it was incomplete. In the fourth quarter of 2012, American women earned seventy-nine cents for every dollar men earned for the same job. It should be plain to this generation that this inequity must end before the torch passes to the next generation.

We should not allow another generation of women to spend their work life in such an unfair system. Over the course of a woman's professional life, she loses over $400,000 because of her gender. That is money that a woman can't spend purchasing a home or sending her children to college.

We need a call to action for women to fight back against this intolerable inequity, reducing the twenty-one-cent gap. The Lilly Ledbetter Act is one tool, but the problem is systemic. Professional organizations like the National Association of Women Business Owners and the International Federation of Business and Professional Women have made closing the gap an urgent priority. On days when they are lobbying on Capitol Hill and meeting with members of Congress in their districts, professional women have pushed representatives to support the Paycheck Fairness Act. This legislation would end the secrecy surrounding pay issues, enabling female workers to have the evidence they need to bring legal action against employers who pay male workers more. Progress is being made with women's wages, a trend that's reflected in public opinion polling. A recent survey of registered voters showed that 84 percent supported the Paycheck Fairness Act.

In a competitive work environment, where the best talent is in high demand, women should research and even question a prospective employer about pay equity for comparable positions. Women CEOs should lead by example by ensuring that their own companies close the gap. The twenty-one-cent gap can be closed, but it will take pressure and commitment to do it. Women need to show up at town hall meetings and ask their members of Congress where they stand on Paycheck Fairness. Most likely, if they are represented by a Democrat, their representative is already supportive. The fact that a 2011 version of the bill had nearly two hundred cosponsors without a single Republican among them tells you where the GOP stands. Women should not let them get away with saying, "This will just create more litigation." That is an excuse and a cop-out. Accountability on pay equity is essential because, sadly, we know that voluntary progress will take too long.

Discrimination doesn't stop at pay equity. In the 112th Congress, the reauthorization of the Violence Against Women Act (VAWA) passed the Senate with new, essential protections for Native Americans and victims of violence related to their sexual orientation. But the Tea Party–controlled House refused to consider the bill with those provisions and those members blocked the reenactment of VAWA for the first time since it first became law in 1994. Finally, after a two-year fight, at the beginning of the 113th Congress, the Senate again passed VAWA. Having attracted the support of 78 senators from both parties, there was new pressure on the House GOP. Those members allowed the legislation to come to the floor for a vote, but not without insisting on a vote on an amendment that would strip out the protections for Native Americans, LGBT Americans, and immigrants. That gambit failed, and the bill passed. It was signed into law by the President on March 7, 2013. For me, it was a proud and historic moment.

Another piece of legislation imperiled by Tea Party extremism was the Trafficking Victims Protection Reauthorization Act. The original law, the Trafficking Victims Protection Act (TVPA) of 2000 was the first comprehensive federal law to address trafficking in persons, a modern form of slavery. Today, 293,000 American children are at risk of being trafficked. It is a crime under federal and international law and it is a crime in almost every state in the United States. The law provided a three-pronged approach of prevention, protection, and prosecution. As a state senator, I was the primary sponsor of Florida's law criminalizing human and sexual trafficking.

The federal legislation to reauthorize TVPA was introduced in 2011 and had bipartisan support, but the bill's Republican sponsor, Rep. Chris Smith (R-NJ), reintroduced it with controversial antiabortion language that stalled the bill's progress. It should come as no surprise that Representative Smith would inject abortion politics into something as universally abhorrent as human trafficking. This is the same representative who was the principal sponsor of House Resolution 3, the legislation that would have allowed for federal Medicaid funds to be used to terminate pregnancy only if the woman was a victim of "forcible rape"—a bill cosponsored by Congressman and former Republican vice presidential candidate Paul Ryan. While it was unclear exactly how "forcible rape" was to be defined, it likely would have exempted statutory rape, incest, and possibly rape taking place when the victim was drugged or unconscious. Fortunately, the TVPA legislation passed as part of the Violence Against Women Act reauthorization, without the offensive antiabortion provisions.

It's sad that in the year 2013 I have to urge women to be more actively engaged in the political process to prevent a few men from redefining rape, or from weakening human trafficking legislation. Yet the threat to women is real, as evidenced by Paul Ryan being chosen as the vice presidential candidate by Mitt Romney, despite Ryan's support for redefining rape and his equally outrageous support for requiring a rape victim to have to carry her pregnancy to term.

There is no more powerful weapon in politics than a message, and women must stand up and tell their stories and, yes, sadly, explain why we need to continue to pass anti–human trafficking legislation and why any rape is rape.

I hope young women were paying close attention in early 2012 to the controversy sparked by the activism of Georgetown Law student Sandra Fluke. As a campus leader, Fluke had sought to convince administrators of the Jesuit school that it was not fair for them to place limitations on health-care benefits for female students, such as denying them coverage for contraceptives. The Georgetown University president, John J. De-Gioia, refused to budge.

But the passage of the Affordable Care Act gave Fluke new leverage, because the reforms made it necessary for all employers, including religious institutions like Georgetown, to offer full medical coverage, including for contraceptives.

There was an uproar among some members of the religious community, who claimed that the health-care reform law was compelling them to subsidize behavior, such as birth control, that was against their religion. The Obama administration put forth a compromise rule that would allow religious institutions, such as hospitals and universities, to avoid directly paying for birth control coverage but required the insurance company providing the policy to include it in the benefits. There are bound to be legal challenges over this issue in the months to come, but I'm glad that the President has made it clear that his administration will do its utmost to protect the rights of women who work for religious institutions to have coverage for contraceptives, if they want them.

Darrell Issa (R-CA), chairman of the House Oversight and Government Reform Committee, staged a "hearing" to discuss what his party considered an unconstitutional violation of the First Amendment. But if it were truly a hearing, then Republicans would have welcomed all opinions. The Democrats submitted the name of Fluke as a witness, but Issa rejected her on the basis that she did not have the "credentials" to speak at the so-called hearing. Issa called ten people to testify on their outrage—and all ten were men.

It was outrageous, and it was a flagrant act of sexism.

Democrats, led by Elijah Cummings of Maryland and Carolyn Maloney of New York, scheduled a special hearing to give Fluke a chance to speak a few weeks later. She spoke movingly of a classmate who had a medical condition that required the use of drugs also used as contraceptives; Georgetown would not cover the cost. Fluke's remarks were succinct and unsensational, marking the beginning of a more nuanced conversation about how U.S. domestic policies interact with religious institutions.

Apparently, that intellectual subtlety was lost on conservative talk-show host Rush Limbaugh. He wanted to talk about Sandra Fluke's private life. "What does it say about the college co-ed Susan [sic] Fluke," he said, "who goes before a congressional committee and essentially says that she must be paid to have sex, what does it make her? It makes her a slut, right? It makes her a prostitute." He went on and on, in that vein and worse. The Web site MediaMatters counted forty-six instances over the course of the next three days that Limbaugh attacked Fluke's character on his show.

The outcry was immediate. Even Georgetown's president, John J. De-Gioia, who opposed Fluke's position on reproductive rights, said in a public letter that he applauded Fluke and her deportment before Congress. A few conservative commentators also stepped up, including Peggy Noonan, who called Limbaugh's remarks "piggish."

Scores of prominent Republican politicians ignored Limbaugh's vile attack. Mitt Romney, then running for President, said only that "he would have said it differently." That statement leads me to the same question that columnist Maureen Dowd printed in *The New York Times*: "Is there a right way to call a woman a slut?"

John Boehner, the Speaker of the House, said only that Limbaugh's slander was "inappropriate." Conservative columnist George Will had a pointed retort: "Using the salad fork for your entrée, that's inappropriate." He continued, "It is the responsibility of conservatives to police the right and its excesses . . . and it was depressing because what it indicates is that Republican leaders are afraid of Rush Limbaugh." And the reason they're afraid of Limbaugh, I would add, is that he gives voice to a set of sexist notions that appeal to Republican voters on the far right.

Several months later, in August 2012, Republicans were more aggressive in condemning another set of incendiary remarks from one of their own, Rep. Todd Akin from Missouri. During his U.S. Senate campaign, Akin told an interviewer that abortions should never be allowed, even in cases of rape, because it's "really rare" that rape victims get pregnant. "If it's a legitimate rape," he continued, "the female body has ways to try to shut the whole thing down."

Despite calls by GOP leaders for Akin to abandon his campaign, those same leaders declined to say what, exactly, bothered them about Akin's remarks, aside from his complete ignorance of the female anatomy. A great many Republicans support a ban on all abortions, including those from rape and incest. It seems they were angry at Akin for doing a bad job at explaining why they favored a policy that is so hideously cruel to women who are victims of sexual assault. It wasn't long before another prominent Republican candidate, Richard Mourdock, sparked a similar controversy, remarking that his opposition to abortions in the case of rape was based on his opinion that every pregnancy was a gift from God. When vice presidential candidate Paul Ryan was asked why he opposed a rape victim being able to terminate a resulting pregnancy, he said, "I'm very proud of my pro-life record, and I've always adopted . . . the position that the method of conception doesn't change the definition of life." I'm sure I don't need to point out to most readers how outrageous it is for the Republican Party to nominate for vice president a man who refers to rape as a "method of conception."

These episodes damaged the campaigns of all three candidates, largely because women stepped forward to challenge the sexist notions at the heart of those remarks. One of the most inspiring moments occurred in

March 2011, after Rep. Chris Smith announced on the House floor that he supported an amendment that would strip funding for Planned Parenthood's health and sex education services. Rep. Jackie Speier (D-CA) rose to speak, and to illustrate the importance of Planned Parenthood, the congresswoman described having her own abortion, for medical reasons, and how it was a grueling decision that caused her to grieve for a child that might have been. The very next speaker, Rep. Gwen Moore (D-WI), narrated her own harrowing chapter—an unplanned pregnancy at age eighteen. Because she didn't have access to Planned Parenthood, Moore didn't even have the choice of whether to terminate the pregnancy. Had she had access to the agency, she might have benefited from the guidance its staff offers to young mothers who are trying to raise a child while at the same time going to school. (Moore's pregnancy kept her from accepting an invitation to study at Radcliffe, which was then Harvard's college for women.)

These brave women lawmakers stepped forward to describe a vulnerable time in their lives, and in doing so they seized power and influence in the debate over reproductive rights: The video of those floor speeches went viral, and the pair soon found themselves on *The View*, discussing these episodes with a national television audience. These are the kinds of conversations that bring about shifts in the cultural paradigm.

In the years to come, we will need more women like Sandra Fluke, who exposed herself to ridicule and derision but who still succeeded in making Americans more sensitive to gender issues. We are strengthened by President Obama, who made the Ledbetter Act such a high priority and had the good grace to phone Fluke to tell her how proud he was of her. I also reached out to Sandra soon after the hearing and resulting firestorm from Rush Limbaugh's appalling character assassination, and we sat down to discuss her future. It was with a great deal of pride that I campaigned with her across the country on behalf of the President. Sandra Fluke is the next generation of young women for whom Lilly Ledbetter and so many others fight.

We will also need more hard-charging, courageous congresswomen

like Representative Moore and Representative Speier who will close
ranks to stand up for women's rights to make decisions that relate to their
health, as well as to close that twenty-one-cent gap that still exists between men and women doing the same job. Finally, we will need something we don't yet have: a champion for women's rights in the Republican
Party.

I'd like to think that all women elected to Congress—regardless of party
affiliation—could unite behind the causes of women's privacy rights and
pay equity. But when nearly all the Republican women in Congress voted
against the Ledbetter Act, which allows women to fight pay discrimination in the workplace, it became evident that party politics remains the
obstacle to progress.

I hear Republican members, regardless of gender, argue that a law
holding an employer accountable for lack of pay equity "would just invite
more lawsuits." That seems to be the one-size-fits-all explanation given
by most Republicans when they vote against a law that has a legitimate
enforcement mechanism. I believe that women who are elected to serve in
Congress have a responsibility not just to their constituents but to their
fellow women. However, I strongly suspect that many Republican women
in Congress cast their "no" votes because they recognize that strongly
embracing women's rights would alienate them from the Republican Party
and its hard-right voters. I serve with many Republican women whom I
like personally, which makes it that much tougher to watch some of
them struggle when they want to stand up for women, but their instinct
for political survival is stronger.

Perhaps they learned this by watching the demise of those few female
Republican legislators who dared to cast votes in support of women's issues. Senator Olympia Snowe had the courage to support two female
nominees to the U.S. Supreme Court, Sonia Sotomayor and Elena Ka-
gan. In 2003, she infuriated the party by voting against a ban on late-term
abortions. In October 2009, she provided the single Republican vote in

the Finance Committee in support of the Affordable Care Act, which contained provisions against allowing insurers to treat being a woman as a "preexisting condition"—that is, a health factor warranting a more expensive premium. Thanks to that moderate record, Snowe was booed lustily by conservatives at a Republican caucus meeting in Bangor, Maine, in early 2012. As it became clear that she would likely be challenged by a Tea Party conservative in that year's primary and faced with the prospect of six more years of polarization, Snowe announced her retirement, saying, "Unfortunately, I do not realistically expect the partisanship of recent years in the Senate to change over the short term."

Alaska Senator Lisa Murkowski, another moderate Republican, supported stem cell research and is pro-choice. During the 2010 election cycle, those "radical" positions earned her a challenger in the primary, which she lost. Murkowski decided to run as an Independent to win back her seat in the general election. The message that Republican voters have sent to female members of their party is that voting as women is to their political peril.

If female Republicans holding elected office can't change the party's outmoded attitudes on women's issues, then I hope the wives of male Republicans will make an appeal, similar to the way Abigail Adams did with her husband. Failing that, the daughters and granddaughters of leading Republicans may be allies in our cause. Although I don't know her personally nor agree with her on many issues, it was heartening to read Meghan McCain's column in The Daily Beast following the election. She said,

> I've spent most of my adult life fighting for change from inside the Republican Party. We Republicans need to look at the future instead of living in the past. We have to learn from what the last two presidential elections have taught us. We must accept each other and the different opinions within the party instead of trying to cannibalize people that diverge from an arbitrary purity test. I refuse to let the extremists win. We can't let the Tea Party bully us any longer. We can't keep

worrying about ultraconservative white male voters. At the end of the day, I still believe I'm on the right side of history, and we can't let this party sink away. We can and we must evolve. I don't know exactly how yet, but I for one am ready to spend the next four years helping us get there.

And if we don't move forward, adapt, and become relevant again, the Republican Party isn't going to survive. It will just continue to alienate more moderate voters like myself. If I don't see some changes in the next four years, I'm going to consider registering as an Independent in 2016.

The longer the GOP clings to its denial of equality for women, it will continue to lose women's precious votes. In the 2012 presidential election, Barack Obama beat Mitt Romney by 18 points among women, who made up 54 percent of the electorate. Had Romney managed to draw even, he may have won the election.

This cause of achieving fairness for women should be so galvanizing that it overwhelms the divisions between women loyal to different parties. I can only speak for myself, but I have never hesitated to work with a Republican colleague in Congress, no matter how conservative, on legislation favorable to women. In that spirit, I collaborated with Rep. Sue Myrick (R-NC) to pass the EARLY Act, a piece of legislation that seeks to raise awareness of the potential for breast cancer in younger women. To make headway in Washington on issues that matter most, it makes a big difference when there are champions on both sides of the aisle.

Even as we fight for women's rights in America, we must be conscious of ours being a global campaign. That's why I am so proud to have had Hillary Clinton represent the United States as Secretary of State. I learned a great deal about her values from a speech she delivered in 1995, while she was First Lady, at the United Nations World Conference on Women. "It is no longer acceptable to discuss women's rights as separate from human rights," she said. Clinton continued,

It is a violation of human rights when babies are denied food, or drowned, or suffocated, or their spines broken, simply because they are born girls.

It is a violation of human rights when women and girls are sold into the slavery of prostitution.

It is a violation of human rights when women are doused with gasoline, set on fire, and burned to death because their marriage dowries are deemed too small.

She went on that way, describing how women are raped as a spoil for the victors of a war, how they're denied the right to plan their families, how domestic violence is a leading cause of death among young women worldwide, and how young girls are subjected to the humiliation and pain of genital mutilation. There is simply no excuse—religious, cultural, or otherwise—to treat women with such brutality. The United States should use the full weight of its diplomatic power to eradicate these crude, inhumane practices.

For example, we should do more to pressure the government of Pakistan to crack down on men who commit "honor killings"—the murder of a woman by her husband, purely because he judged that his wife failed to perform her "wifely" duties. It almost sounds too barbaric to believe, but in 2010, 943 women were slain for the honor of their husbands, according to the Human Rights Commission of Pakistan. In August 2012, a Pakistani man named Muhammad Ismail described how he shot his wife dead, then went next door to kill his wife's mother as well as his wife's sister. Ismail told CNN, "I am proud of what I did. That's why I turned myself over to police." He was imprisoned for the crime, but Pakistan's justice system allows him to negotiate for his freedom by offering blood money to the surviving members of his wife's family.

In Western cultures like ours, discrimination against women is more subtle but no less persistent. And the subtlety of it makes it harder to overcome. But women must not doubt our own instincts; we need to educate people to recognize bias and sexism, then equip ourselves with the skills and resources to confront it. Together, we can reverse popular myths that have lingered in American culture despite overwhelming evidence to the contrary.

The President, with two young girls of his own, understands that meeting those goals will take coordinated action, which is why in March 2009, the Obama administration created the White House Council on Women and Girls, with the charge of examining how responsive federal agencies are to issues that matter most to women. Chaired by Valerie Jarrett, this initiative has worked to close the wage gap, expand the availability of paid maternity leave, and make child care more affordable.

In addition, the council is focused on addressing the underrepresentation of professional women in so-called STEM fields: science, technology, engineering, and math. As Jarrett pointed out during her 2013 speech at the White House Technology Inclusion Summit, women fill nearly half the jobs in America but only 25 percent of those in STEM.

For a long time, girls were socialized to believe that it wasn't cool or becoming of them to be good at math or science, or to be smart at all. But over the years, there have been so many women who flipped that conventional wisdom on its head. Grace Hopper, who was instrumental in the invention of the first modern computer, earned her doctorate in mathematics at Yale in 1935, a time when the proportion of females in math doctoral programs was actually higher than it would be in the 1980s.

Mae Jemison, who received a doctorate in medicine from Cornell in 1981, went on to become an astronaut, flying a shuttle mission in 1992. But it wasn't always easy for her. As an engineering student at Stanford, she told *The New York Times,*

> Majoring in engineering, I would have [been] maybe one of two or three African-American students in my classes; some professors would just pretend I wasn't there. I would ask a question and a professor would act as if it was just so dumb, the dumbest question he had ever heard. Then, a white guy would ask the same question, the professor would say, "That's a very astute observation."

Today, we're fortunate that we have a President who knows how important it is for girls and young women to feel more empowered to explore those fields. A 2012 study by the Girl Scout Research Institute found that 82 percent of girls feel "smart enough for a career in STEM." Unfortunately, the study also found that 57 percent of the girls surveyed said they would have to "work harder than a man to be taken seriously" in STEM fields, which may explain why only 13 percent of girls told surveyors that a STEM industry was their "first priority" for a postgraduate career.

My youngest daughter, Shelby, just might be among them. I'm always thrilled to see the enthusiasm with which she tackles her math homework. She tells me it's her favorite subject. She's constantly daring me and Steve to give her math problems so she can solve them in her head. She thinks that's cool—and so do I. When my oldest daughter, Rebecca, was in elementary school, she would reflexively repeat that she was "bad at math." Not wanting this to be a self-fulfilling prophecy, I wouldn't allow her to say that and encouraged her to work harder. She's in eighth grade as of this writing, and carrying an A in math.

In 1972, the passage of Title IX marked the beginning of a new era in higher education, by mandating gender equality in institutions that receive federal funds, leading the way for more opportunities for women most prominently in athletics, but also to improve their education and broaden their professional prospects. For those of you who were thrilled like I was by the U.S. Women's Soccer Team in August 2012 as it marched to a gold medal, keep in mind that those heroics may not have been possible without Title IX. In fact, the team's star player, Abby Wambach, developed her world-class skills playing at my alma mater, the University of Florida, where the women's soccer team was created specifically to comply with Title IX.

In an article about Wambach and Title IX that appeared on the Web site ThinkProgress, it was reported that there are some 200,000 women playing sports at U.S. colleges, many of them enjoying scholarships that not only helped them gain entry to a university but will allow them to graduate without being plagued by student loan payments. Forty-plus years later, these are accomplishments worth celebrating, but the anniversary is also a reminder to commit ourselves to the work that remains undone.

Before we can succeed in changing opinions about what women can and can't do, we must raise expectations for ourselves. This, I believe, will lead more women to enter politics and join me in bringing women's perspective to national issues that sorely need it.

Leading by example is so important. It would have taken much longer for me to recognize what was possible for myself if I had never met a woman named Cathey Steinberg.

A former member of the Georgia General Assembly, Cathey hired me as her chief aide when she ran for the Georgia Public Service Commission, shortly after I graduated from the University of Florida. My job was to travel with her as she campaigned across the state. Here was a Jewish mother who had the nerve to run for office statewide in a very politically conservative state: I admired her moxie.

My parents had instilled in me the confidence that I could do whatever I set my mind to and Cathey Steinberg was the manifestation of that.

Unfortunately, we didn't win that race. Cathey lost the primary to a good ol' boy who had a cozy relationship with the electric utility company, Georgia Power. It likely didn't help that Cathey was Jewish and originally from the Northeast. (Georgia just elected its first Jewish nonjudicial statewide candidate in 2012.)

Still, the experience made a major impression on me. I left Cathey's staff to return to the University of Florida to begin my graduate studies, and one year later became an aide to a Florida legislator, Peter Deutsch. In 1992, Peter decided to run for Congress and I was preparing to be his campaign manager—until the moment he called with another idea. He suggested that I run for the seat he was vacating in the Florida Legislature.

It was an exciting idea, but the timing wasn't exactly ideal. I was just twenty-five years old. I had only been married for a year, and Steve and I had just bought our first home. To be eligible as a candidate, I would have to leave my job as an aide, forgoing my paycheck. And the dawn-to-dusk rigors of the campaign would mean my husband would have to hold down the fort at home. If I won, I'd then spend a good portion of the year traveling back and forth to Tallahassee, which is 470 miles from our home in South Florida, although that was already a routine part of my job as Representative Deutsch's legislative assistant. Finally, the Chair of the Broward County Democratic Party and other leaders, male and (sadly) female, too, told me that there were other candidates with more seniority and experience, who would have the party's support: "Wait your turn," I was told.

After a month of talking it over with my husband, we decided that there would always be obstacles to our ambitions, and there was no point in waiting for a "perfect" opportunity that might never arrive. I looked around at who was serving in the Florida House and realized that my generation's voice was severely underrepresented. I entered the race, against five other candidates—four of them men—and I won. Not because I had more money or connections than the other contenders (I had far less) but mainly because I knocked on twenty-five thousand doors in the district I wanted to represent, so when those voters went to the polls, they could vote for someone who had taken the time to talk to them personally and know the issues they cared about. What I lacked in resources I made up for in shoe leather.

In 1992, women had to work a little bit harder to overcome societal perceptions that we lacked decisiveness, that we were too timid to push the nuclear button or send American troops to war. It was nonsense then just as now. Given what we have seen of Hillary Clinton as Secretary of State, is there any question that she would have been a forceful, decisive commander in chief on foreign policy matters? She may have lost the 2008 Democratic primary, but I don't think it was because she was a woman. If anything, that campaign demonstrated to me how much American attitudes have evolved. In fact, I think Hillary Clinton should have taken advantage of the historic nature of her candidacy. As a national co-chair of her campaign, I remember feeling frustrated that then Senator Clinton didn't emphasize her strengths as a female candidate. She did so later on in the campaign, but it wasn't consistent throughout. I always thought it was a missed opportunity to capitalize on an advantage.

I'm sure that Hillary Clinton's historic candidacy and stellar service as Secretary of State, and Nancy Pelosi becoming the first woman Speaker of the House, serve as an inspiration for women. This is vital, because we need more women to get involved in public service. In 2006, while preparing for a speech in Nashville before an audience of women, I learned that the United States ranked 69th out of 187 nations in the percentage of women sitting in the national legislature. I recently checked those statistics again, and it's gotten worse. Now we rank 79th! It will take a new generation of ambitious, talented women to reverse that trend.

More than thirty-five years ago, Republican diplomat Jeane Kirkpatrick wrote, "Why, when women in increasing numbers are asserting themselves, training themselves, seeking equal rights, equal opportunities, and equal responsibilities in every aspect of American life, have so few contested successfully in the political arena? How can more women be encouraged to seek public office?" Sadly, these questions have not gone away.

I suspect a lot of women hear the same thing I heard twenty years ago: "It's not your turn." Instead of being encouraged to run for the office they want, too often they're directed toward more modest political goals. They're told to first become a community leader, then a member of their school board, a county commissioner, then a state legislator, and only then should they attempt to run for Congress or statewide office, if they are even thought of at all. Too often, the first thought for an open seat in elected office is a long list of well-qualified men in a community. Men start running for office much earlier than most women, so the ramp of their political career is longer. In a seniority-driven system like Congress, men have more of an opportunity to move up once elected, serve on choice committees, be committee chairs, or rise to legislative leadership. Many women, once they finally decide to run for office, do so after their children are school-age or even out of the house. The consequence to waiting their turn or starting later for family reasons is that each of those rungs on the ladder represents a huge time commitment, and I suspect that many women run out of ramp before they reach their true potential. There is nothing wrong with waiting if that is what they want to do, but they shouldn't feel that they *must* wait.

Nor should they feel guilty about pursuing those ambitions at the same time as being a mother. I remember during my first congressional campaign in 2004, facing a Republican nominee, who was also female but who was losing in the polls and had become so desperate that her main campaign message was that I shouldn't be in Congress because I was a bad mother. She repeatedly said, "My opponent has five-year-old twins and an infant" and that "you can be a good mother or a good member of Congress but you can't be both at the same time." At one point, a reporter called me to recount a story this candidate had told her during a recent conversation: that during a debate I did not have a pen handy, and so I used a crayon instead. This was offered as evidence that my efforts to balance motherhood and politics left me "frazzled." I proudly acknowledged using a crayon to jot notes. And you can believe I challenged the idea that this made me a less effective representative. I told the reporter: "All that proves is that I didn't have a pen. And while as a mother, I'm often without a pen, I am never without a crayon." A resourceful mom makes for a resourceful representative!

Too often, women think they don't have enough experience to run. This is another example of the difference in how women and men are socialized. Can most women imagine a conversation with the men they know regarding whether they should consider running for public office in which the man says, "I'm not sure I'm qualified"? Take it from me: If you want it badly enough, and you're willing to work for it, you don't have to "wait your turn."

But this is bigger than any one woman's personal ambition. In a competitive political arena, we are outnumbered. And as long as we lack the strength in numbers, we will lack the critical mass needed to ensure that policies crafted in Congress account for interests specific to women. This is why it is so important to add more women's voices to policymaking roles. Our issues are far more likely to reach the top of the agenda.

✦ ✦ ✦

Nearly all women, but especially seniors, have fielded a phone call in which a salesman asked, "May I speak to the man of the house?" A more subtle version of that question asks to speak to "Mr. Last Name." The implication, of course, was that the man was not only the one who earned a salary but the only one who made decisions about how to spend the family's money. Today, I'm thankful for the Do Not Call Registry, and neither my husband nor I get those calls!

Of all the myths that hold back our gender, the most outdated is the one that insists women aren't capable of being the family's "breadwinner." That is untrue now and it will be even less true in the future if we succeed in making reforms that ease the burden of being a working mother. In fact, often in today's single-parent families, the woman is the only breadwinner and economic decision maker. A Pew Research Center study released in May 2013 found that in 4 out of 10 American households with kids under 19, the woman is either the sole or primary source of income for the family.

Recent studies show that women fared much better than men during the recession—our unemployment rate rose only by 1.6 percentage points while men's rate rose by 2.8 percentage points, according to a recent report by the Center for American Progress. In a survey by Prudential Financial, 53 percent of women were the breadwinner—that is, the primary money-maker in their home. That figure includes women who are single and widowed, but a quarter of the respondents were married women who out-earned their husbands. And yet the same survey found that of those female breadwinners, only 23 percent felt "equipped" to make financial decisions for their household. That self-defeating attitude needs to be adjusted; if they're earning the majority of the household income, those women are absolutely entitled to make those decisions. Just thinking about casual conversations I have had with my own girlfriends, all of whom should know better, I can't think of one of them who would make a major financial decision or even a major household purchase, without their spouse. Their spouses, on the other hand, would think nothing of coming home with a big-screen television with no prior discussion, my own husband included! Admittedly, since I am married to a banker, I usually defer to Steve on how to structure our finances, but we make major financial decisions, including purchases, together.

It's important for mothers to be mindful of their value within the home and the workplace. Just as they deserve equal say in financial decisions, women should be proactive about negotiating terms of employment that allow them to be available to their children.

With the American workplace becoming more and more virtual, telecommuting is increasingly an option for parents who want to be able to be home for their young children or who can't afford to pay for day care. Some employers are happy to offer flextime, a schedule that can be adjusted every day, if necessary, with a defined set of work-related obligations. Job sharing allows two workers who want to spend more time at home to both work part-time, effectively filling a single position. That option will possibly be even more attractive in 2014, when it will be possible for a worker to forgo his or her employer's health-care package by shifting to part-time, then purchasing health care through the health-care exchange.

Incentives are a way to encourage businesses to help working parents balance. But as always, the question is whether there is the political will to make it a priority. Personally, I love the idea of giving tax credits to businesses who demonstrate a willingness to provide workers with children the flexibility they need to balance work and family. I would like to reward companies who have the foresight to invest in a day-care center. Businesses large and small should have an incentive to make innovations in the workplace that so clearly improve the lives of their employees. One of the biggest reasons for absenteeism in the workplace is related to the needs of an employee's children. Research shows that making a more hospitable work environment for parents to meet their children's and their employer's needs is good for business and the employer's bottom line.

Sometimes it's a simple matter of bringing together groups who may not realize how much they can help one another. In my district, we organized a roundtable for operators of child-care centers so that they could interact directly with the corporations where their clients work. These child-care centers are the glue of a community, but they often have a thin profit margin, making them vulnerable to market conditions. For instance, a small child-care center may not be able to stay in business after a family with two children enrolled at the center moves out of town or if one or two of their parent clients loses a job. The closure of that center could have a ripple effect on the other parents who depended on it. They may have to switch jobs so that they can be closer to another high-quality child-care center. In this way, companies lose valuable employees. Facilitating a dialogue between these interconnected parties so that they can all gain a measure of stability seemed like long-overdue common sense that helps the surrounding businesses, the employees/parents, and the local economy.

Other worthwhile reforms require a more aggressive approach. President Bill Clinton deserves a great deal of praise for using his political capital in 1993 to make the Family and Medical Leave Act a reality. The act provided up to three months of unpaid, job-protected leave for people who need to take care of family members in specified situations (including twelve weeks for the birth of a child). This was an important step in bringing attention to the work-family balance and addressing a need in a tangible way.

The next step, which is urgently needed, is to specify paid leave for these same employees. Some defenders of women's rights argue against paid family leave, on the basis that it will make employers steer away from hiring female employees, knowing that a male employee is less likely to use the leave. That shadow of discrimination has to be acknowledged, but overall, paid family leave will be a positive factor for companies and for the country as a whole.

It is shameful that the United States is one of only five nations, out of 168 surveyed, that mandates no paid parental leave. One of the other four, Australia, mandates a year of unpaid leave; the other three, Lesotho, Papua New Guinea, and Swaziland, are closer to the U.S. model. They offer no leave; we offer twelve weeks, unpaid. As someone who was able to be home for at least the first few months with my babies, I can speak to the importance of that bonding, and it's heartbreaking for me to think about the mothers who have to leave their tiny infants behind as they trudge off to a job.

Our neighbor to the north, Canada, offers an entire year of paid leave (if combined by both parents). For parents to have that much time to bond with their child, not worrying about holding on to their jobs, sharing the responsibilities that come with a baby that's totally dependent on them—that's a family that will have a strong foundation.

I got a dose of how tough it would be to establish required paid leave in the United States when I introduced paid leave legislation as a state senator in Florida. The concept I used allowed employees to use their unemployment compensation for a period of paid leave following the birth of a child. This would have meant that unemployment compensation tax rates would likely increase slightly to pay for it, but the dividends of holding on to a good employee, whose loyalty would be intensified, is quantifiable for most businesses. The legislation passed through one committee by one vote and went no further because of the heavy opposition from business lobbyists. Similar legislation has languished in Congress as well.

There will always be political obstacles. I certainly hope that working parents aren't waiting for the government to convince their employers to improve the workplace for working parents. If so, they may be in for a long wait.

The good news is that businesses big and small are coming to realize that it's in their best interest to make allowances for working parents. A 2002 study by the University of Oklahoma and Lehigh University showed that companies that allowed 10 percent of their workers to switch to temporary or part-time positions saw improvement in their stock prices, by roughly the same percentage. It also showed that those workers remained loyal to their employer. DuPont regularly surveys its employees and has found that those who take advantage of the company's work-life programs, like flextime, are more likely to "go the extra mile" and stay with the company for fifteen years or more. A study by Watson

Wyatt Worldwide found that progressive HR practices, including work-day flexibility, were the biggest factor in determining a company's overall financial performance. Providing child-care services to employees reduces the number of missed work days by up to 30 percent, according to yet another study.

All of this research leads to the same conclusion: Working parents who feel like their employers will help them to balance the demands of child care, or being able to be present for important events for their children, are willing to work extra hard in return for that consideration. They will stick by their employers, providing valuable continuity.

So these policies aren't just the right thing for employers to do ethically. It's also the smartest, most practical approach for those business owners who care about the bottom line.

In the case of my professional life, my bosses are my constituents. Every two years, they get to decide whether I can continue to work on their behalf. So far so good! Often, a working mother will ask me, "How do you do it?" Unfortunately, there's no short answer to that question. The truth is that I balance the challenges of a political career with the demands of raising three young children by not doing a lot of hand-wringing over how I'm going to "do it." I never consider that it can't be done. I just know that I do my very best every single day, both for my children and for the constituents I represent in Washington. That doesn't mean it's easy. It doesn't mean that I don't make mistakes. I have learned that there is no finish line and no such thing as doing it perfectly. There's just a new day with a new day's challenges. And on any given day there are a number of tough choices, but failing my children or my constituents is not one of them. The work, whether parental or professional, is too important.

Some of the strategies that work for me may not work for everyone, but first I must confess to one rather unfair advantage: my husband, Steve Schultz, who I affectionately refer to as Saint Steve. During that first campaign in 1992 for the Florida House, after another set of men had discouraged me from running for office, Steve was my hero. For months I practically lived on the front porches of the West Broward County district I hoped to represent. All that walking, with no time to eat except for the chocolate milk shake that Steve had ready before I left in the morning.

Twenty-five thousand doors later, I got elected, and our lives got even more complicated! But Steve has such an easygoing nature, even when some political emergency makes it necessary for me to change our plans, he rolls with it. Once we had kids, a whole new dimension was added to our lives. Even when my pregnancy with our third child coincided with a sudden race for Congress, Steve was totally supportive and gave me confidence that we would make it work. I'm so grateful to him for that because having a husband who truly believes in equal parenting (and in our case lopsided parenting when I'm traveling) gives me the peace of mind that my kids are in good hands. Every mother knows that all is not right with the world if something is wrong in your child's life. When something fun or unexpected comes up for Steve, I'm there to help him to strike the same balance.

Beyond having a supportive and adaptable husband, I find that it helps to put the kids' events on the schedule first, in permanent ink. Whenever it's possible, I bring them to work with me, which gives us more time to bond, while giving them a glimpse of how hard I work when I'm not with them and what my work is about. I want to instill in my children the knowledge that their mom's job is to help make other people's lives better and see how public service can do that. I find it's also important to not be afraid to ask for help. Too often women believe that "having it all" means doing it all by yourself. I lean on my parents, who live in our hometown, and my best girlfriends, who are also working moms, and they lean on me. We all want each other to be successful, so we pitch in whenever we can.

There will always be days when it's harder to juggle work with parenting, but if your children know about the demands of your job, they will be patient with you. My kids are proud of me, which helps as well. It still amazes me how patient they are when constituents come up to me in restaurants or the supermarket. It is not uncommon for one of my kids to offer to snap a picture when someone asks. Serving my constituents is a family affair!

It has become fashionable to say that working women can't have it all, which was the premise of a July 2012 essay in *The Atlantic* by Anne-Marie Slaughter, a former academic and diplomat who described her struggles to work in the public sector while raising her two sons. I can empathize with her struggle, but I think the better question is whether a demanding career and motherhood are worth the stress that comes with it, and the answer for me is: absolutely. I am proud of the work I have done in my district, in Washington, and on behalf of President Obama and Democrats across the country as chair of the Democratic National Committee. I'm even more proud of the three children I return home to. Everyone has a different definition of "having it all," but making sure my husband and kids are happy and thriving and doing my job really well is all that matters to me.

I'm humbled to hear from girls and young women who consider me a role model. And I hope I will have the opportunity to continue fighting on their behalf. But to improve the lives of all American women, we all have to fight together. Let's not settle for "close enough." Let's make Abigail Adams and all the past generations of women proud by achieving full equality.

◄◦►

TEN

America's Promise to Immigrants

E. *Pluribus Unum:* Out of many, one. The greatness of the United States is found not in our economic wealth, nor in our military might, but in our people. We may come from different lands, speak a different tongue, or practice a different faith; but we celebrate that which brings us together: our freedom to speak, believe, and worship as we choose. And of course our right to vote.

As a member of Congress I am regularly asked to speak at naturalization ceremonies in South Florida. It is always so moving to look out on a room of people from Central and South America, Asia, Africa, the Caribbean, and Europe, who come in identifying as one culture and all walk out as Americans. I always encourage them to fully explore their U.S. citizenship, not only by voting in elections and serving on juries but by speaking out on issues in their community.

But these encounters also remind me about the responsibility I, as an elected official, have to the many potential citizens of this country. We owe them immigration policies that are coherent and that reward those who are honest and eager to work.

America has always been a grand experiment in diversity. The framers of the Constitution had a radical (for its time) notion that the people of this nation should have the right to practice their religion, and that being granted this liberty, they would grant it to others who practiced another doctrine. From that principle flowed aspirations for gender equity and racial equality, as well as the sense that immigrant ethnicities add vibrancy to our society. Ideally, we don't merely tolerate other cultures; rather, we celebrate their contribution to the varied spectrum of American identity. This diversity of both people and ideas makes America stronger.

Of course, in a nation that has seen so many waves of immigrants, there have always been disagreements about what groups get to call themselves American. For example, between 1900 and 1910, millions of immigrants came to America seeking jobs in this nation's emerging industrial economy. Typically, they took low-paying jobs that were often dangerous. They weathered fierce anti-immigrant hostility, and even violence, from a portion of the American population fearful that these newcomers were sowing seeds of destruction for the republic. Those fears were unfounded. On the contrary, the immigrants' willingness to work for an honest wage was an engine of prodigious economic growth. Often with the help of unions, these workers' wages increased and within this expanding economy those immigrants' children found work that paid even better.

These immigrants were almost entirely from Europe, and while the first wave may have lived in neighborhoods of de facto ethnic segregation, those barriers were soon overcome as the groups mixed, learning English, marrying across ethnic lines, and having children of mixed ancestry, who then had children themselves. Within a generation or two, these families' identities were not associated so much with their place of origin but with the place to which they'd arrived. They were Americans.

We have seen this pattern of immigration again and again in American history. In modern America, we have a virtually identical phenomenon. The chief difference between this wave of immigrants and the one a hundred years ago is their place of origin. Today, more are emigrating from Latin America and Asia.

So we have known immigration "crises" before. What's more, groups that vilify immigrants likely owe their own American identity to immigrant grandparents or great-grandparents who braved the ethnic tension of the early twentieth century. With the exception of Native Americans, who occupied this land first, all of our ancestors came to the United States at one point or another.

As always, people come to America with hope for making better lives, and we should greet them with hope for the possibilities of what we can achieve together. At the same time we will continue to strive for rational, workable immigration policies, including policing the borders and stopping people from entering the country illegally. America's immigration policies must be informed by common sense and an abiding respect for the lives of those who seek to join our democracy.

The two political parties agree about the need for immigration laws to be enforced, but we disagree about exactly how to stop illegal immigration.

Of course, no single law or enforcement mechanism will end illegal immigration entirely. For example, there are Haitians so desperate to get to America that they climb aboard rickety boats bound for Florida. When one of those boats capsized in June 2012, eleven people drowned and several children went missing. In the Southwest, it is common for poor Central Americans seeking work to give much of their life's savings to a "coyote" who claims a foolproof method of smuggling them into America. In the case of one coyote, that method involved squeezing twenty-three people into the cab and bed of his pickup truck in August 2012. Investigators suspect that a flat tire was enough to cause the truck to flip, killing fifteen people on board.

To prevent some of these human tragedies, and to slow the tide of illegal immigration in general, we need to do more to discourage people from trying to cross the border in the first place. President Obama's administration has increased enforcement efforts along the border, which has had a deterrent effect.

My close friend, former U.S. Representative Gabby Giffords (D-AZ), was always a passionate advocate for border security, having been born and raised in Tucson, where she ran her family's tire business. Gabby's congressional district went right to the border of Mexico and she regularly brought fellow members of Congress and anyone in a position to help address the issue to tour the border with her. Border security was such an important issue for Gabby and her constituents in southern Arizona that on the day she stepped down from Congress, the House of Representatives passed her final piece of legislation, a bill that imposed tougher penalties on smugglers who use small, low-flying aircraft to avoid radar detection and bring drugs across the Mexican border. Before the bill's passage, the law allowed defendants who use ultra-light, single-seat planes to get a lesser penalty than those who use cars or other types of planes. Now, regardless of the vehicle used, the penalty is up to twenty years in prison and a $250,000 fine.

But we know that no matter how effective our border control is, we'll never stop every immigrant who embarks on a costly, dangerous attempt to cross into the United States. To prevent these people from taking such risks, we must crack down on the U.S. businesses that hire undocumented workers.

The anti-immigration activists in the Republican Party may be surprised to learn that it is a Democratic President who has worked the hardest to enforce current law. At the direction of the Obama administration, the Department of Homeland Security has audited at least 7,533 employers suspected of hiring undocumented workers, according to *The Wall Street Journal*. The paper noted that the administration imposed about $100 million in fines. In Obama's first three years, there were more audits and more fines than during the eight years when George W. Bush was President.

These policies are a priority to Democrats, because we recognize that the broken immigration system is dangerous for undocumented workers themselves. Since undocumented workers are likely to avoid police and federal agents, unscrupulous companies and individuals know that these workers are not likely to report on hazardous work conditions or failure to pay adequately for work. Such workers may accept far less than a minimum wage because it is still more than what they were making in their native country. At the same time, as Americans we must accept that without immigrant workers, businesses' labor costs would be higher, and we consumers would have to pay more for the products they produce or services they provide.

Morally, our government must do its best to prevent potential immigrants from placing themselves in such a vulnerable position, encouraging them to explore legal means of work in this country. It is human nature to survive. Trying to stop people who want nothing more than to earn enough money to feed, clothe, and house their families is like trying to stop rushing water from filling in empty spaces. It makes more sense to control the flow of the water in an orderly way, so it doesn't overflow.

As a further protection for undocumented workers, we should continue to broaden the definition of U visas. Traditionally designed to reward undocumented residents who reported a crime, U visas give an immigrant up to four years of legal status and work eligibility. But in recent years, there have been occasions where undocumented workers were given U visas for reporting on hazardous work conditions. This might also be a means for undocumented workers to alert the government about low wages or harassment by their employers. Broader use of the U visa in this way could deter companies who think they can get away with exploiting illegal immigrants.

It's my hope that opportunities will always be available in the United States for dedicated laborers, but not at the expense of the human rights of those workers. Immigration laws should be enforced with that fundamental American value in mind.

Immigration policy should be about more than just dealing with those who immigrate illegally. It should also be about attracting immigrants who want to come and make meaningful contributions to American society.

People like Maria Siemionow, a talented surgeon born in Poland but eager to learn from American physicians. In her autobiography,

Dr. Siemionow explains how she didn't have the "connections" to earn a visa as a medical trainee, nor the money to fly to the United States to be interviewed for positions available at surgical clinics. And so when she learned that a group of American doctors who shared her interest in microsurgery were going to be visiting the former Yugoslavia to teach courses for a week, she boarded a train for a two-day trip to intercept them. Upon arriving, Siemionow convinced a physician at a Louisville clinic to give her a fellowship, qualifying her for legal residency in the United States. She liked America so much that she decided she wanted to build her career here. In 2008, Siemionow made history as the leader of the Cleveland Clinic surgical team that completed the United States' first face transplant.

Siemionow's story has a happy ending, but I wonder about other doctors, engineers, and scientists who are as talented and persistent as she is but not as lucky about catching a break in their bid to get to America.

The H1B visa program fulfills this purpose. It is essentially a work permit that allows a U.S. company or university to hire a foreign worker or student based on his or her professional specialty, allowing that worker and that worker's family to legally reside in America for at least six years. This option appeals to students and foreign workers who want to avoid the arduous, time-consuming process of applying for a green card.

The H1B visa is not a threat to American workers; the government awards these visas only in industries where it's apparent that there is a lack of qualified native-born candidates. One example is nursing, a field in which the shortage of American nurse candidates has made it necessary to recruit from foreign nursing schools.

But there are a limited number of H1B visas available. Every year the government offers 65,000 to qualified U.S. companies, who then recruit foreign workers. Another 20,000 are available to foreigners who have graduated from American colleges and universities.

By imposing such a small cap on the number of H1B visas, we are denying opportunities to thousands upon thousands of skilled workers. It makes no sense for us to grant student visas, investing academic resources in a future professional, only to kick that student out of the country following graduation because he or she didn't qualify for an H1B visa or win the lottery for a green card. These are folks who want to stay and apply their new skills in the same country where they learned them.

In June 2012, the Citizenship and Immigration Services agency announced that it had already exhausted its annual quota for H1B visas, meaning that companies seeking skilled foreign workers would have to wait at least another six months to offer them jobs, just as those prospective workers would have to wait to qualify for those jobs. But why should they? More likely, those in-demand workers would take job offers from other companies in other countries where they could start earning a salary immediately.

According to a recent study by the Technology Policy Institute, the lack of green cards and H1B visas led to the departure of 182,000 foreign graduates of American academic institutions between 2003 and 2007. The analysts projected that those graduates, who came from the lucrative fields of science, technology, engineering, and mathematics, would have earned over $13 billion annually, generating over $4 billion in tax revenue for America.

Providing more H1B visas is such a no-brainer that even Republicans with protectionist reflexes may be willing to vote in favor, if only because powerful interest groups like the Chamber of Commerce support that expansion. Personally, I'd be delighted to work with GOP leaders on comprehensive immigration reform that includes increasing the quota for H1B visas.

When enforcing immigration laws, we must consider the constitutional principle that protects Americans against unlawful search and seizure, as well as the danger that an aggressive enforcement policy will lead to the harassment of a particular ethnic group. We must strike a balance between the law-enforcement operations aimed at undocumented immigrants and the constitutional protections afforded to American citizens and legal permanent residents.

Nowhere is this issue closer to the surface than along the Southwest border, where Arizonans have been frustrated by the numbers of undocumented workers arriving via Mexico. Immigration enforcement is the responsibility of the federal government, but Arizona Republicans, including Governor Jan Brewer, decided to draft their own legislation to deal with undocumented immigrants.

This is a red herring. As I mentioned earlier in this chapter, the Obama administration has actually increased enforcement, both along the border and through investigations of employers. Nonetheless, the Arizona legislature pressed ahead with Senate Bill 1070, which is the most aggressive policy against immigrants in this nation's history. Signed into law by Governor Brewer in April 2010, it required anyone in Arizona to carry identity documents at all times and gave police the power to detain whoever they had reason to believe was residing in the country illegally.

Since the police are not watching the border, the only way they could develop a "reason" for suspecting a person is by judging that person's appearance. The law was so broadly written that a police officer might be fully entitled to pull over a car just because a Hispanic person was driving. Latino Americans faced the prospect of institutionalized harassment on a scale not seen since before the Civil Rights Act put an end to such practices.

It is an outrageous, offensive law that has no place in America. The Fourth Amendment to the U.S. Constitution protects citizens "against unreasonable searches and seizures . . . but upon probable cause . . . describing the place to be searched and the persons or things to be seized." In a state where 30 percent of the legal residents are Hispanic, looking Hispanic is certainly not a reasonable basis for being detained by a police officer.

Recognizing this grave injustice, President Obama directed the U.S. Department of Justice to sue the state of Arizona, effectively halting the law's enforcement. In 2012, the case reached the U.S. Supreme Court. Fortunately for the millions of law-abiding Latino families in Arizona, the justices stripped SB 1070 of its most egregious provisions, such as the one that gave police permission to define what constituted a reasonable probability that a person was likely an illegal resident. The Supreme Court upheld only one major provision of the bill—that which allowed police to ask a person for identification papers. But the court's ruling means it is illegal for police in Arizona to make a traffic stop exclusively to ask for residency documents. And in instances where a cop's request for papers leads him to discover a minor immigration violation, he does not have the right to arrest the suspect on that basis alone. Even though the bulk of the law was struck down, it continues to be used to racially profile individuals.

In fact, that legislation has been exploited at the expense of a truly heroic individual: Daniel Hernandez, the young Hispanic American man who helped save the life of Gabby Giffords on that terrifying day in Tucson when she was shot by a deranged gunman. In an interview with CNN, Daniel talked about the harassment he receives while driving in rural Arizona:

> I'll get pulled over a lot, but not because I'm speeding but because of what I look like. He'll say, "You were reported as being suspicious," and I'll hand over ID. But then his whole demeanor will change, and he'll say, "Aren't you the guy who helped Gabby?" It's really striking that I went from being a "suspicious driver" to being the "hero" who helped Gabby.

It's a great credit to Daniel's character that he doesn't allow these despicable episodes to intimidate him. On the contrary, he says that they are reminders to him that "if Latinos aren't here to fix these problems, then it's never going to be done."

For Governor Brewer and the Legislature in Arizona, SB 1070 was a political maneuver designed to appeal to their Republican base. The legislation was not a problem solver, but rather a problem enhancer, exacerbating community tensions and feelings on what is already a complex and emotionally charged issue.

When it comes to the problem of undocumented workers who are already on U.S. soil, there is a program that is both effective and morally responsible. It's called Secure Communities. Launched during the last year of President Bush's administration but expanded under President Obama, Secure Communities directs immigration enforcement agents to prioritize the deportation of undocumented immigrants who have committed a crime. By linking local police departments to databases for the Department of Homeland Security, the program makes it possible for federal agents to learn when an undocumented immigrant has been arrested for a crime. Those agents can then act to deport that suspect. Among those ensnared by Secure Communities, priority is given to the most violent criminals with unlawful residency. Given the millions of undocumented immigrants who live in the United States, plus the finite resources of Immigration and Custom Enforcement, it makes sense that we would act first to remove undocumented immigrants who are most disruptive to society. It also gives undocumented immigrants an incentive to obey laws, lest their arrest lead to the discovery of their status, followed by deportation.

This may sound too humane to immigration hardliners, but they have no cause for complaining about the number of deportations since President Obama took office. In each of the last two years, the United States has set new records, with 396,906 undocumented residents expelled in 2011.

There is an urgent need for comprehensive immigration reform—but those reforms must not convey hostility to foreigners and suspicion about their motives for coming to America. Rather, they should express confidence that as history has shown, those newcomers will strengthen our nation.

Some of those newcomers are toddlers and small children born elsewhere, then brought to the United States by their parents, who are undocumented immigrants. These children often grow up believing themselves to be American, having learned English at American schools before earning a high school diploma. Yet due to their place of birth and how they arrived here, these young people lack citizenship, which gives them virtually no chance of landing a steady job and being a productive worker in the only country they've known. What's more, they face the constant threat of being deported to a country where they were born but where they may not have a single memory, relative, or friend.

Monica Lazaro is one of these students trapped in residency limbo. She was born in Honduras but moved to the United States when she was eight. In 2010, Monica's mother was diagnosed with colon cancer and Monica was forced to grow up at a very young age, assisting her sick mother while also caring for her two younger brothers. She not only stayed in school, she thrived there, becoming the president of student government at Coral Gables Senior High. Monica also served as president of an organization called Best Buddies, which partnered young people with peers who had intellectual disabilities, and volunteered with charitable efforts to help low-income kids. She enrolled in honors and AP classes, graduating with a 4.86 GPA.

Despite these incredible triumphs, Monica's immigration status made her ineligible for college scholarships. Thanks to a donation, she was able to attend Miami Dade Honors College, where she continued to combine sterling academics with community activism—she started a chapter of the Best Buddies organization, then earned a 4.0 GPA in college courses. Sadly, Monica's mother recently passed away, but Monica continues to fight for her dream to make a life for herself and her brothers. She hopes to one day become a forensic pathologist.

Consider all that Monica has accomplished, all that she has lived through. Doesn't she deserve the chance to become a full-fledged U.S. citizen?

And there are others like her. Ricardo Wagner moved here from Venezuela when he was eleven. His parents had marveled at their boy's determination, and they wanted him to have the chance to explore his thirst for knowledge. The United States offered a chance at a more secure life. Ricardo started the sixth grade with virtually zero knowledge of English, nor of American culture. But he picked up the language so fast that he earned a release from his English as a Second Language class. He then gained access to advanced placement classes, receiving several diplomas and awards, including a letter from President George W. Bush for his excellent grades. On top of his course load, Ricardo accumulated nearly three hundred service hours by the time he graduated, ranking in the top 30 percent of his class.

He was ready to take on the world—until he was struck with terrible news: Due to his immigration status, he could not proceed with his education. The news shattered him. Ricardo had not known that he was not American by birth. He always thought the United States was his home. He grew up here. It was the land where his dreams were conceived, where he envisioned his future, and now he was being denied the opportunity to make a professional contribution to the country that he identified as home.

The DREAM Act was constructed to help young people just like Monica and Ricardo. It is the kind of sensible, pragmatic policy that could have marked a new era in immigration. A bipartisan piece of legislation coauthored by Sen. Orrin Hatch (R-UT) and Sen. Richard Durbin (D-IL), it proposed to give undocumented young people a six-year path to citizenship following their graduation from high school. Those young people could qualify by entering college and earning a diploma, or by serving in the U.S. military for two years. Every year, there are roughly 65,000 young people who fit the profile for inclusion in the program.

For more than a decade, versions of the DREAM Act have been bandied about Congress, but it has never earned the votes it needed to be sent to the President. Republicans have held it back, claiming that its enactment would encourage immigration and that beneficiaries of theDREAM Act would take jobs that would have otherwise gone to American-born workers.

These claims are pure paranoia, with no basis in fact. In 2010, UCLA researchers examined what the impact would be if the DREAM Act gave legal residency status to the 825,000 high-achieving, foreign-born young people who were eligible for it. The analysis found that this group would generate $1.4 trillion in income over the course of the next forty years. DREAM Act beneficiaries would not only be taxpayers, they would be job creators, contributing to growth of the economy—from which everyone can benefit.

If that study didn't have appeal to conservatives, then they might be interested in the Congressional Budget Office's analysis. It found that the DREAM Act would "reduce deficits by about $2.2 billion over the 2011–2020 period." More jobs, more tax revenue, and a smaller federal deficit: This legislation truly would be a win-win for America.

The DREAM Act was to be a signature issue of the Democratic-controlled Congress that was sworn in with President Obama in January 2009. But by December 2010, as the House passed the DREAM Act, Republicans in the Senate promised to defeat it by filibuster. In the 100-member Senate, it takes sixty votes to overcome a filibuster, and DREAM Act supporters fell five votes shy.

Blocked by the GOP, in June 2012 President Obama did the next best thing, announcing that his administration would no longer deport undocumented immigrants who would have qualified for the DREAM Act. This policy did not give them a path to citizenship, as planned in the DREAM Act, but it would at least free these young people from the "shadow of deportation," as Obama phrased it during a speech in the White House Rose Garden. He also stated the following:

> This is not a permanent fix. This is a temporary stopgap measure that lets us focus our resources wisely while giving a degree of relief and hope to talented, driven, patriotic young people. It is the right thing to do.

Immediately after President Obama announced the creation of the deferred action program, I held a press conference of my own, and I invited Monica and Ricardo to join me. Just before it began, I remember Ricardo telling me how petrified he was, but true to his character, he embraced the challenge. When it was his turn to speak, he said that all he was asking for is a chance. That chance can only be provided through a reform in immigration law. Ricardo said it was not his choice to grow up here, but he did, and this is his home now.

For all the despair that followed the filibuster of the DREAM Act, I hope that its potential beneficiaries take solace in the knowledge that the President and members of Congress such as myself will continue to press for this long-overdue immigration policy reform. On this specific issue, and on immigration in general, much of the Republican Party is on the wrong side of history. If it hasn't already happened by the time this book is published, I'm confident that the DREAM Act will become law in the United States, and it won't take another decade.

After Republicans watched President Obama win 74 percent of the Hispanic vote in 2012, some within the GOP ranks seemed to realize that support for immigration reform was a political necessity. Although immigration reform was not the number one issue for Hispanic voters, it was evident throughout the presidential campaign that the GOP's position on that issue was a source of friction.

During his 2013 State of the Union address, President Obama signaled his intention to keep the pressure on. He outlined three clear objectives that immigration reform must accomplish:

> Real reform means strong border security, and we can build on the progress my administration has already made—putting more boots on the Southern border than at any time in our history and reducing illegal crossings to their lowest levels in 40 years.
>
> Real reform means establishing a responsible pathway to earned citizenship—a path that includes passing a background check, paying taxes and a meaningful penalty, learning English, and going to the back of the line behind the folks trying to come here legally.
>
> And real reform means fixing the legal immigration system to cut waiting periods and attract the highly skilled entrepreneurs and engineers that will help create jobs and grow our economy.

Ideally, American immigration policy should act as a filter, allowing honest, hard-working people a path to citizenship while turning away those who don't respect the rule of law or who don't seek to embrace America's diversity of culture and opportunity.

In my experience, however, recent immigrants have profound appreciation for the freedoms of America, as well as for the economic opportunities that come with hard work and dedication. They have every reason to obey the laws. Meeting with immigrant groups and families in my South Florida district, and officiating at naturalization ceremonies, I always depart with a sense of optimism about the contributions that they and their families are making to our society.

As so many of us are the sons and daughters, grandkids or great-grandkids of immigrants ourselves, we owe a particular debt to our ancestors: that we fix our nation's broken immigration system. We have a moral obligation to change a system where we tacitly accept the economic benefits of cheaper labor while turning our back on abuses of those workers. We cannot continue a system that deports those who've known no other home than America. And we cannot ignore that immigration continues to help strengthen America when immigrants contribute so many of our valuable innovations. It is my sincere hope that by the time this book is published, Democrats and Republicans will have come together to find a comprehensive solution to our nation's immigration problems. In a modern era, this is our way to pay tribute to our ancestors. Whether they migrated here on the *Mayflower*, through Ellis Island, via El Paso, Texas, or along another pathway, they all form the foundation for what has made this country great.

ELEVEN

Civil Rights:
A March Without End

A young woman named Terri Schiavo could never have imagined that she would be at the center of a national debate about an individual's civil rights. Schiavo, from St. Petersburg, Florida, was just twenty-six in February 1990, when she collapsed in her home from cardiac arrest. She slipped into a coma and as the extent of brain damage became evident, she was deemed to be in a "persistent vegetative state."

There was no hope for recovery. After eight years, during which her condition did not change, Schiavo's husband, Michael, asked a Pinellas County judge for permission to remove the feeding tube so that Terri could die of natural causes, a death that Michael believed his wife would have preferred, based on conversations before her heart attack.

Schiavo's parents, Bob and Mary Schindler, opposed that motion, however, wanting to keep their daughter attached to life support. The two sides battled in court for several years before a Florida judge ruled that Michael Schiavo had demonstrated that this natural death is one his wife would have preferred.

When the Schindlers' petition to the Florida Court of Appeals was denied in September 2003, it appeared the case was over, clearing the way for Michael Schiavo to remove the feeding tube. But the Schindler family, frustrated about having exhausted their legal options, took its case to the media—and to Governor Jeb Bush and the Republican-led Florida Legislature. These Republican members had been galvanized by video footage of Terri Schiavo that was edited to make it appear that she was responsive to her parents. This misleading footage was, to Governor Bush and Republican legislators, more persuasive than the opinions of multiple physicians who examined Schiavo and found her unresponsive.

Terri Schiavo's feeding tube was removed on October 15, 2003; but within a week, Republicans in the state House passed "Terri's Law," written by Republican legislators and Governor Jeb Bush and signed by the Governor on October 21, 2003. Terri's Law granted the Governor authority to intervene in the Schiavo case specifically, allowing him to order her feeding tube reinserted. In what he called "an act of compassion," he ordered state police to the hospice to ensure that Terri Schiavo's feeding tube was reinserted.

As a member of the Florida Senate at that time, I was shocked by the wanton disregard that Governor Bush and my Republican colleagues displayed for the constitutional right to privacy, not to mention the separation-of-power principles as well as the system of checks and balances designed to ensure that no single branch of government accumulates too much power. This was a specific, individual family dispute and the appropriate venue for settling that dispute was the courts, which had ruled that there was clear and convincing evidence that Terri Schiavo would not want to be sustained by medical intervention. Neither Florida law nor the U.S. Constitution gives the executive branch authority to overturn a judicial opinion. If the governor, by signing Terri's Law, could essentially negate the intent of the court's ruling, as Bush did in the Schiavo case, then it meant that it was free to do the same in any private family tragedy, including yours or mine.

For these reasons, the Schiavo case was a flash point in the ongoing American debate about civil rights. We enjoy the right to free speech, to freedom of religion. Our Constitution shields us from unwarranted searches and rigged juries. We are protected against discrimination based on our cultural identities. And perhaps the most fundamental civil right in our democracy is the one that entitles us to vote for those who represent us in government. In short, these civil rights shape our lives, defining our interactions with those in power and with one another. Our claim to those rights, then, should last until the very day we die, which is why the campaign to prolong the life of Terri Schiavo was such a grave injustice.

In a letter written from inside the Birmingham jail, Martin Luther King Jr. said that "injustice anywhere is a threat to justice everywhere." To oppose that threat, King understood that there was immense power in the image of people gathering peacefully to march in unison, braving police dogs and fire hoses. It vividly demonstrated the marchers' depth of commitment.

King's warning about the threat of injustice is just as relevant today. We must train ourselves to be attentive to acts of tyranny and oppression, springing to the defense of any individual in need, lest the same injustice be committed against others. But just as our civil rights take many forms, so do the methods employed to trample them. It's up to us to be cognizant of how a criminal suspect deserves due process of law, just as a minority citizen deserves every opportunity to cast a ballot, just as a gay couple deserves the institutional advantages of marriage. Each example boils down to the question of what should be the standard in a fair and decent society. With very few exceptions, the American standard ought to be more civil liberties, not fewer.

And Americans understand this implicitly. But sometimes a force arises that seeks to strip away civil liberties. At such times, an active citizenry and the U.S. courts are the institutions that must protect justice.

This is what I learned from the Schiavo case, which followed me from the Florida Legislature to Washington in January 2005, when I was first sworn in to Congress. By that time, Florida's Terri's Law had been struck down by the state Supreme Court as unconstitutional; however, in March, just ten weeks after I was sworn in to the U.S. House of Representatives, the conservatives on Capitol Hill had decided to make an issue of the Schiavo case, turning it into a national media spectacle.

It was a surreal experience. Thanks to my familiarity with the case, I

wrote a fact sheet about the Schiavo case to assist my Democratic colleagues unfamiliar with the details, which I was distributing by hand to
senior members whom I had previously only seen on television. Suddenly
I found myself on national television news programs, debating the case
across the screen from long-serving conservative Republicans. But perhaps the most surreal moment of all was when Sen. Bill Frist (R-TN), a
physician, performed a diagnosis of Terri Schiavo from the Senate floor,
pronouncing her "responsive" based on that same video that had been
clipped to make it appear that Schiavo was reacting to her parents.

On March 19, 2005, a group of conservatives led by Frist and then
Majority Leader Rep. Tom DeLay (R-TX) announced that they were
going to draft legislation that would utilize congressional authority to
transfer the Schiavo case to a federal court, hoping that a judge would
rule in their favor. I was among the Democrats who rushed back to
Washington on a Sunday night for a House floor debate in which we expressed opposition to the bill on constitutional grounds.

It was a moment when my party—then the minority party in
Congress—needed to take a stand on a civil rights issue that could affect
all Americans. Specifically, the party needed someone with a background
in the case, as well as someone who could relate to the moral decision faced
by the Schiavo family. I remember being called into a meeting in the office
of Minority Whip Steny Hoyer, with only a few other members. They
decided that I would be the party's point person. A thirty-eight-year-
old woman with only two months' experience in Congress. In effect, I
was being called upon to lead this sudden civil rights march.

But I was ready. Having just debated against Terri's Law about a year
before in the Florida Legislature, I could refute many of the distortions
about the case that were being propagated by the Republican members
advocating for the federal bill. Despite our efforts, the bill passed, sadly,
with numerous Democratic members' support. The speed with which the
Republicans pushed this bill through on a Sunday night after Congress
had just left for a two-week recess, didn't give members enough time to
study the facts of a complicated, emotionally charged case. President Bush
flew back from his Texas ranch to sign it.

It was most definitely a precedent: It suggested that if Congress didn't agree with the legal outcome of your family's court case, it would use every tool it had to bring about the outcome it preferred.

Ultimately, Frist's effort failed. A federal court judge came to the same conclusion as the state judge. Terri Schiavo's feeding tube was removed and she died on March 31, 2005. Given the media frenzy whipped up by Republicans, including unfounded allegations of abuse against her husband, it was difficult to imagine what dignity remained to be salvaged from her death.

Words can't express how sorry I am for Michael Schiavo and for other members of Terri's family that the partisan legislatures at both the state and federal level did not respect the objective authority of the courts. But I hope they are consoled in a small way by the knowledge that Terri Schiavo's experience taught the nation some lasting lessons.

Following the Schiavo case, millions of Americans made a living will that explicitly reflected their preference of whether to be kept alive after a severe brain injury. That makes it less likely that another family will have its private decision to terminate life support turned into a public spectacle. The Terri Schiavo case reaffirmed that the right to die with dignity or any private family dispute are not matters to be settled in a political venue, such as Congress. Courts with judges appointed to be objective arbiters of fact are where our Founding Fathers appropriately placed jurisdiction over those types of disputes.

It's reassuring, then, that the separation of powers that are pillars of the U.S. government held firm against this assault. It may be no coincidence that the Republicans who had the highest profile in the Schiavo case have all left politics.

Democracy should hold accountable those who would infringe on Americans' civil liberties. Polls conducted at the time Congress debated the Schiavo legislation showed overwhelming opposition by Americans to the position of those who supported the Schiavo bill. Americans understood that this was an infringement on civil liberties and rejected it. To this day, I have had numerous Democratic colleagues tell me that their vote in support of the Schiavo legislation was the one they regret the most.

✦ ✦ ✦

The real challenge for citizens, however, is to stay focused on the importance of protecting their civil rights and liberties, even in times of national turmoil. Following the attacks of September 11, 2001, the country was gripped by fear. We did not yet know if more catastrophic terrorist plots were in the offing. Lawmakers wanted to protect the country against the next attack. But that objective had the risk of putting them at odds with another duty, to safeguard civil rights enumerated in the U.S. Constitution, which protects Americans against the potential injustices of aggressive law enforcement.

This climate of fear gave rise to the Patriot Act. Signed into law in October 2001, the legislation was a response to claims by then Attorney General John Ashcroft that investigative agencies needed broader surveillance powers to protect Americans from those who would do us harm, even if that meant collecting data from Americans in certain circumstances. Among its many provisions, the law expanded federal agents' capacity to track and intercept communications within the U.S., not just for law enforcement purposes but for the sake of gathering foreign intelligence. U.S. Treasury officials were granted more power to track possible money laundering through domestic banks, while immigration agents were allowed to use broader definitions for what qualified as just cause for holding a foreign visitor they suspected of being involved in terrorist plots.

At a glance, these may seem like reasonable measures, and it's easy to see why the Patriot Act had support from Americans—polls from September 2001 showed that 61 percent of Americans believed that it was necessary for the average person to give up some of their civil liberties to reduce the threat of terrorism. But the Patriot Act's broad language contained potential for violation of Americans' civil rights guaranteed by the Fourth Amendment, which protects us from unreasonable search and seizure. Thanks to this far-reaching legislation, investigators could obtain a warrant for the search of a suspect's home, then conduct a search at a time that the suspect was gone, seizing evidence without having informed the occupant that a warrant had been served.

A 2007 audit by the U.S. Office of Inspector General found that for several years after the Patriot Act became law, the FBI sent to telecommunications companies hundreds of "exigent" letters that contained exaggerated claims of emergencies. An agent merely claimed that he or she had requested a subpoena from the Department of Justice but that the need for the phone records was so urgent, the agent should be given access before the subpoena was granted. The OIG investigation found that in many cases, a subpoena had neither been requested nor granted. Shortly before the OIG report was finalized, the FBI tightened the practice of sending exigent letters.

Still, it is profoundly disturbing to our notion of a civil right to privacy that any one of us could have been targeted by an FBI agent, for any reason whatsoever, and had our phone records scrutinized. A law that allows this to happen does not make us more safe. It most definitely makes us less safe, potentially exposing us to the dangers of false arrest, a costly criminal defense, as well as a conviction and prison sentence.

Since the 9/11 attacks, Congress has debated how best to strike a balance between the need to ensure homeland security and the need to safeguard our civil rights and civil liberties. To be clear, it was important that we as Americans rallied around the flag after the 9/11 attacks, and I don't believe that any agency wanted to infringe on the civil rights of their fellow citizens.

In the course of debating whether to reauthorize the Patriot Act, there have been more limited versions that I actually supported. For instance, in 2011 I voted to extend the agencies' right to conduct "roving" wiretaps, such that they don't need a new warrant every time a suspect dumps a cell phone and picks up a new one. I voted several times for versions of the Patriot Act that did not cast such a broad surveillance net. In my view, the wide-open search of library records flies in the face of our Constitution's First Amendment protections. Rather, I support tightening the Patriot Act's restrictions on when these records could be accessed, specifically when there is a reasonable suspicion that the records would be relevant to a terror investigation. The proper balance has not yet been struck to ensure we don't conduct surveillance on Americans regardless of whether they are suspected of engaging in terrorist activity. That is the reason that in February 2011, I voted against reauthorizing three provisions of the Patriot Act, despite that bill's endorsement by the Obama administration. In September 2012, I voted against the reauthorization of the Foreign Intelligence Surveillance Act for the same reasons. In addition, it's not entirely clear that if the Patriot Act had been in place it would have prevented 9/11, nor that federal agents needed its broad powers to prevent subsequent attacks. Although Americans are willing to give up some privacy rights to improve our safety, we need to be minimalist in our approach so we ensure the most minor encroachment on those rights.

This debate erupted in June 2013, after a former National Security Agency (NSA) contractor named Edward Snowden leaked details of a massive surveillance program called Prism, which gave agents access to the systems of America's major Internet service and telecommunications providers. In my view, there is no doubt that Snowden should be arrested, prosecuted, and imprisoned for revealing highly classified intelligence information. He violated the trust on which his security clearance was based and he violated the law, jeopardizing American lives around the world. However, I found it incredibly hypocritical of some of my Republican colleagues who voted for the Patriot Act, as well as the reauthorization of the Foreign Intelligence Surveillance Act, to criticize President Obama for exercising the authority granted to him by the law. It is ironic that these same Republicans didn't make a peep when their own leadership eliminated the Select Intelligence Oversight Panel in 2011. SIOP was an Appropriations subcommittee recommended by the 9/11 Commission to provide more direct oversight by Congress of expenditures on American intelligence gathering. The notion was to establish a level of accountability that was lacking before the 9/11 attacks. As a member of the Appropriations Committee, I was appointed to SIOP in 2010 and can attest to its necessity. The committee ensured greater transparency because members of Congress were specifically focused on reviewing the intelligence expenditures proposed by the agencies. Prior to SIOP, the Defense Appropriations subcommittee had jurisdiction in this area but it was mostly an afterthought given the major portion of the discretionary budget defense represents. Unfortunately, the Republican leadership reverted to this model, throwing the shroud over intelligence appropriations once again.

As to the NSA program that was detailed in the Snowden leak, people may disagree about whether it constitutes an invasion of privacy or not; but those concerns must be weighed next to the Obama administration's disclosure that more than fifty terrorist plots had been stopped as a result of the data gleaned from the program. There is no question that we need to have mechanisms in place to allow U.S. law-enforcement agents to investigate suspected terrorists, but we must ensure that we are not trampling on or casting aside the civil rights that have been the essential element in what makes the United States the greatest democracy in the world. This is not a trivial matter.

Opinion polls released shortly after the Snowden leak show a nation divided over the question of how far the government should go to protect the public from acts of terror. Some 40 percent of respondents believed Snowden to be a hero, while 45 percent believed he should be punished. As a member who sat on a foreign intelligence committee and has been privy to highly classified briefings, I am confident that the Obama administration has struck the right balance between protecting civil liberties and protecting our nation's security. By the same token, with government programs that contain such a dangerous potential for abuse, it is important to ensure that they cannot be more broadly applied by a future administration that has less regard for privacy.

Clearly, on an issue as complex as this one, it's imperative that members of Congress have access and the ability to review the details of these programs in order to provide adequate oversight, not only on the NSA programs but on the Patriot Act. This is in line with the checks and balances that the framers of the U.S. Constitution had in mind. At the same time, it is incumbent on citizens to make their feelings known to their representatives so that the laws enacted truly reflect the will of a majority of informed Americans.

With respect to the Patriot Act, my personal hope is that it will soon shrink in scope. And fortunately the legislation will remain subject to regular review by Congress, which can assess which of its provisions are still necessary and which need revision. In fact, I would prefer those intervals to be shorter than they currently are.

More broadly, I hope that the legacy of the Patriot Act remains true to our Founding Fathers' principles of liberty as a nonnegotiable, inalienable entitlement of every American. We must recognize that laws that infringe on our civil rights infringe on our liberty.

Because every person in this country has equal claim to civil rights, we share a common bond. So we have cause to be concerned about the state of that bond when there are some individuals in our society who are being deprived of those rights.

None is more fundamental to American democracy than the right to vote. And yet from the founding of the republic to the present day, there has been intense conflict over who is qualified to cast a ballot. It took the Civil War and eventually the Fifteenth Amendment to earn that right on behalf of freed African slaves. It took another half century before that right was granted to women. And over the last century, various diabolical methods have been employed to inhibit certain voters, such as Jim Crow laws that enforced poll taxes and literacy tests as a way to discourage blacks and poor whites from participating in elections.

In the run-up to the 2012 general election, we witnessed a strikingly similar tactic under the pretext of protecting against so-called "voter fraud." Since 2010, dozens of states have introduced or passed bills that claim the intent of preventing a person from casting a ballot based on a false identity. These efforts were invariably pushed by Republicans and they usually seek to require voters to provide a form of photo identification in advance of casting their ballot.

Yet there is nothing to suggest that voter fraud is taking place. Rather, a study by the Department of Justice during President George W. Bush's administration found that between 2002 and 2005, there were only eighty-six cases where an American was convicted or pleaded guilty to voter fraud, and each of them was extremely small in scale. Indeed, Richard Frohling, an assistant U.S. attorney in Milwaukee, was quoted in a 2007 *New York Times* article as saying, "There was nothing that we uncovered that suggested some sort of concerted effort to tilt the election." Considering there were 197 million votes cast during that same period, the amount of fraud is a microscopic fraction. It's safe to say that this is not a crisis worthy of a state legislature's attention.

Undoubtedly, these laws do more to discourage voting among certain demographic groups: By requiring citizens to show a form of photo identification before casting a ballot, the Republican voter fraud bills suppress the turnout of low-income adults, minorities, and young people. These three demographic groups are the ones who commonly lack a photo ID, often because they're unable to pay the application fees or because they don't drive a car. All three demographic groups typically vote for Democrats. To require those voters to obtain a photo ID is to require them to make a payment in exchange for the right to vote, amounting to a "poll tax" reminiscent of Jim Crow vote suppression efforts.

It's no coincidence that Republicans have been especially aggressive in passing voter suppression bills in swing states, knowing that it could make a difference in a close race. A study by New York University School of Law's Brennan Center for Justice found that the Republican campaign had the potential to disenfranchise some five million voters in advance of the 2012 election.

Of course, it stands to reason that this cynical campaign would have the opposite effect, causing voters to be more motivated to go to the polls simply because they knew that they were being coerced against doing so. Indeed, the 2012 elections saw greater than expected turnout among minorities, with African American voters in the battleground state of Pennsylvania exceeding their voting rates from 2008 and with Latino voters growing as a share of the voting aggregate in Nevada. Exit polls showed that voters between eighteen and twenty-nine years old made up 19 percent of the national electorate, an increase over the 2008 election, which conservative pollsters assumed would be the high-water mark among youth. Nationwide, minority voters were 28 percent of voters in 2012, up from 26 percent in 2008, according to exit polling. What's more, hundreds of thousands of these young and minority voters waited for hours in long lines to cast their ballots.

In Florida, during the early voting period, which the Republican Governor Rick Scott and the Republican legislature deliberately shortened from fourteen to eight days and twenty-four fewer voting hours, early voters stayed in line until well after midnight. These were people like Desiline Victor, a 102-year-old woman who had emigrated from Haiti and became a naturalized U.S. citizen. Desiline, who now lives in North Miami, waited for three hours at a poll on the first day of early voting before leaving with a family member, only to return later that evening, when the line was a bit shorter. Emerging from the poll with her "I voted" sticker, Desiline was greeted by cheers from the other voters—a scene that President Obama described to all of America during his January 2013 State of the Union address.

It was an inspiring, if bittersweet story, because casting a ballot in a democracy should not be such a grueling chore. There is no reason to have scenes like those in Miami-Dade County, where on Election Day voters had to wait until after 1:00 A.M. to reach the polls. The 2012 election offered a reminder of the necessity of early voting. Nearly 50 percent of voters had cast their ballot between early, in-person voting and absentee ballots before Election Day on November 6, 2012.

My home state is always one of the biggest prizes in a general election. Besides narrowing the early voting period, Governor Scott and the Republican-controlled legislature created restrictions for voter registration volunteers, insisting that applicants provide photo identification and requiring that volunteers submit registration forms within forty-eight hours of being completed by a prospective voter. These logistical requirements were so burdensome, it prompted a lawsuit by the League of Women Voters. For about a year those groups largely stopped registering voters, as they waited for a judge's ruling. When, in early September, a federal court threw out the state's restrictions on voter registration, the voter registration groups had only two months to embark on registration efforts.

Misguided laws have a way of penalizing good intentions. A high school civics teacher in New Smyrna Beach, Florida, named Jill Cicciarelli, discovered that she had run afoul of those laws. Her crime? Helping seventeen-year-old students prepare to practice their civic duty by voting after their eighteenth birthday. A May 16, 2012, article by the Brennan Center for Justice summarizes what the state required of Cicciarelli:

> To comply with this new law, even before setting up a voter registration table in the school auditorium, Ms. Cicciarelli would have had to register online with the state as a "third party voter registration organization," and to sign an affidavit warning her about all the possible felonies involved in voter registration. She would also have had to ensure that each of the students who were helping her with the drive signed that affidavit, so that she could submit their affidavits to the state. She would then have had to wait for the state to assign her a special number. Once she got the number, that number would have had to be stamped or written on all the forms she used for her drive. At that point, she could have set up her table to help students register to vote. But that's not all. She would also have had to track the forms that she and her student volunteers handed out so that she could report to the state each month what happened to those forms, whether or not they were used for voter registration. And after helping students fill out registration forms, she would have had to ensure that each form reached state election officials within 48 hours, no matter how far in advance it was of an election. If she was even a minute late, she would face a $50 fine per form.

At the same time, the Florida Republican Party hired a vendor of its own to register voters, Strategic Allied Consulting, which had been accused in the past of trashing registration forms that had been filled out by Democrats. None of those allegations led to criminal charges, but Strategic Allied Consulting came under suspicion in the 2012 campaign after a number of registration forms appeared to be in the same hand-writing, except with different addresses and birthdays. The Palm Beach County State Attorney launched an investigation into the activity of one worker who submitted 106 registration forms suspected of being fraudulent. In September of 2012, as elections officials in nine counties discovered questionable voter registration forms from Strategic Allied Consulting, Florida Republicans fired the vendor, which made $1.3 million through its deal with the party. The firm also had contracts with the Republican National Committee, which cut ties with Strategic Allied Consulting shortly after the State Attorney's investigation was announced. The GOP suggested that party officers in four other states do the same, ABC News reported.

Apparently, Republicans need look no farther than the mirror to find evidence of voter fraud. Widespread efforts by Republican governors and legislators to pass voter suppression laws were designed to shape the electorate to achieve victories they could not win on their merits—a point that prominent Republicans conceded to *The Palm Beach Post* following the election. The former chair of the Florida GOP, Jim Greer, told the *Post* that "The Republican Party, the strategists, the consultants, they firmly believe that early voting is bad for Republican Party candidates." As for the party's claim that early voting made elections more vulnerable to fraud? Greer told the paper that this was nothing but a "marketing ploy." (In March 2013 Greer was sentenced to eighteen months in prison for stealing from the party's coffers, but his remarks were supported by two influential GOP consultants and former Republican Governor Charlie Crist.) Going forward, I sincerely hope the party does not respond to losses in 2008 and 2012 by devising more tactics for disenfranchising voters who are unlikely to vote for their candidates. Rather, party members ought to do a better job crafting policy that appeals to those groups. That is how a democracy is supposed to work.

If that sounds like too much of a hassle, then I hope that Republicans learned a valuable lesson in 2012. For all their efforts to suppress turnout among minorities, the percentage of minority voters in the general election actually rose compared to 2008, from 26 to 28 percent, based on the exit polls I mentioned on page 195. I suspect minority voters were inspired, not discouraged, by efforts to inhibit their participation.

I am confident that my positions on the issues appeal to the majority of Americans and, having respect for the democratic process, I favor any legislation that expands citizens' ability to vote. I support early voting, as long as there are structures in place to guarantee those votes will be handled properly by elections officials. I support the idea of voting on the weekend or by mail, making it more convenient for people who work long hours during the weekday.

There must be reforms in elections to spare voters a repeat of the long lines of 2012. Rather, the legacy of this past election should be widespread efforts to enhance, not limit, the franchise. A writer for *The Atlantic* had a whimsical idea that voting receipts be turned into lottery tickets, giving those who did their civic duty the chance of getting filthy rich in the process. On a congressional delegation trip to Australia, my colleagues and I learned that an eligible Australian citizen is fined $15 if he or she fails to show up at the polls. Compulsory voting in Australia was adopted in the state of Queensland in 1915 and subsequently adopted nationwide in 1924. With Australia's compulsory voting system comes additional flexibility for the voter—elections are held on Saturdays, absent voters can vote in any state polling place, and voters in remote areas can vote before an election (at pre-poll voting centers) or via mail. As a result, voter turnout in Australia is consistently above 90 percent. (Voter turnout of those registered to vote in Australia was as low as 47 percent prior to the 1924 compulsory voting law.)

Compulsory voting has its supporters and detractors, but that policy still seems more fair than the de facto poll tax that comes from requiring a voter to show photo ID. A fine for not voting is a penalty. Reasonable people can debate whether this goes a step too far, but a payment required to cast a ballot or the effort to secure a legally required identification is undoubtedly a barrier to access.

Another reform that needs to be seriously considered is universal, same-day voter registration. The 2012 election also saw attempts by Republicans like Governor Scott to purge voters the state deemed ineligible using unreliable databases. Indiscriminately purging voters is an infringement on the right to vote. A positive step to address inconsistent, confusing voter registration laws would be a uniform voter registration process, even if maintained by each state so as not to incite the fury of conservatives who oppose national databases.

I realize that many Americans feel so desensitized by the partisan dysfunction in Washington, it's hard to be surprised about anything, even a brazen campaign to suppress votes. They may think that elections can only be stolen in Third World countries ruled by dictators. But seeking to win elections by disenfranchising voters is a tyrannical act. Until the nation's citizens make their objections known, those cynical forces will grow bolder. No matter one's party affiliation, the appropriate position is zero tolerance for voter suppression.

There are clearly systematic, active efforts to disenfranchise certain groups of voters, even in 2013, forty-two years after the Voting Rights Act of 1965 was enacted. In June, the U.S. Supreme Court, in *Shelby County v. Holder* struck down section 4 of the VRA in a 5–4 decision, saying that the Congress failed to take into consideration the current conditions for minority voters protected by sections 4 and 5 when they reauthorized the VRA in 2006 and should have made revisions to take those conditions into account. Given the widespread voter suppression efforts by states in the 2012 election, this was a colossal mistake on the part of the Court. I was a member of the House Judiciary Committee in 2006, which was then led by Chairman James Sensenbrenner (R-WI) and Ranking Member John Conyers (D-MI). After the decision, former Chairman Sensenbrenner, an arch-conservative in every sense of the word, released a joint statement with Ranking Member Conyers and Judiciary Committee members Steve Chabot (R-OH) and Mel Watt (D-NC). All of them disagreed with the court majority, with Representative Sensenbrenner saying:

"The Voting Rights Act is vital to America's commitment to never again permit racial prejudices in the electoral process. Section 5 of the Act was a bipartisan effort to rectify past injustices and ensure minorities' ability to participate in elections, but the threat of discrimination still exists. I am disappointed by the Court's ruling, but my colleagues and I will work in a bipartisan fashion to update Section 4 to ensure Section 5 can be properly implemented to protect voting rights, especially for minorities. This is going to take time and will require members from both sides of the aisle to put partisan politics aside and ensure Americans' most sacred right is protected."

I could not agree more, but this will be a delicate matter and as of this writing, the House Republican leadership does not appear to be in a hurry to take the Court up on their invitation in the majority opinion, that "Congress may draft another formula based on current conditions." States like Texas that were previously subject to Justice Department pre-clearance review of changes to their election laws have immediately moved to implement laws that suppress minority voting rights, and others will undoubtedly follow. We must update section 4 of the Voting Rights Act of 1965 as soon as possible before the 2014 election to ensure that all voters continue to have their sacred voting rights protected.

It is easier to make a persuasive argument in favor of a civil right or liberty when it applies to all of us. We are all affected by the outcome of elections, just as we are all potentially affected if a government feels empowered to violate our rights to privacy, whether in the course of a criminal investigation or to influence a family dispute, as with Terri Schiavo.

But it requires a great deal more empathy to consider your own opinion of a civil right that may not directly affect you, like gay marriage. There is simply no legitimate reason that same-sex partners cannot be legally married, enjoying the same security and benefits as heterosexual partners. It is time that the archaic, oppressive, and unconstitutional state and federal laws banning same-sex marriage be struck down. The fact that in early 2013 the majority of states and the federal government still prohibited recognition of same-sex marriages is certainly not due to a lack of public support. Americans' opinions on gay marriage have evolved a great deal in the last two decades, and recent polls consistently show the majority favor the right be granted.

I am grateful for having represented a large population of gay men and women in my congressional district. I have no doubt that their love is as real as any heterosexual couple's. Lesbian, gay, bisexual, and transgender (LGBT) Americans' long-term relationships deserve legal recognition. It is offensive, oppressive, and eventually will be deemed unconstitutional to treat LGBT relationships differently than heterosexual relationships under the law.

For most of the past two decades, these Americans' civil rights have been eroded, thanks to the passage of the federal Defense of Marriage Act, along with scores of state ballot measures that go even further to preclude any possibility of a gay couple being legally married. The promoters of these hateful pieces of legislation have learned to be slightly more politically correct in their language. They largely avoid ascribing homosexuality to mental illness, and they generally avoid links to sadistic organizations that seek to "cure" gays with therapy that amounts to brainwashing. More often, the campaign will make vague statements about how a marriage between a man and a woman is the most "natural" union, and how it ensures a child born of that marriage will have a father and a mother.

Of course, "natural" is a subjective term, which is why it should be defined by individual adult couples and not the law. There is simply no denying the authentic nature of attraction and love between a pair of gay men or lesbian women. I have had the privilege of meeting and knowing many same-sex couples who are raising happy, well-adjusted children. In fact, a girlfriend I've been close to since my youth is raising two children with her partner. Each of them carried a child conceived through in vitro fertilization by the same sperm donor. Their daughter, who is their oldest child, is the same age as my twins, who were also conceived through IVF. All three had their Bat and Bar Mitzvahs last year, the milestone event in a Jewish child's life, when they read the Torah for the first time and are recognized as adults in the eyes of the Jewish faith. Our families are living parallel lives. The difference? My husband and I have been married for twenty-two years, and the state where my girlfriend and her partner live only allows recognition of marriage between a man and a

woman. The traditional, one-man, one-woman marriage defense plati-
tudes gloss over the central question of the debate: How would allowing
gay men and women to get married harm the marriage of heterosexual
couples? How is my childhood friend's relationship and family any less
valid than mine and my husband's relationship and our family? They
are not.

Anti-gay leaders have greeted that question with intolerance and prejudice. And yet prior to the 2012 election, all thirty-two states that have
held votes on same-sex marriage have rejected it. I suspect that most of
those who voted against gay marriage have never known an openly gay
couple, because I can't imagine how else they could deprive these partners
this basic civil right. Unfamiliarity breeds ignorance, which leads to intolerance.

Fortunately, that is changing. A generation of young people has grown
up knowing openly gay people, or at least seeing gay characters on television. A set of data from the Pew Research Center creates a vivid illustration of how American attitudes on gay marriage have changed. Whereas
only about 33 percent of the nation's elderly population, sixty-seven and
older, approve of gay marriage, 63 percent of Americans born in 1981 or
later support marriage rights for gay couples. That support loses about 13
percentage points among Generation X and then another 10 points among
Baby Boomers. The younger the respondent, the more likely he or she is to
favor gay marriage.

Considering how the U.S. military consists primarily of young people, it wasn't that surprising when in 2010 Defense Secretary Robert
Gates and Admiral Mike Mullen, chairman of the Joint Chiefs of Staff,
revealed that in a survey of 115,000 troops 70 percent expressed belief
that the repeal of "Don't Ask, Don't Tell" would have either a positive effect on morale or no effect at all. This finding undermined the claims of
those who supported the policy, which forced U.S. soldiers to live double
lives, fearing that discovery of their sexual orientation would lead to the
end of their careers. The repeal became official in September 2011.

But the 2012 general election was the most powerful statement yet of
the nation's evolving views. In Maine, Maryland, and Washington state,

voters legalized gay marriage, while in Minnesota the electorate voted down a ballot initiative that would have denied same-sex couples the right to marry. Months later, Minnesota's governor and Democratic legislature legalized same-sex marriage in the state. As of early 2013, all but three members of the Senate Democratic Caucus have expressed support for gay marriage. The real milestones happened in June, when the Supreme Court struck down the Defense of Marriage Act, allowing same-sex married couples to enjoy the federal benefits and protections they've been denied for years. At the same time, the court ruled that activists for so-called traditional marriage did not have the legal standing to defend California's Proposition 8, a 2008 ballot measure that barred same-sex marriages. Thanks to the court's decision, gay partners will again be allowed to marry in the nation's largest state. Social progress this dramatic could not have happened without the help of progressively minded parents.

I would wager that many parents had an "Aha!" moment like I did with my son, Jake. He was seven at the time and he was spending the week with me at work in Washington, D.C. A segment about gay rights came on the television news. He asked me, "Mommy, what does being gay mean?" I realized that this was a defining moment for my child that would shape his opinions for years into the future. I thought about the parents that choose to instill intolerance and hatred in their child instead of the choice I made. I remember explaining to Jake in terms that a seven-year-old could understand that some men are attracted to and love other men and some women are attracted to and love other women, just like mommy and daddy love each other. This is how we are born.

In more recent years, I've brought Jake and his sisters to gay pride events and parades and like all the parades we march or ride in, they have a blast. The first few times, I discussed with them that they would likely see men kissing men and women kissing women—I didn't want them to be surprised or uncomfortable. Today, they are no more uncomfortable around an affectionate gay couple than kids generally are around affectionate adults. More recently, I was driving then twelve-year-old Jake and his sisters home from school when a report came on the radio related to the controversy over gay marriage. Suddenly, Jake shouted, "Who cares?" at the radio.

"Why is it anyone's business if gay people get married?" As my heart burst with pride, I couldn't help but think, my sentiments exactly.

Gay rights has been the civil rights movement of our time. It has been a difficult struggle for so many. But hearing my kids, I know that their generation will be the one that witnesses the most dramatic milestones in that struggle and we will reach the day when LGBT Americans are truly equal in the eyes of the law. As my friend and fellow South Floridian, Republican strategist Ana Navarro, said on CNN earlier this year, "There's no putting this genie back in the bottle. This is now undeniable. The shift is here. We're not going back." I truly believe that equality is not an aspiration, but a destination and we will get there. It is inevitable.

As citizens of this country, we each derive great power from the civil rights and liberties granted to us under the Constitution. It is our solemn responsibility not to abuse that power. For instance, Americans' First Amendment right to free speech can be used for good when making a conscientious critique of government or culture. But it can be a force of destruction when that right is used to slander people of a particular group.

I can only empathize with the pain that is felt by African Americans and Hispanics when they hear racial and cultural epithets, and I cannot know the anger and hurt that LGBT Americans feel when they see signs like "God hates fags," among others that the infamous Westboro Baptist Church brings to public events. But as a Jewish woman, I can appreciate the awful sensation of being hated for no reason but for belonging to a minority group.

I was brought up in a secular Jewish household on Long Island with a strong connection to that aspect of my identity. I was certainly conscious of Jews being a small minority group by the numbers nationally, but in my world growing up, there was diversity and a large Jewish population. Being Jewish, I knew I was a little bit different from my Christian friends. My best friend, Dawn, who I grew up with and who remains my friend to this day, is Catholic. We spent both of our traditional religious holidays at one another's homes. I chose Dawn as the matron of honor at my wedding, which was held at Great Neck Synagogue, a modern Orthodox shul. In fact, of my six bridesmaids, three were Christian and three were Jewish. But other than celebrating different holidays and knowing we thought about Jesus in a different way, I didn't feel much different than anyone else in our community.

I was in high school when I first realized that some people looked at and thought of me in a different way. I had been dating a boy I met while working as a food server in a restaurant called Family Affair, located near my home in Melville, New York. While we certainly both acknowledged the difference in our religions (he was Catholic), we were two American high school kids and we didn't talk very much about things we didn't have in common.

One day the woman who was the assistant manager of the restaurant and who had never been very nice to me, took my boyfriend aside and "warned" him that I was Jewish. Her exact words: "Why are you dating that Jew bitch?"

When I learned of this, the light bulb went on for me as far as why she always treated me badly; but I was shocked, confused, hurt, and angry. It was my first direct experience with anti-Semitism, which I knew occurred, but to other people, far away (or so I thought) from my community.

My first year at the University of Florida I remember meeting a girl who told me, "I've seen pictures of Jewish people before but I never actually met one in person." It was mostly an innocent, ignorant remark made by someone who simply grew up in a town in Florida with no Jews at all, but it made me very uncomfortable. As a young person, these small, personal encounters made me realize that throughout my life, as a member of an extreme minority group (Jewish people are approximately 2 percent of the U.S. population), I would always be viewed by some people as a Jewish person first, which depending on their stereotyped view, would color their opinion of me.

I went with that awareness on my first visit to Israel and the experience was truly a revelation. It was early in my career as a state legislator, part of a program sponsored by the American Jewish Committee, which invited young, promising American Jewish leaders to spend time in Israel so they could internalize why the existence of a strong, Jewish, democratic State of Israel was so important for Americans, but particularly for American Jews to support. Young Jewish leaders were selected for this program in part because the younger American Jewish population at large was less likely to be affiliated with a synagogue or the organized Jewish community, a trend that caused concern among older Jewish, pro-Israel American leaders. Having grown up in a secular household myself, I was not socialized to automatically join a synagogue or be involved in Jewish organizations. But around our family's dinner table, my parents always instilled in me and my brother a sense of pride in our heritage, reminding us of the importance of continuing our Jewish values.

During the three-week trip, I spent some free time exploring the streets of Jerusalem by myself, when suddenly I realized that every person I had encountered that day, from the man who bagged my groceries to the one who drove the bus, was Jewish. It was a profound moment. Virtually every Jewish person in the U.S. lives with the daily reality that most people they encounter are not Jewish, and there are fairly regular reminders, whether it is an invocation at a public event that ends with the refrain, "In Jesus Christ's name, we pray," or the cornucopia of Christmas that is everywhere, with only token, "because they must," acknowledgments of Hanukkah.

That day on a street in Jerusalem I realized how important it was for Jews throughout the world to always know we have a haven in Israel. Jews have faced thousands of years of persecution too overwhelming for most to comprehend. The refuge that is Israel ensures any Jew anywhere in the world will always have a place to go if they faced persecution in another land. In Israel, we can look out for each other, like every community does. And Jews around the world look out for Israel.

Of course, I seek that same sense of connection at home in Florida, and I always find it; but every now and then there is a report of a Nazi swastika spray-painted on the wall of a synagogue, and with that, the connection to the broader community frays ever so slightly. The same effect occurs when an ethnic slur comes at me through Twitter, or when I see a Facebook poster make a crack about Jews that contains a crude stereotype. In the comments sections of online articles, posters hiding behind online pseudonyms can be their genuine spiteful selves, hurling all the racial invective that is kept bottled up while talking to neighbors and coworkers.

These are all acts of free speech, but they are abusive because they create divisions and hostility in communities. When we're attacked that way, the reflex is to attack back with judgments about the group the offender belongs to. We must resist that impulse. That is the beginning of a cycle that divides communities. We mustn't let prejudice lead to more prejudice.

But I do not propose that we crack down on this speech. Even if that were practical, it would inhibit debate in our society—a cure that's worse than the disease. Rather, let us recognize that bigotry and hatred often occur from lack of understanding. Enhancing that understanding is a key to promoting tolerance and reducing bigotry. Serving in the U.S. House of Representatives gives me the opportunity to represent my constituents by bringing my unique perspective as a younger Jewish woman to the work I do on their behalf.

When I was a freshman member of Congress, Jewish community leaders in Miami approached me about wanting to establish Jewish American Heritage Month. Much like Black History Month in February and Hispanic Heritage Month in mid-September to mid-October, it would be an annual month dedicated to educating Americans about the important contributions that Jewish Americans have made to our country throughout American history, which would lead to more tolerance and less hatred.

Normally, the odds of a freshman member of Congress in the minority passing legislation during their first year would be between slim and none. But I had the help of my resourceful and experienced Chief of Staff, Tracie Pough. Early one morning before work, Tracie called me to say she noticed that that day's legislative calendar included a bill to express the House of Representatives' "support for the symbols of Christmas." It was a resolution sponsored by the late U.S. Representative Jo

Ann Davis (R-VA) in response to Christian groups' perception that the Christmas holiday was being watered down. The examples they used were store policies directing employees to wish shoppers the more sensitive "Happy Holidays" rather than assuming the shopper celebrated Christmas; or using more than just red and green in holiday displays in order to appeal to more customers.

There was a bit of controversy to this resolution and Tracie saw this as an opportunity to push the House Republican leadership to balance the legislative calendar with my Jewish American Heritage Month (JAHM) resolution. I took the idea to House Democratic Leader Nancy Pelosi, who agreed and went to work making it happen. Fortunately, I had taken the time to secure 250 bipartisan House cosponsors, including House Majority Leader Tom DeLay, so passage would be assured. In December 2005, it was the first piece of legislation I passed as a member of Congress. Two months later it passed the Senate, where it was sponsored by the late Senator Arlen Specter (R-PA).

In April 2006, President George W. Bush issued the first JAHM proclamation, and it has been proclaimed annually in the years since. In 2009, President Obama held the first White House reception in honor of Jewish American Heritage Month and has held a reception or a JAHM event at the White House each year. Programs occur every May across the country designed to educate and raise awareness about the 350-plus years of Jewish life in America and the many contributions Jews have made to our nation's history.

Through these events and celebrations, it is the hope of Jewish leaders like myself that our society sees increasingly fewer instances of bigotry and anti-Semitism. In America, most people live in communities with very few, if any, Jewish families. Jewish American Heritage Month programs are designed to reach these Americans so that even innocent, yet ignorant comments like the one my hall mate made to me in college don't occur.

We have an opportunity through outreach and education to find the good that lies within each person, bringing them closer into our communities so that they can know the harm they cause by using words that create a rift between us. In this way, the racial and ethnic barriers between us will dissolve, along with those relating to sexual orientation, religion, age, and so many others. America has always been a balancing act between people of various identities; if any nation can achieve a single identity that binds us together, let it be this one.

With every passing year, we are drawing closer to a more free and enlightened society. As I look back over my life, there is no question that Americans today have more civil rights and liberties than they had when I was a child. This is what makes me optimistic for the future. As those freedoms were fought for and secured, there were some who warned of slippery slopes and dangerous precedents. Those fears have all been proven wrong.

This is not a zero-sum game. That is, giving more rights to those who lack them does not leave fewer rights for everyone else. In a complex world, giving more freedom to the individual human being makes us all more free.

It is exciting to imagine that the civil rights battles fought by my generation will be remembered by history and that equality will be more commonplace by the time my son and daughters become adults. They are learning from us, marching alongside us for the cause of human freedom, and they will be joined by their sons and daughters, who will be marching long after we're gone.

TWELVE

Aiming for Sensible Policy
on Guns

On the morning of January 8, 2011, my friend Representative Gabby Giffords (D-AZ) was outside a grocery store in her hometown of Tucson, staging an event called Congress on Your Corner, in which her constituents were welcome to talk to her about whatever issues were most important to them. Tensions had been running high in Gabby's district, which goes right to the border with Mexico. Traditionally, immigration is a combustible issue there, but at that time, so was Obamacare. At one point during the debate over the health-care policy, the glass front door to Gabby's district office had been shot out. But Gabby has the remarkable capacity to see the good within all her constituents, no matter how strenuously they have disagreed with her. Besides, she is not one to be intimidated into silence, and she would not let such incidents get between her and the people she represented.

But on that day, from within the crowd, a man stepped forward and began firing a gun at Gabby at point-blank range. Gabby suffered a gunshot wound to the head, and she narrowly survived. Six others were killed, including a nine-year-old girl and a federal court judge. Thirteen were injured.

When I heard the news that Gabby had been shot, I was stunned and utterly grief-stricken for my friend and for the pain and suffering felt by her husband, Mark Kelly, and her family. Our families had become close, with Gabby, Mark, and Mark's daughters sharing time with me and Steve and our kids—we even took vacations together.

The shooting was the act of a deranged man who several weeks before went to a sporting goods store in Tucson to purchase a Glock 19 semiautomatic handgun. Despite having been suspended from a community college based on concerns over his mental health, the man had passed the store's background check. (The killer entered a guilty plea to the crimes and in November 2012 was sentenced to life in prison without the possibility of parole.)

Americans have the constitutional right to own a gun, but that freedom must be treated with responsibility. The larger question is, can we adopt commonsense measures to limit gun violence, such as keeping guns out of the hands of violent offenders and the mentally ill? Are there commonsense restrictions that can be placed on the type of gun?

We have a precedent in this country of banning certain types of arms already, like machine guns—we can certainly agree that we shouldn't just allow someone to walk around with a shoulder-fired missile. But there are some who are offended by any suggestion that there should be constraints on the type of gun one can own, or on the amount of ammunition a gun magazine clip can hold. This is a very narrow-minded point of view, and it's not shared by all gun owners. I've held my own roundtable meetings with hunters who are members of the National Rifle Association (NRA), I've learned that they see little need for these types of weapons or ammunition clips and in our discussions they all consistently agree with me on the need for universal background checks. I've heard similar sentiments from other hunters who've engaged in this debate.

Given the risk of a gun getting into the wrong hands, the most patriotic Americans ought to recognize that their right to own a firearm must be balanced against the community's interest in keeping innocent people safe from shooting sprees, which have become all too common.

Every year in the United States, more than thirty thousand Americans are killed by firearms.

The tragedy in Tucson could have been a new beginning. We could have recognized that the time had come to reform the laws on gun ownership and to be more civil when we speak to our political opponents. Sadly, we missed that opportunity. And over the two years that followed Tucson, there would be even more deadly mass shootings—in Aurora, Colorado, in Oak Creek, Wisconsin, and then in Newtown, Connecticut.

While guns will always be available to law-abiding, mentally competent persons, we must take care that they don't end up in the wrong hands. We cannot erase the horrors that have already been committed with guns. And as long as guns exist, there is no law that can protect us from them completely. But we can bring reforms that make it significantly less likely for innocent Americans to become victims of gun violence. If we can accomplish this, the world our children inherit will be safer than the one we inhabit today.

Like so many Americans, when I heard the news of the shootings at Sandy Hook Elementary in Newtown, Connecticut, I could hardly breathe. My first thought was of my own children at school and how, as a parent, you just automatically assume they are at the safest place they could be. How could this happen? It shocked the conscience, the idea that a human being could kill twenty children, all age six or seven, along with a principal, teachers, and his own mother. The pain created by this single, cowardly act is simply impossible to comprehend.

It seems absurd to suggest that it took such a horrific event to make reducing gun violence and passing commonsense gun safety laws an urgent political issue, because that would imply that it wasn't urgent after a madman used assault weapons to massacre innocent people in an Aurora, Colorado, movie theater. Or that it wasn't urgent in the days that followed all the other mass shootings we've witnessed, from Columbine High School to Virginia Tech. But the awful truth is that none of those mass

murders were able to generate the political will for reforming gun ownership laws. We cannot allow the killings in Newtown to go unanswered.
We can and we must build a broader consensus for change.

To demonstrate how many Americans have been affected by gun violence, Rep. Jim Langevin (D-RI) suggested that lawmakers each invite
victims from their districts to be guests at the 2013 State of the Union
Address. I invited Megan Hobson, a seventeen-year-old girl from Hia-
leah, outside of Miami. Megan was only sixteen when the car she was
riding in was riddled with bullets from an AK-47 in a drive-by shooting.
When she heard the shots, she grabbed the two-year-old riding next to
her in the backseat and put him on the floor of the car, likely saving his
life. Megan, however, was shot through the pelvis, damaging her intes-
tines and bladder. Near death, she was operated on through the night at
Memorial Regional Hospital and required more than thirty pints of
blood. She would return for three more surgeries and now walks with a
limp. Megan is a hero, but she is just one of roughly 78,000 Americans
who are injured in gun-related incidents each year. While Megan was in
Washington with me, I was able to introduce her to Gabby Giffords,
who Megan credits with helping her get through her own ordeal. She
told me, "I knew that if Gabby could do it, I could, too." I am so proud of
both of them.

In January 2013, about a month after the bloodshed at Sandy Hook,
Senator Dianne Feinstein (D-CA) drafted legislation that would reestablish the ban on military-style assault weapons, as well as the high-
capacity magazines that make it possible for shooters to fire off dozens of
rounds without having to reload. (In the Tucson incident, the shooter
was reportedly able to get off thirty bullets in less than thirty seconds.)
Those measures had the support of President Obama, who shortly after
the Newtown tragedy asked Vice President Joe Biden to chair a task
force that would bring back recommendations for reforms designed to
reduce gun violence. In 1994, when the Vice President was in the U.S.
Senate, he authored legislation that brought about a ten-year ban on
nineteen types of assault weapons, but in 2004 Congress failed to reauthorize that legislation. Senator Feinstein's legislation, as well as the pro-

posals brought back by Vice President Biden's panel, would broaden the range of assault weapons banned by defining them as any gun that has a single cosmetic feature or accessory reminiscent of guns used in combat. The 1994 legislation banned only assault weapons that had at least two of those features.

In introducing her proposal, Senator Feinstein pointed out that the ban would have no effect on guns that were legally purchased prior to the bill being enacted. She added that the legislation's passage would still allow for gun enthusiasts to choose among 2,258 legitimate hunting and sporting rifles and shotguns. It is, in my opinion, a measured, reasonable approach to the need to reduce the scourge of gun violence. But, to be clear, no one piece of legislation will solve this crisis—we need a comprehensive approach.

Toward that end, on January 26, 2013, the Obama administration issued twenty-three executive actions aimed at improving gun regulations and safety, without needing congressional approval. Based on that initiative, federal agencies were required to enhance their disclosures to the federal background check system, while the U.S. Attorney General was ordered "to review categories of individuals prohibited from having a gun to make sure dangerous people are not slipping through the cracks."

Another problem is that criminal background checks are legal requirements that apply only for purchases made through a licensed firearm dealer. That only accounts for about 60 percent of firearm transactions, according to a study by the Campaign to Stop Gun Violence. Much of the remaining 40 percent occur at gun shows and flea markets, where people deemed by law to be "occasional sellers" can trade weapons for cash without having to do a background check at all. As a January 2013 *New York Times* editorial points out, this is "a gaping loophole that has allowed teenagers, ordinary criminals, terrorists, Mexican drug cartels and arms traffickers to have easy access to weapons." The President needs congressional support to close that loophole, and he can certainly count on my voice and my vote.

The reforms necessary must go beyond access to guns. There are too many gaps in the nation's mental health system—people who are suffering from psychological disorders but who can't get treatment, usually because it isn't covered by their health-care plans. With the inception of Obamacare, we have the opportunity to make mental health treatment and counseling available to more Americans, which would allow professionals to treat people who might otherwise develop violent tendencies. I'm pleased that the Obama administration has identified improvements in the mental health-care system as a key to reducing gun violence, but it is essential that Congress act to make sure it happens. It will need to be made a priority and given funding.

In addition, the administration has called for more research to help answer the questions that haunt all of us: What causes someone to amass a vast supply of weapons and ammunition, then turn them on innocent people? It is not enough to say that these tragedies are "incomprehensible." Federal funds ought to be made available to dedicated social scientists who can help us understand this distressing dynamic, because that's the first step toward taking political action and bringing about cultural changes. Personally, I'm skeptical of the claim that the violence in movies and video games breeds violence among viewers—the studies I've seen have been largely inconclusive in linking one with the other. Nevertheless, I've found the entertainment industry to be very responsive to suggestions about tightening access to their products depicting serious violence so that they aren't available to children. But more extensive research is necessary as part of a comprehensive approach to reducing gun violence. We must avoid adopting simplistic solutions to complex problems that need a multifaceted solution.

As the President underscored in his January 2013 report, *Now Is the Time to Do Something About Gun Violence*, the thirty thousand suicides and homicides related to firearms every year clearly suggest a public health crisis, making this a legitimate field of inquiry for the CDC. But, as the report points out, a Republican-led Congress has blocked every effort to fund those studies through the CDC and other agencies. The NRA has consistently opposed any funding for research by the CDC as well as the Bureau of Alcohol, Tobacco, Firearms, and Explosives, even going so far as securing legislation prohibiting such research.

✦ ✦ ✦

In anticipation of U.S. Senate hearings on gun control, CBS News and *The New York Times* asked Americans in January 2013 for their opinions on the issue. More than half (54 percent) said that they supported stricter gun laws. The survey found that nine out of ten respondents favored background checks on all gun buyers and nearly 80 percent supported the idea of a national database that tracked the sale of guns.

In late January 2013, the first Senate Judiciary Committee hearing since the shootings in Newtown began with a rousing call to action from my friend Gabby Giffords. As her husband, Mark, clasped her left hand, she read a short speech handwritten on a loose-leaf piece of paper:

> Speaking is difficult. But I need to say something. Gun violence is a big problem. Too many people are dying. Too many children. We must do something. It will be hard. But the time is now. Be bold. Be courageous. Americans are counting on you.

To hear it from a victim of gun violence, who had once been on the other side of the congressional dais, it was hard not to be moved—and to feel a sense of hope. Gabby has retired from Congress, but she and Mark remain active in trying to shape American policy, especially on issues relating to gun violence. They recently launched an organization called Americans for Responsible Solutions with the mission of encouraging members of Congress to be bolder in their efforts to revise gun ownership laws so that deadly weapons don't end up in the wrong hands. Gabby and Mark are gun owners and strong supporters of the Second Amendment, and their organization will work to ensure that, whatever reforms may come, Americans will still be entitled to own guns for collection, recreation, and protection. In essence, Americans for Responsible Solutions will be able to give voice to this majority of the American public that favors commonsense solutions to protect our communities—the same solutions that are thwarted by special interests like the NRA, which uses political contributions, advertising, and lobbying to block legislation that the vast majority of Americans, including gun owners, agree upon.

New York mayor Michael Bloomberg and Boston mayor Thomas Menino cofounded Mayors Against Illegal Guns, which has worked extremely hard on the effort to stem the tide of gun violence in America. They're focused on closing the gun-show loophole, but also the Craigslist-style sales of guns made through the Internet without a background check. Founded in 2006, Mayors Against Illegal Guns has grown to include more than 850 mayors from across the country.

Mayor Bloomberg's effort isn't limited to policy—it also has a political influence through his Independence USA political action committee, which poured more than $2 million into helping to defeat Debbie Halvorson, the former congresswoman from Illinois who ran in the Democratic primary to fill the Chicago seat vacated by Rep. Jesse Jackson Jr. Initially considered the front runner in that race, Halvorson had a mixed record on gun control. Bloomberg's PAC endorsed gun control supporter Robin Kelly in the Democratic primary. Given the Democratic registration in that district, Kelly's win in the February primary all but assured her of defeating all challengers and she was elected to Congress. This was the first time I can remember that a pro–gun control group worked to elect a pro–gun control representative, the reverse of a tactic commonly used by the NRA to elect anti–gun control representatives.

It is clear, however, that these types of efforts will continue to be an uphill battle while the NRA wields huge influence in pressuring members of Congress, especially in politically conservative districts. The NRA makes it clear to every member of Congress that should they support even seemingly reasonable restrictions on gun ownership (like closing the gun-show loophole, or limiting high-capacity magazines), not only will they not get the support of the NRA, but the NRA will actively work to defeat that member in the next election.

At the same Senate hearing where Gabby Giffords and Mark Kelly appeared, NRA CEO Wayne LaPierre was called to testify. There had been widespread speculation about the possibility of LaPierre endorsing universal background checks, particularly since in 1999 Senate testimony on behalf of the NRA he said, "We think it's reasonable to provide mandatory instant background checks for every sale at every gun show. No loopholes anywhere, for anyone."

But LaPierre was in no mood to revisit those remarks. He expressed frustration about having to appear at the hearing at all. And he vehemently refused to consider endorsing a plan for enhancing background checks for gun buyers, suggesting that the fragile political consensus forming on that question would be short-lived. A universal background check, said LaPierre, "ends up being a universal federal nightmare imposed upon law-abiding people all over this country."

Apparently, he has a different definition of "nightmare" than most of us. If we allow the memory of another mass shooting to fade without doing anything to make the next one less likely, that would be much worse than a nightmare. Because the waking reality is in a first-grade classroom in Connecticut. It is in a movie theater in Colorado. At a Sikh temple in Wisconsin.

I understand there's no guarantee that gun control legislation would have prevented all of those massacres. Still, it's unconscionable to compare the inconvenience of background checks with the possibility of saving innocent lives. However flimsy the current standards are, consider how many more Americans may have died if not for the Brady Handgun Violence Prevention Act, passed in 1993. Since that law required background checks for many gun purchases, the FBI has run over 150 million names through its database, and in 1.7 million transactions that background check blocked a gun transfer, largely because the prospective buyer had a criminal conviction. Imagine how many American lives were saved thanks to this single reform. And imagine how many more can be saved if we continue to craft sound policy that keeps guns away from dangerous people.

Given the entrenched power of the pro-gun lobby, the political odds have historically been stacked against meaningful reform. But I believe change is on the horizon. There is a longtime supporter and constituent in my district who is an avid hunter, a Second Amendment supporter, and Life Member of the NRA. He has a large gun collection—at least 150 of them—and for years I've known him to be an opponent of gun control laws. But shortly after the slayings at Sandy Hook Elementary, he e-mailed me to say that enough was enough, that the time had come to adopt some basic, commonsense reforms. His e-mail ran through five items he felt must be addressed: universal background checks for all gun purchases; banning high-capacity magazines that hold more than ten to twelve rounds of ammunition; banning military, assault-style weapons; banning armor-piercing bullets; and improving the mental health system. He then said that the NRA and Wayne LaPierre didn't speak for him on this issue. This constituent told me that he found LaPierre's press conference following the Newtown tragedy "disgusting," and he knew many NRA members who felt the same way.

Following the Newtown shootings, I organized a series of roundtable discussions in my district with law enforcement, elected officials, mental health advocates, gun control groups, and health-care professionals, seeking opinions from different experts who deal with guns or gun violence. I knew that it was important to hear from gun owners myself, so I reached out to my friend and asked him if he would be willing to pull together a group of fellow gun owners, hunters, sportsmen, and NRA members to discuss with me what they believed should reasonably be done to reduce gun violence. The gun rights supporters and I got together at one of their offices and almost to a person, they agreed on the five items which my friend had e-mailed me. In particular, they felt strongly that no one single item would solve the problem by itself. They also felt strongly about the need to invest in improving our nation's mental health system. Some felt that addressing violence in entertainment was an important part of reform that required more study. They all agreed that the NRA was taking an extreme position on what most NRA members believe were important, commonsense reforms. By the end of our meeting, the eight men joined me at a press availability to share their point of view publicly— which they originally had all said they would not do. They all felt that it was time they took a stand.

For a moment in early 2013, it appeared that we finally did have the consensus in Congress to make significant policy change on gun control. There seemed to be a bipartisan agreement in place that would expand background checks on individuals who purchase guns to prevent purchases by those who the law prohibits from owning a gun. But on the afternoon of April 17, that agreement evaporated, as the background check compromise negotiated by Democrat Joe Manchin (WV) and Republican Pat Toomey (PA) along with measures that would ban assault weapons and high capacity magazines, were all defeated in the Senate, where they failed to garner 60 votes.

Shortly after that vote, my friend Gabby posted her reaction on her Twitter account, saying, "I'm not giving up." Neither am I—because I have seen for myself how attitudes have evolved.

It takes a great deal of character to change one's opinion on an issue as important to some citizens as gun ownership. I understand that the right to self-defense is an early, sacred feature of our U.S. Constitution. But an even more fundamental attribute of the American character is our desire to avoid exposing innocent lives to unnecessary risk. And that is the reality of the current state of our nation's gun laws. We already know that the NRA and other extremists will be forceful in lobbying for the status quo; those of us who recognize the threat of loose gun safety policies must be just as forceful in opposing them.

In his press conference outlining his administration's plan for reducing gun violence, President Obama promised, "I will put everything I've got into this—and so will Joe—but I tell you, the only way we can change is if the American people demand it." Those demands must be heard in conservative districts, where members of Congress ought to be asked, pointedly, why they oppose a ban on high-capacity magazines or why they oppose a universal background check. Polls tell us that the majority of Americans favor these measures, which suggests that the lack of political will is due to that majority's silence in the debate.

As politicians, we can only do so much. It is up to every American to help change attitudes toward the culture of gun violence in our country. What can individuals do? Megan Hobson used her experience as a victim of gun violence as an opportunity to speak out in favor of gun control. Doctors and nurses have come to me to talk about the public health impact of roughly 11,000 gun deaths and 78,000 gun injuries each year, and how this should be treated as the national health epidemic that it is. Hospitals, doctor's offices, and health insurers could more widely disseminate gun-safety information and raise awareness on gun violence among the public and legislators. Individuals can and should voice their own opinion by reaching out to their local, state, and national legislators and by supporting organizations who focus on ending gun violence.

It is too late to save the lives of all those who have perished as a result of firearms falling into the wrong hands. But if we can pass meaningful reforms, we will honor those lost with a profound gesture of respect for those victims and their families.

THIRTEEN

Discourse, Not Discord

I t seems long ago, but for most of 2009 and 2010, the Tea Party was all the rage, literally. In 2010 mid-term elections, a cast of ultra-conservative Republicans won election, powering the GOP takeover of the House. Republican Minority Leader, Ohio congressman John Boehner, was elected Speaker, but he was forced to deal with a combative, intransigent pack of Tea Party freshman legislators. Nearly all of them had signed the "Taxpayer Protection Pledge," a document circulated by the fiscally conservative political operative Grover Norquist in which the signer forsakes one of the most sacrosanct responsibilities of his office: their independence to use their judgment to make the best decision to ensure the welfare of the American people. How on earth can you hope to negotiate with a colleague who has already committed, by signature, to an absolute position?

The congressional term that followed was one of the most acrimonious in recent history, marked by a debt ceiling showdown that brought the U.S. government to the brink of shutting down.

In May 2011, Speaker Boehner announced that House Republicans would not agree to the President's request to lift the debt ceiling. As I explained in chapter 1, this was a measure that was necessary for the government to pay our bills and meet our legal obligations for paying out benefits in programs like Social Security and Medicare, as well as tax refunds and military salaries. In all the years that Congress has debated the merits of spending, lifting the debt ceiling was a mere formality; never before had a party resorted to such an extreme tactic.

In essence, the GOP had decided to hold the nation's economy hostage to extract spending cuts from Democrats, a course we objected to because those cuts were certain to shatter an economic recovery that was still fragile. The simplest way to explain the Republicans' refusal to raise the debt ceiling is to compare it to your family's credit card. Imagine if you had a large credit card balance and when you saw that balance you were so outraged, you simply decided not to pay it. Clearly, that's not an option.

This brinksmanship unleashed a fresh round of tirades on the House floor and on cable news shows. Over the course of that summer, consumer confidence tumbled, sending ripples through the economy. The impasse was resolved in August in a deal that raised the debt ceiling and made a down payment on reducing the deficit with budget cuts of $1.2 trillion and no additional revenue. A provision of the deal called for the creation of a bipartisan committee that came to be known as the Super Committee. It earned that moniker because it was bipartisan and bicameral and the result of their deliberations, unlike the normal legislative process, would go directly to the House and Senate floors and not be able to be amended. Members of Congress would then take an "up or down" vote on their work product. The Super Committee was tasked with identifying at least $1.5 trillion in future spending cuts or else face a forced "sequestration"—huge, automatic cuts to a host of domestic programs like education and health-care research and massive cuts in defense spending. The theory behind the bipartisan deal was that both sides would have enough "skin in the game" to avoid the fiscal cliff it would cause without an agreement. To almost no one in Washington's surprise, the Super Committee failed to reach agreement.

The day before the vote on the deal, I got a call from Gabby Giffords's husband, Mark. He told me that Gabby had been following the debate while continuing her rehabilitation, as part of her recovery from the shooting in Tucson several months before. She was considering flying back to the capital to make sure the debt ceiling legislation didn't fail by one vote because she wasn't there. She knew what was at stake for the country and for her constituents in particular. Gabby wanted to make sure she was there to cast her vote on their behalf. Mark asked me whether I thought her vote could make a difference and I told him it was definitely a possibility. They made plans to fly back.

Our staff arranged for me to meet Gabby, Mark, and her Chief of Staff, Pia Carusone, in the carriage entrance of the House side of the Capitol so that Pia and I could walk Gabby into the House Chamber to cast her vote. We went up to the second floor in the elevator and slowly walked toward the chamber, with me holding Gabby's elbow and Pia right behind. As we approached the entrance and climbed the few steps into the chamber, members gradually recognized Gabby, realizing that she'd returned to cast her vote. The symbolism of that moment hit each House member and the entire chamber erupted in a thunderous ovation. Republicans and Democrats alike shed tears of joy and gratitude.

At the same time, each of us had a solemn responsibility to safeguard our nation, both from those who would do us harm and from financial ruin. A group of members were crowding around Gabby, offering to take her voting card from her to help her cast her vote. But since she still had more progress to make in her recovery, I realized that this might be the last vote Gabby cast in Congress. I knew she wanted to do it herself, so I cleared the way for her to be able to insert her voting card in the slot where members record their vote. The debt ceiling legislation passed, 269–161. The vote was expected to be closer, but I am certain that Gabby's presence changed some hearts and minds that day. It was, for me, one of the most emotionally powerful scenes I have witnessed on the floor of Congress.

Unfortunately, thanks to the conflict and uncertainty that led to that deal—and for the game of chicken that preceded it—the United States had its credit rating downgraded for the first time in history. In a news release, Standard & Poor's stated, "The downgrade reflects our view that the effectiveness, stability, and predictability of American policymaking and political institutions have weakened at a time of ongoing fiscal and economic challenges."

Among the major factors cited by credit rating agencies was the unlikelihood that Republicans would agree to let the Bush tax cuts expire in 2012, combined with Republicans' unwillingness to identify new sources of revenue, such as increasing taxes on the wealthy. It was the most vivid illustration yet of the consequences of two parties being unable to work together. Sadly, there would be more of these instances to come, many of them vitriolic.

But we must not give up hope. It is within our power to change. We can be a society that settles its differences with words, respectfully. We cannot take back words that were spoken in a reckless rage. We can, however, act with more civility in the future, letting our children see that this is the most appropriate, effective way of resolving conflict.

One of the greatest privileges of being elected to serve in Congress is that it provides an opportunity to speak directly to the American people. The words we choose reflect on the voters who elected us, as well as our respective political parties. That awareness should lead us as members of Congress to hesitate in the moment before we let anger dictate our language. And given the necessity of working together to pass legislation that benefits the American people, we should avoid ad hominem attacks.

Members of Congress, candidates, and political operatives don't have to like each other; but as democratically elected representatives, we have an obligation to rise above partisan name-calling so that we can debate contentious subjects with an even temper. If elected officials demonstrate this maturity, it would be an example to our constituents to show more restraint. Instead, too often we've seen members of Congress like Representative Bachmann and former congressman Allen West (R-FL) fan the flames of large crowds of Tea Party supporters with supercharged rhetoric that does nothing to add to the legitimate differences of opinion we have on policy. To be fair, there are Democrats that engage in this behavior as well, and of course it's inexcusable from either side. It simply ratchets up the intensity of the moment and encourages more heated words, unproductive shouting, and worse—the potential for escalation. Beyond the fact that this lack of civility adds nothing of substance to our political discourse, much would be added to the comprehension of the gravity of important issues if the media devoted less coverage to the personality clashes in politics and more to the substance of the conflict.

This problem is not only the result of the advent of news channels with an ideological tilt, but local news coverage as well. When was the last time you recall hearing political news coverage that focused on the substance of the issue rather than the conflict between the parties or individuals?

I'm reminded of one particular instance: During the floor debate in the House on the budget in July 2011, after Representative West spoke in favor of the Republican budget legislation, I was the next House member to speak. I spoke against the bill, focusing particularly on the provision in the budget that would end the guaranteed health-care program for seniors as we knew it, by turning Medicare into a voucher program.

Florida has the second-highest population of Medicare beneficiaries in the country, with more than 3.5 million senior citizens on Medicare. For a House member from Florida to support ending Medicare's guaranteed benefit after seniors spent a lifetime paying into it was just irresponsible. Before Medicare, many seniors faced medical bankruptcy when they dealt with a catastrophic illness. Medicare ended that crisis for seniors in America.

In my statement in opposition to the bill, I respectfully disagreed with Representative West, suggesting it was irresponsible for the "gentleman from Florida" to support turning Medicare into a voucher system, given how many seniors both he and I represented in our South Florida districts. A short while after finishing my remarks, I received an e-mailed tirade from Representative West, which took umbrage with my criticism of his position. Having never spoken with or met him in person, it was a little disturbing that he tracked down my personal e-mail. His e-mailed message included a torrent of name-calling in which he referred to me as "the most vile, unprofessional, and despicable member of the U.S. House of Representatives." He continued by saying that "if you have something to say to me, stop being a coward and say it to my face, otherwise shut the heck up." He concluded his tantrum by telling me that I was "not a lady" and would "not be afforded due respect" from him. West had copied the House Republican and Democratic leadership on his e-mail to me and it leaked to the media later that day. By that point, the press was familiar with Representative West's track record for making incendiary comments.

There was a frenzy of coverage about his e-mail and its contents. I was interviewed by NBC's Andrea Mitchell, a class act and a seasoned reporter who asked me what I thought about the content of West's e-mail. I replied that I thought his e-mail spoke for itself and also that it showed how much pressure he must be feeling, given how problematic his position on Medicare was for his constituents. Other news outlets focused on the tirade and the conflict between West and me and not the core of our disagreement: which was that Democrats supported preserving Medicare as a health-care safety net for seniors, and Republicans supported ending the Medicare health-care guarantee and turning it into a voucher, which would provide only a fixed amount to a senior on Medicare and they would need to make up the difference in the cost themselves. Most seniors live on a fixed income and the added expense would be cost prohibitive for millions. In fact, the nonpartisan Congressional Budget Office did an analysis of the Republican budget and what its effect on Medicare would be and estimated it would cost the average senior citizen on Medicare more than $6,000 per year in additional premiums. While the offensive e-mail sent to me by Representative West was definitely a newsworthy story to cover because it was so over the top, the coverage never really illuminated the subject matter on which we disagreed. The news stories focused on the tirade instead. While titillating, I doubt many viewers were educated about the subject on which we differed.

Undoubtedly, a spirit of good sportsmanship in Washington and in the media would improve the quality of political discourse among individual Americans. In particular, I worry about parents who listen to the political shock jocks on the radio or who speak disrespectfully in front of their children without context or explanation about the elected officials with whom they disagree. What kind of example does that set to impressionable kids who are forming ideas about political interaction? I do my fair share of talking back to the talking heads when I'm watching television, but when my kids are around, I explain to them why I agree or disagree with what I'm hearing to help them formulate their own opinions on various issues. Now that the twins are fourteen and my youngest is ten, they have grown up with this discourse in our family room. I find them talking to the television, too, often giving voice to their own informed opinion on a news item.

We must get better at communicating with those with whom we disagree, because if we get any worse, the American people are going to feel even more alienated and cynical about the state of national politics, refusing to participate or pay attention. This would inflict damage to the very core of our democracy.

Differences of opinion are natural and healthy aspects of a democracy governed by two parties, and we must be able to express these differences with civility. But as anyone who has observed Washington knows, we are not always able to hold ourselves to these standards of conduct. The modern political climate is nastier than any in recent memory, marked by party members who tend to hector one another when they should be engaged in constructive debate. An important example of civility we should be setting is common decency in our political discourse, particularly when elected officials are interacting with one another and at public meetings where constituents have the opportunity to interact with their elected officials.

President Obama could not even get through his 2009 State of the Union address before Rep. Joe Wilson (R-SC) shouted "You lie!" in the middle of his speech. During a town hall event in February 2012, then Rep. John Sullivan (R-OK) told constituents that "killing a couple" U.S.

Senators would be the only way to pass the budget. Former Mississippi governor Haley Barbour, speaking at a fundraiser outside the Republican National Convention, said that he hoped that the event's keynote address would "put a hot poker to Obama's butt"—a remark that had racial overtones, given the historic practice of branding slaves.

These reckless statements all prompted apologies, with the political figures explaining that they were simply caught in the heat of the moment; but some of the most offensive behavior in Washington has occurred over the course of years, with plenty of time to consider the broader consequences. During most of President Obama's first term, Republicans and their acolytes in Washington trafficked in racially loaded speculation that the President had been born not in Hawaii but in Kenya. The President finally had to stage a press conference and release his Hawaiian birth certificate—and that still hasn't stopped these scurrilous allegations from floating around the party's fringes. These mercurial members actually seem proud of their impolitic remarks, which are far from being heat-of-the-moment gaffes. Former congressman Allen West, for instance, highlighted the intemperate comments he made about me in a fundraising letter to supporters. Considering the $17 million he raised in his ensuing campaign, it seems there was some method to his madness, although I suspect that his extreme style was ultimately the reason he lost the 2012 election.

Granted, every era in American politics had moments of indecorous rhetoric. In 1800 Alexander Hamilton circulated among his friends a scathing critique not just of President John Adams's politics, but of his character as well. Its discovery by then Senator Aaron Burr escalated tensions between the two powerful figures, who would finally settle their dispute in a gun duel. Hamilton was slain and Burr became a fugitive.

The modern era of incivility began with the culture war of the late 1960s, with young antiwar demonstrators and civil rights activists on one side, Nixon's white conservative "silent majority" on the other. The Nixon tapes reveal the depth of contempt the President felt for the protesters, who he likened to "little animals" with a communist agenda, and it was Nixon's former aide Pat Buchanan who delivered one of the most memorably divisive speeches, claiming at the 1992 Republican National Convention that there was "cultural war" in America between liberals and conservatives, the outcome of which was "as critical to the kind of nation we will one day be as was the Cold War itself."

Still, there is something qualitatively different about the tenor of our postmodern political climate—the language is more violent, more personal. And I can speak from firsthand experience. In 2009, a Republican candidate running against me scrawled my initials, "DWS," on a piece of paper, fastened it to a target, then blasted it with gunfire at a shooting range. During the 2012 campaign, another Republican opponent doctored a photo of me, depicting my neck with a studded dog collar, in order to illustrate that, as chair of the Democratic National Committee, I was the President's "attack dog."

I won't pretend that Democrats don't occasionally go too far in our rhetoric. In September 2012, the chairman of the California Democratic Party compared Republican speeches to Nazi propaganda, issuing an apology later. Also in September 2012, during an interview at the Democratic National Convention in Charlotte, North Carolina, then Palm Beach County Democratic Party chairman Mark Alan Siegel, a former New York State assemblyman, went on a tirade against Christian voters who profess support for Israel, saying they were "the worst possible allies with the Jewish state." Christians, he added, "just want us to be there so we can all be slaughtered and converted, so they can bring on the second coming of Jesus Christ." In the furor that followed those remarks, Siegel resigned his chairmanship. And my colleague in the Florida congressional delegation, Alan Grayson, had a tendency to go overboard in his first term, in criticizing the GOP's position on health care, saying in one floor speech highlighting Republican opposition to the Affordable Care Act, that our GOP colleagues' solution for Americans who get sick and could not afford health care insurance was "Die quickly."

Since becoming the chair of the DNC, a portion of my political voice has been in service to President Obama. So I have tried to use more measured words in my policy discussions in interviews, speeches, and debate on the House floor. It is natural for us, as politicians, to try to call attention to our message. Choosing stronger words will make it more likely that those words are heard by a wider audience. However, the adage to think before you speak is always advisable, both to ensure that what we say will lend credibility to our argument and also because we should set a good example of constructive debate that adds to the discussion and makes it more likely to result in good policy.

I am not guilt-free when it comes to choosing my words carefully. During the debate on the Republican budget, I joined a press conference in which the participants criticized the Republican position on Medicare. The Republican budget in the 112th Congress included a provision that would have turned Medicare into a voucher system, ending Medicare as we know it and eliminating guaranteed coverage that seniors have paid into for a lifetime. In my remarks, I pointed out that seniors would pay more and more each year for their health insurance, that Medicare would no longer be a guaranteed health insurance coverage program. Then I added, "Instead Medicare would become little more than a discount card. This plan would literally be a death trap for seniors." In hindsight, even though I felt strongly about the harm of the proposal, the words I used were unnecessarily harsh. I could have gotten my point across without going as far as I did.

I'm sure there will be instances in the future when I say something I later regret. I wear my heart on my sleeve and I wouldn't make all the sacrifices that come with serving in Congress if I didn't feel passionate about issues. Still, I do my very best to treat my congressional colleagues and others with whom I disagree with respect and to act in good faith.

As we consider the consequences of the deterioration in political discourse and how we can reverse that course, it's helpful to ask ourselves: How did we get here? My more tenured congressional colleagues tell me that while there have always been moments of discord in Washington, this era is especially vicious. I find a variety of opinions for why that is. Some blame the media for stoking verbal clashes colorful enough to carry the 24/7 news cycle. Others blame the millions that are spent by

PACs on negative advertisements, which air over the course of campaigns that last longer than they ever have before.

One of the more interesting theories I heard came from a senior member of Congress, who noted a seemingly innocuous shift in the lifestyle of congressional members: It used to be that when a representative was elected, he or she would move to Washington, D.C., with their family, living there roughly half the year. So it wasn't uncommon for a Democratic member to have a child on the same baseball team as a Republican member. They were more likely to run into one another in the grocery store or the bank or out at dinner with their spouses. These past generations of congressional members were more civil in Congress because they had a sense of being part of the same community, sharing at least one attribute even if they disagreed about every political question. Plus, calling a rival a name on the congressional floor would make it awkward to encounter that same rival in the stands at their children's ballgame.

In more recent years, most of the congressional action has been condensed, with the House meeting in session about 3.5 days a week, alternating between Monday night through Thursday, or Tuesday night through Friday, meaning that often members need spend only three evenings in Washington before flying home for a four-day weekend. The 112th and 113th Congresses, with a Republican majority, also have seen a very light schedule, with Congress in recess many more days than in recent history, making it more difficult for members to spend time getting to know each other and building trust.

Consider the Republican members of Congress who were swept into office in 2010 on a wave of Tea Party support. This class of legislators has been widely criticized for using excessively harsh language in the course of debating issues—and it so happens that many of these same members are rather reclusive when they come to Washington. A CBS News report in January 2011 found that nineteen of the eighty-seven new Republicans from that class slept in their congressional office, rather than rent a home in Washington. As Rep. Joe Walsh (R-IL) told the news station, "I think it's important that we show we don't live here, we are not creatures of this town."

Maybe if Representative Walsh were more of a social creature in Washington, he wouldn't have accused his Democratic opponent in the 2012 election of exploiting her service record in Iraq as a way to get votes. That opponent, Tammy Duckworth, flew 120 combat hours in Iraq before her Black Hawk helicopter was hit by a rocket launcher in 2004, blowing off portions of both her legs. Duckworth had the poise to try to help her copilot land the helicopter safely before passing out from her injuries. She narrowly survived and now uses two prosthetic legs. Today, Tammy Duckworth is a member of Congress (D-IL).

You probably wouldn't expect to see me socializing in Washington with a Republican like Rep. Dan Webster (R-FL). When we served in the Florida Legislature together, he was the Speaker of the Florida House of Representatives and we disagreed on many issues, including women's reproductive health, tax policy, and education reform—he authored a Florida Senate bill that would have required women to have an ultrasound before terminating the pregnancy. Despite these political differences, Dan has always been genial in his dealings with me. He's fair-minded and we were able to work on several things we did agree on, like funding for the HIPPY program in Florida (discussed in the chapter on education) as well as the decennial redistricting process in 2002 when we both served in the state Senate. So, after he was elected to Congress in 2010, I teamed with him to host a bipartisan dinner. We each invited five members from our respective sides of the aisle. It was such a success that Dan and I decided to host more of these get-togethers. For the subsequent dinners, we asked every member who joins us to bring a member of the other party. We've had four of those dinners as of this writing, and we're up to thirty members. We have no specific agenda other than to get to know each other, because there are really no opportunities in Washington, other than committee hearings, when Democrats and Republicans spend time together. The good news is that if our dinners get any more popular, we'll be accused of holding clandestine sessions of Congress!

Truly, these efforts at developing rapport between political rivals go a long way, and it's a shame that recent House leadership—of both parties—hasn't done more to encourage these bipartisan events.

I've made a concerted personal effort to organize events that I think will help heal the partisan rancor that accumulates during a congressional session. For instance, in 2009, I collaborated with Rep. Jo Ann Emerson (R-MO) and Sen. Kirsten Gillibrand (D-NY) to create the congressional women's softball team, which in the 2011–2012 session of Congress had thirteen Democrats and seven Republicans between the two chambers. We play an annual charity game that raises money for the Young Survival Coalition, a breast cancer advocacy group that helps women under forty diagnosed with breast cancer. We play against the female Capitol press corps and we practice for three months, several times a week, at 7:00 A.M. We've found being out there together as friends and teammates with a common opponent helped us develop camaraderie that carried over to the legislative process. None of us are surprised that the women members of Congress have literally stepped up to the plate to reach across the aisle and play together so we can work together.

These are the small gestures that can, over time, make a big difference in how members of Congress behave toward one another. To make the most dramatic change in the political discourse in Washington, however, individual members will have to engage in some introspection and examine whether they are part of the problem. The Republican Party will have to look within itself. The infection from their Tea Party wing has damaged our civil discourse. It is unproductive, unhelpful, and doesn't foster consensus-building. While one political party does not bear sole responsibility for the lack of civility, as I have detailed here, there are many more recent examples of Republicans using inflammatory language.

This vitriol predated President Obama. At the very start of President Clinton's presidency, there were vicious and prolonged attacks by GOP members and their surrogates, beginning with Whitewater, then the politically motivated Kenneth Starr investigation and Monica Lewinsky scandal.

Granted, as the chairperson of the Democratic Party, I can't be an objective judge. So I'll just ask: In modern times, can you imagine a group of Democrats in Congress using such insidious tactics to take down a Republican President? Because I cannot. I certainly would never enlist in such an unsavory cause. Even if it worked, the end simply doesn't justify the means. That is why, ultimately, the scandal reflected more poorly on Republicans in Congress than it did on Clinton, who remains wildly popular with Americans and has enjoyed a very productive post-presidency humanitarian career.

It is no coincidence that the partisan rancor increased after the next Democratic President took office in 2009. When President Obama came into office, the Republican Party was not driven so much by a victory-at-any-cost attitude at the top but by angry-as-hell grassroots conservatives: constituents who took their politics with a spoonful of Fox News, stoking and amplifying their contempt for bailouts, taxes, and illegal immigration. This provided the seeds for the Tea Party, of course, and from my view, its members were bound together by their anger rather than by any coherent vision for how to improve the quality of government.

Still smarting from their defeat in the 2008 election, Republicans were eager to bring these very active Tea Party members into their base. But those Republicans soon learned that anger toward "big spending, big government" liberals and moderates was the attribute that unified this Tea Party coalition. Detailed discussions about issues would not lead to the discovery of how Tea Party members differed. Rather, to enjoy support from this group, Republicans were obliged to echo that fury. This led to more vitriol in Washington, as Republicans strove to prove they were "Patriots"—true conservatives rather than the moderates the Tea Party blamed for the excesses of past congresses. For the same reason, GOP leaders had no inclination to preach restraint among their constituents.

Then health-care reform came along. Members of the Tea Party brushed aside all the objective evidence that reforms could reduce rather than add to the federal deficit; in their view, this was "socialized medicine" that would lead to more taxes and more debt. So they boarded buses and demonstrated in Washington, carrying signs that compared President Obama and Speaker Pelosi to such noted socialist dictators as Joseph Stalin and Adolf Hitler.

The Affordable Care Act legislation was pending when Congress went into recess in July 2009. Traditionally, the month of August offers members the time to hold town halls that allow them to interact directly with constituents. Then Sen. Jim DeMint (R-SC), who had emerged as a favorite of Tea Party protesters, warned that health-care reform would be Obama's "Waterloo"—a reference to the bloody battle that ended Napoleon's career as a general.

Right on cue, Tea Party members showed up at town halls in a belligerent cose frame of mind. Nearly every day a new viral video appeared, showing Tea Party protesters shouting down members of Congress. Internal memos made clear that theirs was a coordinated strategy meant to obstruct dialogue. A memo from a Tea Party–affiliated group in Connecticut, for instance, advised protesters to "rock the boat early in the Rep's presentation," to "yell out," to "rattle him," to "stand up and shout and sit right back down." Of course, that kind of disruption is an American's constitutional right, but clearly it is a counterproductive method for debating a problem as complex as health-care costs.

But Democrats in Congress would not be bullied. Our members pressed ahead with health-care reform, and as we marched to the Capitol to vote on it in March 2010, the Tea Party protesters greeted us with an ugly scene. Rep. Barney Frank (D-MA) was heckled with anti-gay chants, while Rep. John Lewis (D-GA) heard racial epithets. "I have heard things today that I have not heard since March 15, 1960, when I was marching to get off the back of the bus," he said later. Rep. Emanuel Cleaver II (D-MO) was spat upon.

Republican members should have been outraged and embarrassed. It is our responsibility as leaders to condemn despicable behavior like that, without equivocation. The GOP's silence spoke volumes.

It was discouraging, but if you believe like I do in the importance of having a dialogue with your constituents, you must be willing to face hatred and hostility. So I pressed ahead with a town hall event of my own in April 2010, at Fort Lauderdale city hall. The majority of the crowd had legitimate questions about how the Affordable Care Act would apply to them, but a vocal minority castigated me, as well as any constituent who showed support or an open mind toward the reforms. One woman, a special education teacher who supported the reforms, rose to speak, only to forget her question. She explained to us that she had been struggling to gain health-care coverage in the years since she had been hurt in a playground incident, where a student had hit her in the head with a metal ball. The woman said that ever since, she has had difficulty with her short-term memory. "Good!" proclaimed an angry protester sitting a few rows behind the woman.

Meanwhile, on the plaza outside city hall chambers, Tea Party protesters managed to scream Joe Wilson's immortal phrase "You lie!" every time the door swung open. I was called a "Nazi" and "Stalin." One man screamed at me from the courtyard and held a sign that said that breast cancer was God's way of punishing me for my politics.

Fortunately, I've developed a thick skin, but what disappointed me most was the inability to have a civil conversation with the people in my congressional district, including those who disagreed with health-care reform.

I do not believe that the Tea Party extremists who vote for Republicans are the majority of their base, but they sure act like they are. And they are the voters who show up reliably in Republican primaries. Because Republican leaders have been reluctant to criticize the Tea Party, the GOP is being defined by those extremists. As long as that's the case, it will be extremely difficult for Democrats and Republicans to work together to solve the problems facing this country.

By the time this book is published, I hope we will look back on the health-care reform debate, as well as the debt ceiling deal, and acknowledge it was rock bottom in the modern era of American political civility—I don't want to imagine how it could get worse.

As I acknowledged earlier, the blame for the deterioration of political discourse is in the eye of the beholder. Surely, there is a Republican member of Congress whose own text on this subject explains how Democrats started this conflict and how every act of incivility by the GOP was merely a reaction to an even more vile act by Democrats. But the important question is what we can do next to repair the state of bipartisan politics. It's not something any single politician can achieve—if President Obama rolled over whenever he was challenged by Republicans, he wouldn't be doing a very effective job representing the majority of Americans. Nor is it realistic to expect the media to change their ways. They respond to the articles we click and news programs we watch, although I believe that they bear some responsibility for the emphasis they place on confrontation and controversy.

It is up to us, individually, to change the nature of the way political issues are discussed, the way problems get solved. When you see an offensive comment on an article or blog post, better to ignore it than to respond with a spiteful comment of your own. On Facebook and Twitter, consider the harm that occurs within that online community when you allow an argument to escalate. There are so many people who witness these conversations, so doesn't it reflect better on you to check your temper, step back, and merely say that you disagree but that the other person is entitled to his or her opinion?

These attitudes should extend to the relationship we have with the media. By relying on just a single program or news outlet to shape one's political perspective, a person's critical thinking skills can stagnate. To stay healthy and lively, our brains need a balanced diet, with intellectual nourishment from a variety of sources, including those that may seem biased. Without making this effort, we will be ill equipped to understand opponents of our point of view and how to respond and eventually achieve consensus. For most Americans, consensus, agreement, and mutually agreed upon compromise is a laudable goal. Often, the media coverage of political conflict seems to be rooting for permanent division. Conflict sells.

If we can summon this discipline, to mix it up in our viewing habits, the political media will be compelled to strive for fairness in their coverage. Political figures will have to abandon the shortsighted strategy of demonizing their opponents with emotional arguments. Instead, they'll have to make their case with reason and clarity. Even PACs that have bottomless pockets for airing political advertisements would quickly learn that slinging mud doesn't pay.

But most of all, we must strive to improve the civility of political discourse because young people are watching us, learning about the ways we react to those with whom we disagree and how problems are resolved. However upset we may get about a policy or a candidate, it is important to show children how to process that frustration in a productive, conscientious way. For the future of our country, let our children see through our words and actions that the bond we share as Americans is stronger than any single issue that divides us.

——◦——

FOURTEEN

To Belong to Something

At least once every year, as troop leader of my daughters' suburban girl scout troop I would load the girls into a van and head to the southeast corner of Broward County, crossing the train tracks along a shabby industrial section of Dixie Highway to park near a low-slung building with steel bars around the windows. This is the Jubilee Center of South Broward, a nonprofit organization that provides a wide range of social services to the county's homeless and working poor, from legal aid to haircuts. Lined up behind a row of folding tables, the Girl Scouts would serve the folks that file in for a hot lunch.

It always inspired me to see how the girls in my troop responded to serving the poor and less fortunate. The most memorable moment for the volunteers occurred the day that a family came to Jubilee, with two daughters who were approximately the same age as the girls in my troop. I could see a look of confusion and concern in the eyes of my own daughter and the other Girl Scouts as they imagined how different life must be for their peers. We had discussed poverty and hunger with them, but until those two girls came in with their mother, I'm sure that my Girl Scouts only imagined homeless and less fortunate individuals as being adults—that is, people they couldn't really relate to. Seeing someone their age in need of help gave them pause, a new perspective. My Girl Scouts could eat whatever they liked, whenever they wanted it, whereas these two girls had no choice but to eat exactly what was served. It was likely to be the only hot meal they would have that day. In this instant, the Scouts learned a new and profound appreciation for how fortunate they were. They gained a new comprehension of the importance of volunteer work: that it is a way of expressing gratitude for what they have by serving those who have little.

Such is the mind-broadening power that comes from an act of service to the community. Volunteers forget their own problems for a moment, gaining insight into those faced by others, as well as the satisfaction of knowing that they have lent a hand. *Tikkun olam* is the way we express this mission in Judaism. The Hebrew phrase translates as "repairing the world." That may seem overwhelming to one person—the world is so huge, and there is so much that needs fixing. But the way I wrap my mind around this important responsibility is to take the view that if each one of us devotes a small part of our lives to performing deeds that are driven purely by this desire to help others, then there is no problem we can't solve.

This was evident in the days that followed Hurricane Sandy's destruction on the East Coast, as millions of dollars in donations and supplies flowed toward the region. There were many tales of individual sacrifice and heroism that followed the storm. In particular, I was moved by the story of Terri Lannan, a Lincoln, Nebraska, volunteer who stayed in the Northeast for weeks and spent Thanksgiving handing out boxed meals to those made homeless by the disaster. "I can always have Thanskgiving with my family, but these people need help right now," Lannan said to the *Omaha World-Herald*. "I have food and a nice warm home to which I can come back. They don't."

Much was made of the government's poor response to the devastation that followed Hurricane Katrina, but we should also remember the spectacular outpouring of donations and supplies that followed the disaster, preventing it from becoming an even more colossal human tragedy.

I think we can all identify on some level with Lannan's generosity, but it may be hard to know where to start, or how we can help solve a problem so huge in scale. At the same time, there are constant temptations to shrink the world down to a more manageable size, to concern ourselves exclusively with our closest friends and family. Without realizing it, we create a bubble between ourselves and the rest of society. Technology can exacerbate this problem. Just glance around any public place: You'll see a large percentage of the people will be either talking on their smartphones, texting on them, or listening to music stored there. Or they may be peering into the screen, surfing the Web, or using social media that effectively transports them out of that public setting and into a private one, populated by more familiar faces.

This is not purely the fault of technology. It's also a consequence of rising income inequality and a political movement that celebrates the pursuit of one's own interest at the expense of others. The retro moment being enjoyed by author Ayn Rand is an outgrowth of this phenomenon. In *Atlas Shrugged* and *The Fountainhead*, Rand lauds the heroism of one talented person struggling to overcome the stifling mediocrity of the surrounding society, represented by a government that regulates businesses into submission. Viewed through this lens, the Great Recession separated the winners from the losers, the producers from the dependents. Rep. Paul Ryan is one of Rand's most famous admirers, and so when in 2011 Newt Gingrich called the Ryan budget "right-wing social engineering," he was simply reading between the lines of a document that would engineer the survival of a ruling class of elite, while callously abandoning those who need government and charity to bridge the gap for their survival. Charity work is for dupes, according to Rand, who named one collection of her essays *The Virtue of Selfishness*. Since President Obama's 2008 election saw conservatives react with the rise of the Rand-influenced Tea Party, *Atlas Shrugged* has sold roughly two million copies—more than it sold when it was a bestseller in 1957. Selfishness is, to borrow a term from Twitter, trending.

Compare that ethos with *tikkun olam*. One would have you reward yourself; the other would have you repair the world. Consider, which of those is the more courageous? Which will build more character? Which will build a stronger community?

I was pleased that during the 2012 campaign, *Rolling Stone* asked President Obama for his opinion of Rand and her disciples. He suggested it was a book that might appeal to "misunderstood" young people not yet aware of how much human connections matter.

> Then, as we get older, we realize that a world in which we're only thinking about ourselves and not thinking about anybody else, in which we're . . . developing ourselves as more important than our relationships to other people and making sure that everybody else has opportunity—that's a pretty narrow vision. It's not one that I think describes what's best in America.

The America I know is united by a collective sense of purpose in which we root for the success of one citizen, knowing that it will help many more of us succeed. We are all members not just of the nation's economy but of its society. So a business that makes ingenious innovations doesn't just produce profits for its owners, it is generous in creating jobs in the surrounding community, just as volunteering in one's community creates immeasurable value both for the volunteer and for the beneficiary.

As our country recovers from the Great Recession, I am hopeful that we will rediscover an enduring truth: that the more we give to others, the more others will give to us, and the more there will be for us to share. This social compact was enshrined in the Declaration of Independence and has been a fixture in our democratic republic ever since: We teach our children that we are individuals, each of us entitled to life, liberty, and the pursuit of happiness, but also that each of us ought to belong to something, a cause that transcends one's own self-interest and brings us closer to our fellow Americans.

There will always be a culture of activism in this country, because it has always been the animating principle for progress. For those who are uncertain about how best to serve their community in the future, it may help to look to the past for clues.

If history is any indication, the most generous Americans will be guided by the recognition of society's most pressing need. This tradition of altruism can be dated at least to 1727, when a young Benjamin Franklin organized the Junto, a Philadelphia club consisting of local tradesmen and intellectuals who gathered every Friday to discuss the issues of the day. In particular, they considered how general welfare of people in the American colonies could be most improved. Among the topics, Franklin mused over the city's approach to fire fighting, which relied largely on good Samaritans pitching in with buckets of water. His consultation with the Junto led him to publish an article in *The Pennsylvania Gazette* describing the need for a "Club or Society of active Men belonging to each Fire Engine; whose Business is to attend all Fires with it whenever they happen." His fellow colonists responded to this call, and the nation's first volunteer fire department was formed.

When bloodshed from the Civil War led to shortages of bandages and soldier supplies, ladies' aid societies formed in the South, while courageous women like Clara Barton toiled to supply soldiers of the North, a humanitarian cause that would produce the American Red Cross. In more recent years, Jimmy and Rosalynn Carter brought national attention to the dearth of affordable homes for low-income Americans, leading to a volunteer surge at Habitat for Humanity. The most iconic call to service by a U.S. President was the one that John F. Kennedy made in his inaugural address, challenging Americans to "ask not what your country can do for you—ask what you can do for your country." President George H. W. Bush's own inaugural did not have the same historical echo, but he deserves credit for highlighting in his speech "a thousand points of light, of all the community organizations that are spread like stars through the nation, doing good." Today the Points of Light Institute connects hundreds of volunteer-driven groups, allowing them to share their resources and talents, amounting to more than 30 million volunteer hours in 2012. It was also Bush who signed the National and Community Service Act in 1990, authorizing grants to schools and charities that rely on activists to perform good deeds in their cities.

Government can and should be a partner in the cause, but legislation alone cannot achieve the necessary momentum. Rather, the driving force must come from individual citizens compelled by a sense of duty to do one's part to improve society. I believe that the sight of people in need strikes a chord within each of us, leading us to offer our help. For those unsure where to start, I would recommend joining a charitable cause or a nonprofit institution that focuses on an issue that is personally important to you. Doing so gives you an opportunity to work side by side with people who share the same personal stake in the mission as you. It's distressing to read reports about how membership in the PTA has dropped from six million ten years ago to less than five million today. This is an institution that gives parents a voice in shaping the curriculum, teaching style, and administration of the school and the educational system that serves their children, and I have no doubt that the quality of that education would be improved if more parents actively participated in the PTA.

Volunteerism comes in many shapes and sizes, and it can also be a natural extension of one's sincere interest in a particular cause.

My daughter Rebecca adores animals, so she volunteers at a shelter that seeks to match orphaned dogs and cats with trustworthy owners. I can see in her glowing face how much she gets out of it.

One doesn't have to be wealthy to make a meaningful contribution. Museums, ballets, environmental groups, and countless other organizations are constantly in need of volunteers to staff events. By contributing your unpaid time, it's possible for these organizations to put more money into their charitable efforts, giving those who volunteer their time the satisfaction of having made a small but valuable contribution.

For those who have an itch to travel and who want to promote American goodwill in the developing world, the Peace Corps is a deeply enriching enterprise that is attracting a more diverse group of volunteers than ever before. Women's health is an issue that is very close to my heart, and I know that Planned Parenthood and other local clinics would be grateful to have the assistance of those who understand how important it is that women have a place to go that is affordable, when they need their healthcare needs met.

We're all blessed with unique talents and special expertise; I believe we have a duty to share these blessings with our community. Ultimately, sharing brings society closer together. It's a personal investment of the individual for the sake of a larger cause.

Ironically, though, these acts of goodwill have the most powerful impact on the giver, not the receiver. That is, performing selfless acts leads to unexpected benefits. Of course, it is difficult for researchers to isolate volunteerism, specifically, as a leading factor in improving the volunteer's quality of life, but the correlations are so consistent that they're hard to ignore.

A 1999 paper by John Wilson and Marc Musick, "The Effects of Volunteering on the Volunteer," is still widely cited as a reference on this question. Among the studies it selected for analysis was one that compared women at two dates, thirty years apart, finding that those who had volunteered at least "intermittently" during those three decades scored higher across a wide variety of physical and mental health indicators. Similar longitudinal studies found that "volunteers were less likely to die than non-volunteers, regardless of level of church attendance, age, marital status, education, or gender."

Young people enjoy even more immediate benefits. The paper noted a study finding that students who had been active as volunteers during eleventh and twelfth grades were less likely to be arrested within four years after graduation. Another study tracked students who joined a school-based teen outreach program that linked them to volunteer opportunities, finding that these students were significantly less likely to get pregnant, fail a course, or be suspended from school, compared to those students who didn't join the program.

I can speak firsthand about how volunteerism increases focus and success in a young person. During high school I volunteered at the Plainview Animal Hospital in Plainview, New York, and was dual-enrolled in high school at the local agricultural and technical college, SUNY Farmingdale, in Farm Animal Health and Introduction to Animal Science. I spent my freshman year at the University of Florida as an Animal Science major. Then a friend of mine recruited me to apply for an open student senate seat representing my residence hall. Because of my positive experience with volunteering in high school, I was open to the idea, and soon I was introduced to the world of politics, Florida Gator–style.

It was like being hit by a lightning bolt: I realized that public service and politics was something I loved. It enabled me to give voice to my views and the views of those I represented. It was also fun! The strategy and work ethic necessary for success in politics was a stimulating challenge that proved quite addictive. Because of that experience, I decided to change my major to political science, taking my life in a 180-degree turn. My parents always taught me to "reach for the stars" and I eventually realized that I would one day run for public office in the "real world." So I interned for a city commissioner in Gainesville, which led to an internship with a state legislator in my original home state of New York. In 1992, just two years after completing my master's degree in political science, I was elected to the Florida House of Representatives at the age of twenty-six.

Given my own experience, I was not surprised to learn of a study that tracked alumni of another university, Florida State. It found that students who had been active in community service during their time on campus had mostly remained active both ten and twenty-five years following their graduation. Like me, I suspect they liked how volunteering made them feel and they were going to keep at it.

By convincing young Americans to become active we're liable to get lifelong activists. And I take an optimistic view of those generations and the prospects for their commitment to public service.

Much has been made about the time that our young people spend on social media sites, but Facebook, Twitter, and similar pages can be a way for them to learn about volunteer opportunities, or about causes that are worth donating their time and money. It's been derided as "slacktivism" among the more seasoned volunteers, who worry that those who "like" a charity's page or re-Tweet a post are doing so instead of making a more time-consuming contribution offline. But research shows that those who use social media to promote favored causes are largely doing so in addition to more traditional modes of volunteer work. For instance, if a teenager tells his or her friends about the fulfillment gained through community service via social media, then maybe next time those friends will come along.

The media is certainly paying attention to issues that are trending online. Ask anyone who staffs a nonprofit, and they're likely to tell you they support any technology that makes it easier for them to get their message out, reach prospective volunteers, and attract donations.

When it comes to developing advocacy among younger generations, the more difficult question in my mind is how strong a hand our society should take. In some districts, students are required to perform a minimum number of community service hours before their high school graduation. I know that in Florida there is a minimum community service requirement in college or vocational scholarship programs.

But when young people are required to perform community service, the students often participate because they must, not because they feel personally compelled or passionate about a cause. I've noticed that the competence, drive, and motivation of a young person interning in my congressional office is dramatically different when a student voluntarily seeks to work, versus the kid whose parent calls and says their child needs a certain number of hours to complete their community service requirement. The teenagers who regard volunteer work primarily as a means for improving their chances at earning a scholarship or being admitted to a favored college may have a slightly different mentality than those students who are motivated by interest in the cause. To others, I suspect that the term "community service" suggests an activity that was mandated by court order, as if volunteer work is so awful that it constitutes punishment. In fact, a young constituent once told me that the first time he showed up at a volunteer event, the organizers assumed that he would be asking them to sign paperwork from his probation officer. They were surprised to learn that he'd volunteered purely for unselfish reasons.

If we can achieve more widespread encouragement for students to participate in community service, our society would reap rich rewards. It would not only give charities access to millions of extra hands, it would have the potential for inspiring some of those young volunteers to continue being active later in life. Creating incentives to participate, taking a carrot-rather than a stick-based approach, is a good way to draw young people into service and help them realize the impact their participation has on the work they are performing. It makes it more likely that a young person will discover a lifelong commitment to activism and to making a difference in the community.

This leads me to the conclusion that the best way to advance the cause of service is for those of us who know how meaningful that activity is to lead by example. Let other people see, through words and actions, how much we value our roles as community activists. In particular, parents should let their children observe them in that capacity, leading those kids to grow up with a sense that it's simply the way a conscientious and considerate society operates.

There are plenty of reasons for us to seek out opportunities to volunteer. But to really make a difference, it's important to confront the obstacles that prevent folks from lending a hand. Not that they make excuses; rather, I suspect they want to get involved but honestly don't believe they have the time.

Throughout my years of public service and running for office, I've found that most people perceive that the most precious and most difficult resource to part with is money. The reality is, the most precious resource that most people have is their time. Think about your own life and how you react when groups ask for your help. Speaking to crowds during the 2012 Obama campaign, I told these prospective volunteers that I recognized how valuable their financial contributions were, but I also emphasized how important and impactful it would be for them to invest their time in this cause. To illustrate this, I like to tell a story about the requests I receive from the PTA at my youngest daughter's elementary school. Often, the group will send out an e-mail or a notice home asking for parents to volunteer some time to help with an upcoming event. Of course, they usually ask for a small donation toward the event, as well. Given what my average day with three kids and a full-time job is like, writing the check is easier and makes me feel like I helped. For many of the moms I know, whether they stay at home or work, it's much tougher to find the time to stand behind the table at the bake sale. But the time devoted by volunteer parents is essential for the success of that bake sale, whether it's taking the time to bake something or helping sell the items. The project fails without the volunteers.

In 2008, the Corporation for National and Community Service staged focus groups around the country to investigate attitudes about volunteering. They found that people who don't volunteer tend to think that those who do have an excess of leisure time. They assume that the volunteers are retired or that they are adults without children. In fact, research shows that the opposite is true—American professionals volunteer at a higher rate than those who don't have a college degree, and often they volunteer for an activity related to their children, as I did with my daughters' Girl Scout troops. Not surprisingly, the nonvolunteers told surveyors that they didn't want to commit to a public service that would prove time-consuming. On the other hand, they did say that they would be more likely to volunteer if they were encouraged by friends to do so.

This offers valuable clues for how to increase volunteer turnout, but let's zoom in to see demographic data. Research shows that in recent years adult volunteering has increased among three age groups: late teens, middle-age Americans (aged forty-five to sixty-four), and adults sixty-five and older. That's great news, but it begs the question of why young Americans, from twenty to forty-four years old, have not shown similar increases.

Since we know that many volunteers participate in service that pertains to their children, researchers suspect that this trend is related to the fact that couples are getting married and having children at an older age than they have in the past. That lack of children, or the demands of having an infant in the home, may explain this group's falling behind others in volunteering. My own hunch is that young Americans who are just entering the workforce or considering how to provide for children that may arrive in the future are especially anxious about finding a job and then keeping a job. That focus may lead them to regard volunteer work as a "luxury" they can't afford.

To reach these individuals, we can encourage their employers to participate in workplace volunteer activities. Deloitte, a research consulting firm, conducts an annual Volunteer IMPACT Survey, and in 2011 it targeted working adults aged twenty-one to thirty-five. Surveyors found that workers in this age group who volunteered through their employers were twice as likely to say their corporate culture was positive, as well as being significantly more inclined to be proud of their company and loyal to it. The trendy term for this is "employee engagement" and one of the more common examples is the Dollars for Doers Program, in which a company makes a donation to the charity where their workers volunteer. (A typical rate is $10 per hour of employee service.) Among 214 major American firms surveyed by the Corporate Giving Standard in 2011, 63 percent offered this program. Many companies also offer to match donations made by their employees to nonprofit causes, or allow workers paid-release time so that they can volunteer while still being paid their regular wages.

MicroEdge, a company which provides software to an array of charitable causes around the world, offered this analysis of the many benefits that come from service, both for the employer and the employee:

> These programs help to build brand awareness and affinity, while strengthening trust and loyalty among customers. They put a human face on the company, reinforcing the idea that the company is comprised of real people that just happen to be organized around a particular product or service. It's almost like a singer coming down off the stage and into the audience as he or she continues to sing. By doing this companies become more approachable while enhancing their corporate image and reputation.
>
> But it is really on the employee side where the benefits are most, well, meaningful. Employees that volunteer tend to

experience greater job satisfaction, and improved morale. This, in turn, leads to a more positive attitude which constructively impacts job performance, teamwork and many of the other intangibles that make good companies better. As a result, the companies doing this see both improved employee retention and productivity.

Clearly, these activities provide great value to companies that want happy, devoted workers.

But the Deloitte survey turned up evidence that the millennial generation is particularly mindful about the personal benefits they'll reap from volunteering through work. Of those who declined the opportunity to do so, lack of time was by far the biggest reason. So it's evident that employers need to do more to incentivize these activities, making it worth their employees' time. Deloitte researchers concluded that "companies that view their volunteer programs as strategic assets and incorporate service into the business planning may have a distinct advantage when it comes to engaging millennials and capturing their minds, hearts and spirits."

I hope that workers who are ambitious within their professional field recognize that participating in charitable functions gives them the chance to build stronger relationships with their supervisors in an untraditional work setting. At Procter & Gamble, for instance, hundreds of employees team with "brand leaders" for an annual service day. In one recent case, these groups spent that time cleaning a high school and building a baseball diamond for underserved children in Cincinnati. Imagine the bonds formed between workers on these service days, as well as the feeling of pride they feel for their accomplishment.

We can't rely entirely on self-starters and civic-minded employers to drive volunteer participation, however. The charities and various nonprofit causes must be willing to meet prospective activists halfway, crafting opportunities for those folks to volunteer in a way that minimizes the hassle. For instance, a typically busy person may occasionally discover that he or she has a few hours in the middle of the day to donate to a charity. These are called "serendipitous volunteers" and an organization ought to have a list of activities ready for the moment such a person telephones or walks into the office.

In addition, agencies must welcome assistance from "entrepreneurial volunteers." These are people whose passion for the cause aligns with a charity, but who are more comfortable defining the terms of their involvement, rather than being told what to do. A 2006 article by volunteer consultant Nancy Macduff points out that disaster relief missions appeal to this style of activist. Others favor entrepreneurial volunteering because it may allow them to stay at home and work online.

In short, if there's a will there is definitely a way. As long as I have a vote in Congress I will do everything I can to promote a spirit of community service, rewarding those individuals, businesses, and charities who display creativity and hustle. No matter what may be a person's cause, working toward it will bring him or her closer to neighbors, making that person think less in terms of self and more in terms of community. We all respond to inducements of money and prestige, but what really defines character is what we're willing to do with no expectation of pay or recognition.

———◄◦►———

Change . . . What Happens
Next Is Up to Us

Over the course of our lives, each of us has moments of clarity, when we know exactly what matters above all else. That flash of insight gives us a sense of purpose, and in that moment we have the capacity to reorganize our lives so that virtually every decision we make from that point forward serves that overarching purpose. In my own life, there have been two such moments: giving birth to my children and being diagnosed with breast cancer.

One was exhilarating. The other was devastating. But both of these events made me realize that I absolutely must make the most of my opportunity to have an impact on what matters most to me while on this earth, sharing whatever knowledge and skills I have for making it a better place.

That had always been my mission in life, but when I had children, this mission came into sharper focus, becoming more urgent than ever before. My husband and I brought into the world three babies who depended on us completely and who we could not imagine living without—meaning that we were dependent on them, as well. Caring for those children immediately became the most important thing in our lives, and with that came a sense of vulnerability.

This is why my breast cancer diagnosis gave me such a dreadful jolt. Even though my doctors were confident that the disease could be defeated through aggressive treatment, I knew how pernicious cancer could be. There was no guarantee that I would survive and no guarantee that it wouldn't come back if I beat it. All the experiences I imagined having with my children, all that I wished to teach them and do for them, all of that was in jeopardy.

At the same time, I learned that I was not alone. There was a sisterhood of women whose lives had been interrupted just like mine had, who felt the same fear about the future. Women like Maimah Karmo, who was only thirty-two when she received her own breast cancer diagnosis, in 2006. Maimah's daughter was three years old at that time. With her breast cancer at stage two, Maimah didn't know whether she would live long enough to see her daughter go to kindergarten, much less graduate from high school and college.

In the midst of a grueling chemotherapy regimen, Maimah promised God that if she was given the strength she needed to outlast the disease, she would devote her life to helping other young women battle breast cancer. Maimah won her battle—and then she made good on her promise by creating the Tigerlily Foundation (tigerlilyfoundation.org).

Even before my own diagnosis, I had always been a proponent of breast cancer research and awareness, but when I developed breast cancer, that work became even more important to me. In 2009, after I shared my own breast cancer experience publicly, I teamed up with Maimah and her foundation to craft legislation that directed the Centers for Disease Control and Prevention to launch a national education campaign designed to raise awareness of breast cancer in young women. That bill, called the EARLY Act, was incorporated within the Affordable Care Act (Obamacare) that passed into law in March 2010, thanks in large part to a diverse coalition of more than forty organizations who rallied in support of the bill. Today, the EARLY Act Task Force at the CDC, through appropriations passed as part of the EARLY Act, have awarded grants to organizations like Sharsheret (sharsheret.org) and FORCE (facingourrisk.org), which help younger women deal with the unique challenges they face when diagnosed with breast cancer. The EARLY Act Task Force will be creating a national education and awareness campaign targeted at young women so they are more likely to catch breast cancer early and survive.

Taking these actions, knowing that I had a role in helping future girls and women prevent breast cancer, was incredibly empowering. With the help of Maimah and other breast cancer activists, we managed to turn personal adversity into universal good.

Every person has the capacity to empathize with others and to be their champion. For instance, not all of us have children, but all of us were children at one time, so we can understand the consequences of decisions made by adults responsible for children's well-being. We must recognize our responsibility and our obligation to make decisions in a way that will improve children's welfare. Similarly, not all of us will receive a cancer diagnosis, but we will all have to come to terms with our own mortality. When that day comes, we will face the question of whether we did enough during our lives to make a difference in the lives of others.

Having considered that question myself, I can say that there is no room for doubts or regrets. Each of us must be able to answer that universal question by saying that he or she absolutely has made a positive impact on the world. We cannot fool ourselves; we must truly believe this. And we cannot afford to postpone the purpose that defines our lives, because we do not know how long we have. For the sake of our children, for our fellow human beings, and for the tranquillity of our own individual souls, we must begin to take action right now.

Nothing in the universe is more powerful than a group of people willing to make personal sacrifices in service to a greater purpose. This principle has been a guiding force in my life, and certainly in my political career.

In 2005, after I was first sworn in to Congress, I immediately volunteered to help the political arm for the House Democrats, the Democratic Congressional Campaign Committee (DCCC) to recruit and to raise money for promising Democratic candidates for the House of Representatives. I led and participated in fundraisers that raised millions of dollars for each election cycle and did news interviews to get our message out, all for the cause of helping Democrats achieve a majority in the House. These activities took extra time beyond my normal congressional duties and even took me out of town to campaign in the home districts of other candidates and incumbent colleagues facing difficult reelections. I felt that electing more people who shared a vision of achieving a fairer and more just society, moving away from the policies of President Bush, would do more to advance the goals of my constituents in South Florida than anything I could do alone.

It was with that in mind that I accepted President Obama's request in April 2011 to take on what was, as I like to only half-jokingly say, a third full-time job. My first responsibility is being the mom to my three incredible kids. As I said earlier, my primary professional responsibility is serving my constituents in Congress. And I now have a third full-time job as chair of the Democratic National Committee. When Steve and I talked about the extra time this role would require and that it would take me away from our family a bit more than my day job does—every week back and forth to Washington, D.C.—we knew the right thing to do was to say yes to the President of the United States. We knew that the 2012 presidential election had more at stake than any election we had seen in our lifetime. We felt that the impact of voters making the wrong decision on November 6, 2012, would affect our kids and the children of the families I represent in South Florida and all across the country, for decades and, in reality, for generations.

But as the chair of the Democratic Party, I also knew it would not be easy to secure the reelection of our Democratic President during a time of slow economic growth, no matter how much Republican policies were at fault for the Great Recession. It appeared certain that unemployment would remain high through the election, and since FDR, every President who ran for reelection with an unemployment rate over 7.2 percent had been defeated. What's more, the presumptive nominee, Mitt Romney, and his supporters had embarked on an aggressive fundraising schedule, giving

Republicans the means to blanket the media with fierce and often misleading criticism of President Obama, through Election Day.

If one person can make a difference, then many people can make a big difference. And so, more broadly in the 2012 election, as Republicans tried to dominate the airwaves, Democrats ruled the ground game. While the GOP's negative ads ran on a continuous loop, funded by billionaire-fueled super PACs, we had real people engaged at the local level who were contacting likely voters, informing them about how the party's policies would affect their lives, building relationships that would last through the fall and beyond. The time that these activists gave to President Obama and to other Democratic candidates was far more valuable than the hundreds of millions that flowed through Romney super PACs. We always expected the election would be close, but we trusted that our investment in grassroots activism would put us over the top in the crucial swing states.

On the day before the election, Republicans in Ohio boasted that they had knocked on 75,000 doors in the twenty-four hours prior. What they didn't know is that Democratic activists had knocked on 376,000 Ohio doors that day. In Florida, there were 122 Obama field offices, compared to Romney's 48, and nationally Obama had 755 to Romney's 283. They were the center of action leading up to and on Election Day, and they made the difference in Democratic turnout, as our party won every swing state for Obama but one, while tallying a million more votes than Republicans for Democratic candidates in the House. In the end, the election wasn't very close. President Obama won the Electoral College vote 332 to 206 and the popular vote by more than five million votes.

The decisive factor was that regular people from a wide variety of backgrounds all were willing to take time out of their lives to achieve a goal that was far bigger than any individual ambition. Every single person who played a role in that 2012 campaign can feel a sense of ownership pride: We knew that President Obama's reelection was important to the cause of progress in the world's richest, most powerful country. Together, we affected the course of history.

◆ ◆ ◆

In the journey to becoming an actor, not an observer, in world events, the first step is often the most difficult. Typically, a person is provoked by a sense that "something should be done" about a particular issue, and in the next instant recognizes an opportunity, saying: "Maybe I'm the person who should do it."

"It" may be going to a city government meeting to express concern about a dangerous intersection in your neighborhood. It may be spreading the word among residents of your state about a major oil company seeking to drill in a protected wildlife habitat. Or it may be deciding that it's not enough to merely sign a petition expressing your support for gay marriage, that you will join the campaign so you can work in concert with others who see this is a civil right that has gone unrecognized for too long.

Truly, there is no problem, no crisis so severe that we cannot resolve it together.

To an individual American, for example, the national economy may seem as vast as an ocean, and just as impervious to a single person's influence. So while we may be concerned about the economy's health, we typically express our opinion with one vote, for the candidate who we most trust to manage that economy: a pebble tossed into the ocean, creating a small ripple before vanishing into the expanse.

Still, that experience of voting and the knowledge that our vote is equal to the one cast by Bill Gates or Oprah Winfrey, which is equal to the one cast by Barack Obama, gives us faith in our democratic society. Voting is a contribution to society and being conscious of that gives us a deeper investment in it.

But there are so many other methods available to us as we seek to improve this country for the next generation of Americans. For instance, every dollar an individual person spends is a political act, influencing the nation's economy at a molecular level.

So just as we scrutinize politicians before heading to the polls, we ought to consider the kinds of businesses with whom we invest our hard-earned incomes. If you own a small local business or if you think like I do, that they are the backbone of America's middle class, then consider paying a little bit more for their goods and services, versus a major corporation that is shipping its jobs overseas, whose executives are investing their income in offshore tax shelters and who might eventually force that local small business to shut its doors. If you are upset about the treatment of seasonal farm workers, then be careful not to buy from the companies that engage in their mistreatment. Those who share my frustration about the salary disparities between men and women as well as the challenges of balancing work and family should check out the companies who are highly rated by *Working Mother* magazine, a publication that spotlights the best companies with family-friendly workplaces, and go out of your way to do business with them. If you're worried about the state of the environment, then buy foods from responsible producers, a car with an efficient engine, and check out the wide range of energy-saving tools to reduce your home's carbon footprint.

You can also have an impact on the causes that matter to you by "voting with your feet." As a pro-choice woman, when I learned years ago that the owner of Domino's Pizza contributed millions of dollars to anti-choice organizations whose mission was to limit a woman's access to reproductive choices, I never ordered another pizza from Domino's again. When I learned that the CEO of Outback Steakhouse before the 1996 elections had stated it was his mission to ensure President Clinton's defeat, I stopped going to Outback.

More recently, during the 2012 election cycle, when it became public knowledge that the president of Chik-fil-A restaurants regularly donated to organizations with an anti-gay agenda, like many Americans, I let my kids know that we would not be eating there anymore—even though Chik-fil-A had just opened a location in our hometown. When they asked me why, I told them about the company owner's donations and although Shelby mourned the loss of their french fries, they understood. In this way, I instill our family's values in my children and pay it forward so they use their belief system to make personal economic choices in the future.

We must be aware of the consequences our actions have, but we must also be aware of the impact of a lack of action. Action and inaction can be equally powerful. If we are not paying attention, there is a danger that we're promoting a cause we don't actually support. We may produce consequences that are harmful not only to ourselves but to society as a whole.

I am hopeful about reforms that will empower broad-based citizen action, but the wheels of change often turn too slowly. I am asking Americans not to wait for legislation. With our children's future hanging in the balance, there isn't a moment to lose.

Instead of waiting, I would suggest that Americans who are impatient for progress give their time and talents to the many altruistic organizations that have already established a sophisticated, effective system for advocating in Washington. I point you to a few here and elsewhere in this book, but this list is by no means exhaustive. There are many effective organizations out there.

For example, there are many strong environmental advocacy groups, but I have come to admire the work being performed by the Everglades Coalition (evergladescoalition.org). They are the major advocacy organization supporting the restoration of the Florida Everglades, the only ecosystem of its kind in the world. Decades ago, former governor Napoleon Bonaparte Broward made a decision to dig canals throughout these swampy, massive wetlands and interrupt the sheet flow of water throughout the ecosystem. As a result, much of the original Florida Everglades became dry enough to develop. However the expanse that remained, which is vital to Florida's need for drinking water as well as its wildlife, plant life, and environment, was parched in some places and too wet in others. In the 1990s, thanks to the leadership of then Governor Lawton Chiles, the Florida Legislature passed the Everglades Forever Act, the most ambitious wetlands restoration act ever planned or attempted. The state-federal project, for which I have repeatedly and proudly cast my vote in the Florida Legislature and in Congress, requires billions of dollars and has created thousands of jobs. It continues today, pushed forward by the determined advocacy of the Everglades Coalition. People who share my concern for the preservation of this natural wonder can go to the coalition's Web site and scan the fifty-seven member organizations who form this alliance, joining the one that is closest to their home.

As I discussed in chapter 10, women's issues are near and dear to me, especially when they overlap with health-care policy, which is why I encourage constituents to give their time to Planned Parenthood, an organization that has been viciously attacked by ultraconservative groups and could benefit from activists to spread the word about how much good the organization does across a wide variety of women's health issues. During the onslaught by Tea Party–backed members of Congress against Planned Parenthood, one thing became clear: Millions of American women have used a Planned Parenthood clinic for basic health-care services at some point in their lives, which is why this organization had so much support in their fight to preserve their federal funding.

Too many times we have heard gut-wrenching stories about children dying from poisoning, or drowning, or another avoidable tragedy. Each year, there are roughly a million such deaths around the world. Much of my career has been devoted to making children's safety a higher legislative priority. I am aware of the importance of this issue, particularly preventing children's accidental injury and death thanks to Safe Kids Worldwide. In 1997, I had recently joined the board of my local National Safety Council chapter. During my board member orientation, NSC brought in Safe Kids Worldwide (then known as National Safe Kids Campaign) to brief me on the important safety issues on which they were working. Organization members told me that the number one killer of children under five years old in Florida was accidental drowning in residential swimming pools. This was also a significant problem nationally. Safe Kids staff described how infants and toddlers who were temporarily unsupervised would wander out the back door of the home or into a neighbor's yard with an unlatched gate and fall into the pool. I was not yet a parent, so children's safety had not become personal by this point in my legislative career. During that orientation briefing, however, one of my signature legislative agenda items was born. After inquiring during our discussion if the group had ever discussed pursuing legislation to reduce and prevent childhood drowning, we developed our plan to introduce the de Ibern/Merriam Pool Safety legislation. I would encourage parents and non-parents alike to volunteer with Safe Kids and similar organizations so that they can enjoy the comfort of knowing that they have done their part to protect the youngest, most vulnerable members of society.

As the debate continues to rage around our government's continuing efforts to improve health-care coverage and strengthen safety net programs, you can bet that the AARP (aarp.org) will be at the table, which is why I would encourage seniors to take an active role with this organization. Programs like Social Security and Medicare have weathered near-constant assaults from Republicans with a cuts-only approach to deficit reduction. Members of Congress like myself depend on the intelligent, informed citizens at AARP to educate their members about the dangers of privatization and other misleading proposals that would take the "security" out of social programs. We are buttressed by the strong voices of AARP's membership.

It's important to remember that you don't have to agree with every policy position of a group to join it. You may have a slightly different position on some education issues than the PTA, but perhaps you can do your part to bring that powerful organization toward your point of view by getting involved in your local school PTA chapter or even at the county or state level.

There are gun owners who support reasonable gun control policy and perhaps they could work within the NRA to move that organization closer to the center. Or they can join the organization founded by my friends Gabby Giffords and her husband, Mark Kelly, called Americans for Responsible Solutions (americansforresponsiblesolutions.org), which I discussed in chapter 12. Sometimes new organizations are more responsive to their newest members. I certainly know the value that Gabby and Mark put in dialogue with constituents and I have faith that their group will have a grassroots style for promoting commonsense solutions to violence and gun control.

In the course of joining these activist groups, you'll meet people who feel the same way as you on similar issues, and you'll learn how much more persuasive you are as a group.

I sympathize with those who feel isolated and powerless against the tide of so-called moneyed special interests that seem to have their way with the American political system, but those groups are composed merely of individuals who share a common purpose and put their money behind it. So I would challenge frustrated citizens to identify the causes that mean the most to them and to seek out the interest groups who fight in Washington on their behalf. Join them. With the help of everyday Americans, those groups will grow stronger, with a more persuasive power over policymaking.

If there is no organized group that promotes the specific cause that matters most to you, then create it! Connie Siskowski, a resident of the Palm Beach County congressional district just north of the one I represent, noticed that there was no one advocating on behalf of children who struggle in school because they have to care for a relative who is disabled or has health problems. So she founded the American Association of Caregiving Youth (aacy.org) in 1998. Since then, according to a CNN report, Siskowski's organization has provided assistance to over five hundred young people in South Florida, enrolling them in special classes that allow them to deal with the stresses of caregiving while making sure that the students' teachers are sensitive to the responsibilities those students have at home. Siskowski understands the students' plight because she remembers being eleven years old and having to start looking after her grandfather. More than a million kids in America are taking care of sick and disabled relatives, but they're too young to have a voice in politics. Thanks to Siskowski, they now have someone looking out for them. Her program has spread to seventeen high schools and eight middle schools in Palm Beach County. Bolstered by media coverage of the program's success, Siskowski has established an affiliate network of partners throughout the United States. As the organization grows, so will public awareness. Educational policies will be crafted that are responsive to this young, vulnerable population of American school-children.

Democracy rewards those who take action, serving those who apply its principles methodically and constructively. As a result, democracy is our partner in this crusade to make the lives of our children and all children better tomorrow than they are today.

If nothing else, I can assure you that your personal involvement on issues that matter to you the most can have a direct impact on the direction those issues take. I spent several years as an adjunct professor at Nova Southeastern University in Davie, Florida, lecturing graduate students all over the country, from teachers to speech pathologists to medical students, on how they could best influence public policy. Within each of these professions there exist codes and regulations subject to changes in state and federal law. My overarching advice to these students was that it certainly *was* worth their time to convey their opinion to their elected officials, particularly those who regulated their profession, and that the amount of time they take to influence the outcome of an elected official's decision is directly proportional to the weight that lawmaker will give to their opinion.

During lectures, I would often ask my students to raise their hand if they had ever signed a petition. All the hands would go up. When I would ask about other forms of more time-consuming advocacy, like attending a town hall meeting, far fewer hands would go up. Over the years, more hands would go up when I asked whether students had ever sent an e-mail in support of or in opposition to a particular bill pending. Often, these e-mails would be generated by the professional organization that lobbied in the state capital or in Washington, D.C., and required little more effort than filling in the person's name and address to the signature portion of the e-mail and hitting send.

As we've discussed in this book, our most important resource is our time. If an issue is only as important to you as the time it takes to quickly scrawl your signature on a petition someone has likely shoved in front of you on the way in or out of a supermarket with little explanation, then how does an elected official give more weight to that opinion than dozens of handwritten letters that likely took a good thirty minutes to write, then stuff, steal, stamp, and mail? A phone call, attendance at a town hall meeting, going down to city hall or traveling to the state or national capital to meet with elected officials, even sending a personalized e-mail rather than just hitting send on one that is automatically generated shows the elected official you are trying to persuade that you feel strongly enough about the issue to expend what is most valuable to you: your time. If an issue matters to you enough, an elected official knows you will spend the time it takes to try to influence the outcome and they will likely pay more attention to that message than one that required little to no effort.

Another important element of enhancing your influence is to focus your communication toward elected officials who represent you and for whom you can vote. It is human nature to be more easily persuaded by people who affect our lives. (It stands to reason that an elected official whose election is affected by the votes of their constituents is going to be more responsive to the people who vote in their jurisdiction than those who do not.) When faced with the need to influence a decision maker for whom you cannot vote, reach out through professional organizations or join an organization with a broad reach so they can coordinate communication with constituents in the decision makers' community.

As someone who receives a great many solicitations from a wide range of constituents and interest groups, believe me when I tell you that I can tell the difference between those who are truly committed to effecting an outcome, versus those who only have a casual interest in it. When something really matters to you, don't be shy about letting people in power know exactly how much!

To more fully illustrate the value derived from a life of service and community action, I will leave you with the story of Rixys Alfonso.

Having been born in Cuba, Rixys came to understand that the most effective way to challenge a dictatorial regime was through nonviolent action. In 1980, she was among the thousands of Cubans who flooded the Peruvian embassy, seeking asylum. That demonstration convinced Fidel Castro's communist government to allow Cubans who were frustrated by the country's lack of economic development to leave by boat, through

Cuba's Mariel Harbor, an exodus known as the Mariel Boatlift. This was the way that Rixys and her parents came to settle in the United States.

The Alfonso family was grateful for being warmly received by the South Florida community that would be their permanent home and they soon came to regard themselves as Americans. Rixys took work as a receptionist and enjoyed her job. The freedoms of this country were so abundant, however, that Rixys did not feel nearly the same urgency to take political action or be involved in her community. She was not apathetic, but she had become so comfortable that she was not compelled to get intimately involved in social causes. On some level, I think we can all relate to that feeling.

Then something terrible happened. In 1997, Rixys's newborn son, Devin, was diagnosed with a severe form of scoliosis, which caused a significant spinal deformity. She was told by doctors that Devin's condition was terminal. He was given six months to live.

This dire threat to her son's life gave Rixys a focus like nothing had before. Similar to the way that I, like so many others, reacted to my breast cancer diagnosis by doing research, Rixys read everything she could about Devin's scoliosis. Soon she came across Dr. Robert Campbell, a medical researcher in Texas who was performing experimental treatments on patients who had spinal conditions like Rixys's son. Called Titanium Rib, it might not save Devin's life, but it would give him a chance that he didn't have without the procedure.

Knowing she didn't have a moment to lose, Rixys mailed Dr. Campbell every relevant test that had been performed on Devin. After studying those tests, Campbell's team determined that Devin qualified as a candidate and after an initial visit, he was made eligible for the Titanium Rib treatment.

There was still one colossal problem. Because the surgery Campbell performed was not yet approved by the FDA, the $150,000 expense could not be paid through Medicaid. To save her son's life, Rixys would need help. She called me.

Prior to that phone call, I don't believe Rixys even realized that I was her Florida state senator. But immediately I understood how desperate her situation was, and I vowed to do whatever I could to help. That meant phone calls to state bureaucrats who made decisions on Medicaid coverage, as well bringing other political figures into the crusade. Rixys located three more children in the state who suffered from severe scoliosis and needed treatment, proving that this obstacle was not unique to Devin.

Thanks to that activism, we prevailed. Medicaid agreed to pay for the surgery, and it saved Devin's life. He must return periodically for new surgeries—he's had forty-one of them so far. He's now sixteen years old—a junior in high school who has played golf and softball, and has even participated in his school's Navy ROTC program.

It may have seemed like a miracle, but the lesson that Rixys took away from this experience is how seemingly impossible endeavors can be made possible through advocacy. Knowing this, Rixys felt compelled to use her newfound skills for the sake of other parents whose children had life-threatening disabilities. After several years of local advocacy, Rixys came to Washington to offer emotional testimony at a congressional committee considering the Pediatric Medical Device Safety and Improvement Act of 2007. Since then, Rixys's heroics have been featured in *Good Housekeeping* magazine and on CBS's *The Doctors*, as well as in a documentary on the Learning Channel. Not one to rest on her laurels, in 2010 Rixys initiated a petition that led to the passage of a U.S. House Resolution, which I sponsored, honoring Dr. Campbell and compelling the FDA to "continue to support and incentivize other medical advances to save children's lives threatened by rare disorders." That same year she was appointed by then Governor Charlie Crist to the Florida Developmental Disabilities Council. Named a "Hispanic Woman of Distinction" in 2012, Rixys estimates that that year she raised $2 million for charity.

Every time I encounter Rixys, I'm inspired by her tireless enthusiasm. The cause of helping disabled children has brought so much more meaning to her life. She is an example to all of us.

But there is no rule that says we must wait for some personal calamity— like a sick child or a cancer diagnosis—before we get involved. If we are conscious of how deeply fulfilling it will be to work on behalf of a cause that matters to us, then let us give ourselves to that cause without hesitation so that we can begin a new, more rewarding phase in our lives and begin constructing a future that will improve the outlook for kids.

The changes I've discussed in this book will not come easily. On the contrary, there will be moments in the months and years to come when our faith in progress is tested. There may be occasions when we become cynical, suspicious that the American political system has been hopelessly corrupted and polarized and that energized citizens are powerless to make changes that are universally good.

But if we give in to that despair, if we give up on these principles that we know are right, then how will we explain it to our children? How would we justify our inaction?

We can't! There is no excuse for failing. Let us not allow ourselves to feel overwhelmed by the weight of the problems that face this country and the uncertainty of our future. Rather, let us regard them as opportunities to inspire ourselves and partner with others in the cause of progress.

I was in Chicago the night of the 2012 election to congratulate the President on his victory and to share in the joy of our supporters. But celebration lasts only as long as it takes for a piece of confetti to travel from the ceiling to the floor. It will be swept up and carried away, and then we are faced with the task of making good on the mandate given to us by voters. If we have clarity of purpose and use the knowledge we've gained to take direct action, then there can be no doubt that we will succeed in making this nation stronger for the next generation.

Acknowledgments

After going through the painstaking process of writing, fact-checking, and rewriting this book what felt like a thousand times, I have even more respect for authors than ever. An enormous amount of work went into this manuscript, and now I know that authorship is a group effort. This book has been a "work in progress" for a long while, particularly when in the middle of writing, I was nominated by President Barack Obama to chair the Democratic National Committee. As I said many times, it is an incredible privilege to be asked by the President to do anything, but particularly to be asked to take on the role of watching his back and helping to bring him across the finish line for a second term. Thank you, Mr. President, for your confidence and for your vision of an America that will ensure the well-being of the next generation, for whom this book is written.

Any member of Congress will tell you that he or she could not possibly succeed without the help of their staff. I am no exception. However, I pride myself on what one former staffer once said about the environment in our office: "Debbie Wasserman Schultz runs the toughest sweatshop that no one wants to leave." I am fortunate to have a team that has an all-too-rare quality in Washington—longevity. Some of them have been with me since I was running for Congress, some since the start of my first term. And in three cases, there are staffers who have worked with me from all the way back to my days in the Florida House of Representatives.

They are the finest group of professionals with whom any member could hope to work. They work grueling hours, have very little personal time, and pride themselves on my favorite work ethic: being "no task too small" individuals. They just get it done in spectacularly successful fashion. If I look good on any given day or achieve something significant, the credit goes to "Team DWS."

Tracie Pough, my chief of staff, who is really the sister I never had but always wanted, is a remarkable leader, mother, daughter, and friend. She nurtures our team and ensures they can develop professionally, and always seems to know how to make things right when everyone is convinced "it can't be done." We have finished each other's sentences or hit send on the identical e-mail so many times through the years, it has ceased to surprise us. "Thank you" is simply inadequate for my gratitude to Tracie. Thanks go to Tracie's husband, Terrance Ashanta-Barker, for being another partner like my husband, Steve, who supports his wife 100 percent while, like my family, they juggle a two-city family life.

My political career has been capably managed for many years by Steve Paikowsky, who bears the brunt of jokes in our office as the oldest staffer. Steve is generous with his time and a trusted and respected political adviser across my home state of Florida, and has advised many politicians across the country as well. He is always there looking out for me and I'm glad I have the opportunity to thank him here in permanent ink so I can point him back to it when we're going a thousand miles an hour.

Other longtime devoted congressional staffers are Ian Rayder, who proved his mettle by surviving his interview to be my deputy campaign manager in 2004, when I nursed Shelby all the way through our meeting and he didn't flinch. He has been rock solid ever since and has risen to be my deputy chief of staff. Jonathan Beeton has been my voice from the day in 2005 when he came for a "tryout" as my press secretary on the day of the State of the Union address and had a job by the end of the night. He's always gone the extra mile for me and given valuable advice and insight, working long, unpredictable hours, particularly when sudden news stories have plunged us into the mix unexpectedly. Coby Dolan (who also did a stint as my legislative aide in the Florida House) has been a smart, loyal, passionate, and hardworking policy team leader as my legislative counsel and director. His judgment and commitment to thorough research and attention to detail always ensure I am prepared, and then some! Dani Gilbert started with me in the state senate during high school as an intern, and proved so capable that when she graduated, she temporarily filled in for my legislative assistant during the summer before she went to college. I jokingly made her promise that when she graduated from Yale, she would come work for me when I was elected to Congress someday. And that is exactly what she did, serving as my expert on foreign policy, health care, the Jewish community, and women's issues. Jason O'Malley had the distinction of being hired as the first employee in my first race for Congress when I was seven months pregnant with my youngest daughter, Shelby. We just marked ten years of working together and he has been an integral and critical part of my success. I've watched him mature and grow as a professional and as a wonderful father. Kate Houghton, who has been with me in multiple roles in both my congressional office and the DNC, is like my kid sister. Starting as an intern and rising to become deputy director of the DNC Chair's office, Kate is organized, capable, creative, and compassionate. In 2012, we were all devastated when she went through leukemia. It was like losing my right arm. Happily, she came back stronger than ever and we are all so thankful and proud of her.

More recent members of Team DWS in D.C. are Hannah Lerner and MacKenzie Smith, who make up my incredible scheduling team and are responsible for Herculean feats with helping me balance work and family every day. Joe Leskody, Mara Sloan, Seth Extein, Stacy Eichner, Lindsey Melander Schulte, and Jacqueline Thomas, who round out the D.C. team, all seem to be headed toward being longtimers, too!

My district staff in South Florida does an incredible job helping me serve my constituents. Jodi Bock Davidson, my district director, has been with me from the beginning of my first term. She has become my alter ego in the district and my constituents know that when she speaks, they can count on me to be there for them because she knows me so well. She's also a great mom! My deputy district director, Laurie Flink, has been a longtime friend and my eyes, ears, and voice in Miami-Dade County. She is a compassionate, empathetic friend and professional whom I am lucky to have in my life and on my team. My district staff is rounded out by Reva Britan, Vivian Piereschi, Bettyanne Gallagher, and Mike Liquerman, all of whom are incredible public servants, who are always there for me and my constituents.

My amazing husband, Steve Schultz, makes all that I do possible. He is my best friend, the best dad, and the most patient, supportive, wonderful husband, who has made our twenty-two years of marriage the best years of my life. There is no possible way I could balance everything in my life without his love and full support. Every woman should be as lucky as I am to have a spouse that believes in equal parenting like Steve does. We are also grateful that Steve's employer, Bruce Keir, the president of Community Bank of Broward, is so supportive of enabling his employees to balance work and family.

I was raised by incredible parents, Ann and Larry Wasserman, who are always there for me, Steve, and our children. They are always on standby for car pool duty and when our kids were smaller, babysitting, too. They have always been the two people whose advice I've needed and trusted the most. I benefited from an idyllic childhood full of their unconditional love that continues today.

My brother, Steven Wasserman, is a funny, smart, wonderful sibling who fortunately works as an Assistant U.S. Attorney in Washington, D.C., so we see each other often. He's been a great uncle to our kids and one of my best friends throughout my life.

My husband's brother, Henry, and sister-in-law, Connie Schultz, have always been there for me. Connie even traveled to D.C. with me on my first trip as a congressional candidate so I could nurse Shelby, who was only four months old. They are incredibly special.

My three incredible children, Rebecca, Jake, and Shelby, are the best kids any mother could ask for. Rebecca is vivacious, smart, and athletic. She is good to her friends and has shown early on that she has a gift with young children. Her twin brother, Jake, is athletic, smart, low-key, and thoughtful. He has a natural kindness and is a giving person, just like his dad. Shelby, our little one, is kind, smart, athletic, and always happy. People comment that she always has a smile on her face. My children are the lights of my life, whom I love with all of my heart.

No woman can really succeed in life without girlfriends. I am fortunate to have devoted friends who help me juggle all the balls I have in the air. Diane Weinbrum, Rebecca's godmother; Robin Bartleman, Shelby's godmother; and Mindy Chmielarz are my best friends, my confidantes, and second mothers to my children. Marla Dolan, one of my college roommates, bridesmaid, and Coby's sister, is always there for me, Steve, and the kids, even though she lives in Boston!

Tom Francis gave me critical assistance in getting the manuscript into final form and has been a pleasure to work with. I have appreciated collaborating with Julie Fenster and thank Joelle Delbourgo, my agent, for shepherding this project from beginning to end. Kathy Huck, my editor, has held my hand throughout this process and been incredibly patient and understanding about my time constraints arising from my congressional, DNC, and parenting responsibilities. Thank you for your help, guidance, encouragement, and assistance. Thank you as well to the staff at St. Martin's Press for your support throughout.

Finally, thank you to my constituents for giving me the greatest professional privilege of representing our community in the nation's capital. This book, ultimately, was written for you and reflects the values and priorities our community shares.

Selected Sources

Introduction: The Future Our Children Deserve

The statistics on women in Congress came from Congress itself, which has a page on its Web site devoted to that topic, http://history.house.gov. On it you'll find statistics and profiles of women who have been in Congress through the years. Nancy Pelosi was quoted in a *USA Today* article by Nancy Kiely, "Nancy Pelosi Talks About Being a Mom," May 10, 2007.

One: Strengthening the Economy (So Our Children Don't Have To)

The CRS provides nonpartisan background information on issues facing the government; this research is sometimes available to the public. The source for the data regarding sequestration was found in the CRS online report *Budget "Sequestration" and Selected Program Exemptions and Special Rules*, by Karen Spar (Washington: CRS, January 13, 2013). Figures on the cost of the Iraq War were calculated by *The Christian Science Monitor* in Dan Murphy's article "Iraq War: Predictions Made, and Results," December 22, 2011. Congressional criticism of President Bush's spending can be found in Tom Daschle's speech, "America's Economy: Rising to Our New Challenges" (Washington, DC, January 4, 2002), available at http://www.angelfire.com/rant/sstewart/News/daschle.html. Further comments can be found in the *Chicago Tribune* article by William Neikirk and Bob Kemper, "Daschle Unveils Economic Plan for Democrats," January 4, 2002). Alice Gomstyn's October 2, 2008, article on ABC News.go.com, "Bailout Bill Basic: From TARP to Tax Breaks," helped explain how new "sweeteners" were the key to passing TARP legislation. Information on the government bailout of the automobile industry came from a CRS report by Baird Webel and Bill Canis available online, *The Role of TARP Assistance in the Restructuring of General Motors*, January 3, 2013.

The Obama economic team's proposal on stimulus monies is discussed in two articles that vary somewhat on the figures, but not on the intent: Noam Schieber's article in the February 22, 2012, *New Republic* article "The Memo that Larry Summers Didn't Want Obama to See"; and Ezra Klein's long post on the *Washington Post*'s Wonkblog, "Could This Time Have Been Different?," October 8, 2011.

The opinion of leading economists on employment is cited from the University of Chicago's Booth Business School; on February 15, 2012, its Initiative on Global Management Web site hosted an experts panel to discuss the impact of the stimulus program on employment. My Fox News appearance regarding the stimulus was covered in Susan Jones's September 12, 2011, article at CNSNews.com, "Debbie Wasserman Schultz: It's 'Baloney' to Say Stimulus Didn't Work."

The Consumer Fraud Protection Bureau is described on their Web site, www.consumerfinance.gov. The fact that some Senate Republicans opposed nominations for that agency was investigated by Edward Wyatt in *The New York Times* in his article "Dodd-Frank a Year Later," July 18, 2011. The data showing that income inequality has increased over the past twenty years was offered by *The Economist* on its Web site on October 26, 2011, under the title "The 99 Percent." The source for President Obama's success in slowing the growth of federal spending is MarketWatch.com, which posted the Rex Nutting article, "Obama Spending Binge Never Happened" on May 22, 2012.

Two: Safety Nets, Built to Last

The figures on senior citizens in the poverty ranks came from a speech made in the House on August 14, 2012, by my colleague in Congress, Eddie Bernice Johnson (D-Texas). Those figures were verified by the *Tampa Bay Times*' Polifact.com. The Social Security financial figures were found at the Social Security Administration Web site in two charts called "Social Security Income, Outgo and Assets" and "Size of Income, 1962 and 2010." The projection that SS trust funds are available to pay full benefits to eligible Americans through at least 2036 is discussed, along with legislative responses to address any shortages thereafter, under the heading on the same Web site, "Proposals Addressing Trust Fund Solvency."

The opposition to Bush's privatization plans was covered in the *Washington Post* article, "Skepticism on Bush's Social Security Plan Is Growing" by Jonathan Weisman, March 15, 2005. Paul Ryan's opinions were quoted on the *Huffington Post* site, in Stephen Ohlemacher's article "Paul Ryan's Social Security Plan Slammed by Democrats," August 19, 2008. The quote from the *Los Angeles Times* is from Michael Hiltzik's article "Proposal to Privatize Social Security Rears Its Ugly Head Again," August 21, 2012. Peter Orszag wrote about the Ryan plan in his op-ed "Five Myths About Paul Ryan's Budget" in the *Washington Post*, August 23, 2012. That paper also provided information on Romney's Medicare proposal in Ezra Klein's article, "The Republican Ticket's Big Medicare Myth," August 12, 2012.

The remarks by Senator Bernie Sanders were made in a 2011 speech before the United Steel Workers and were quoted in the ThinkProgress.org article by Zaid Jilani, "Bernie Sanders Introduces Bill to Lift the Payroll Tax Cap," August 25, 2011. The figures on improper payments came from the White House Office of Management and Budget and were available at the whitehouse.gov blog: see Jeremy Zients, "Improper Payments Progress," November 16, 2010. The details of the alleged fraud by Jacques Roy were covered by Jack Cloherty and Pierre Thomas in their ABCNews. go.com posting "Biggest Medicare Fraud in History Busted," February 28, 2012.

Three: Health Care: A Right Worth Fighting For

Ted Kennedy's regrets about opposing Nixon's health-care plan were discussed in the New York *Daily News* article by Richard Sisk, "Reforming Health Care Was Sen. Ted Kennedy's Unfinished Life's Work," August 26, 2009. The Heritage Foundation comments are from its November 19, 1993, report *A Guide to the Clinton Health Care Plan* written by Robert E. Moffitt. Much of the data in this chapter is available at my Web site, www.wassermanschultz.house.gov, under the tag for health care. The statistic on uninsured Americans came from the CNN.com article by Lee Christie, "Number of Americans Without Health Insurance Climbs," September 13, 2011.

The accounting and consulting firm, Deloitte L.L.C., makes its periodic studies of health-care attitudes: see "U.S. and Global Survey of Health Care Consumers," available on its Web site. The projections of life expectancy for Americans came from a 2007 CRS report, *U.S. Health Care Spending*, by Chris L. Peterson and Rachel Burton. Limbaugh's claim regarding the tax increase was reported by *Business Week* in the July 3, 2012, article by Elizabeth Dwoskin, "Why Obamacare's Tax Increase Isn't the Biggest Ever."

The Heritage Foundation's role in defeating Clinton's health-care reform was covered by Paul Krugman in *The New York Times* article "Hurray for Health Reform," March 18, 2012. Facts surrounding the effect of health-care reform on the budget can be found in the Congressional Budget Office report *Estimates for the Insurance Coverage Provisions of the Affordable Care Act Updated for the Recent Supreme Court Decision* (Washington: CBO, July 24, 2012), http://www.cbo.gov/publication /43472.

The Department of Health and Human Services operates the Web site Healthcare.gov, which provides updates for consumers, as well as trend analysis. It confirmed the data on Medicaid's viability through 2024. A good summary of the effect of the

Affordable Care Act on those with medical needs is "Health Care Reform Bill 101: Rules for Pre-Existing Conditions" by Peter Grier, which appeared in *The Christian Science Monitor* on March 24, 2010.

Four: A Superpower for Peace

Dick Cheney made his comment about Americans being "greeted as liberators" on NBC's *Meet the Press*, March 16, 2003. The exact amount of the national debt is updated regularly at the Treasury Department Web site, http://www.treasurydirect.gov/NP/BPDLogin?application=np. Background on the Afghanistan surge was offered in Peter Baker's "How Obama Came to Plan for 'Surge' in Afghanistan," *The New York Times*, December 6, 2009. The Democratic Party statement on Iran was posted on the party's Web site, www.democrats.org, within the 2012 platform, which was titled "Moving America Forward." The 1963 quote from Kennedy can be found at the National Endowment for the Arts Web site, http://www.arts.gov/about/Kennedy.html.

Five: We Know the Drill: It's Time to Explore Alternatives

OPEC's market manipulation in the 1970s was traced in a report by Jahangir Amuzegar, *The 1979 "Oil Shock": Legacy, Lessons, and Lasting Reverberations* (Washington: Middle East Institute Viewpoints, 2009). The quote from Obama's inaugural speech can be found in the *New York Times* article "Obama's Second Inaugural Speech," January 13, 2013. The Michele Bachmann quote is taken from a video posted on washingtonpost.com on August 29, 2011.

The discussion of global warming is based on several articles: Michael E. Miller, "All Wet: Geologist Warns Miami Might Be Headed Six Feet Under," Miami *New Times*, September 8, 2011; Susan Solomon, Gian-Kasper Plattner, Reto Knutti, and Pierre Friedlingstein, "Irreversible Climate Change Due to Carbon Dioxide Emissions," *Proceedings of the National Academy of Sciences of the United States of America* 106, no. 6 (February 10, 2009); and James G. Titus, ed., *Greenhouse Effects, Sea Level Rise and Costal Wetlands* (Washington: U.S. Environmental Protection Agency, 1988).

Cap and trade, as utilized in the past, is explained in the report by the U.S. Environmental Protection Agency titled *Cap and Trade: Acid Rain Program Results*, http://www.epa.gov/capandtrade/documents/ctresults.pdf. Bush's stance on cap and trade is discussed in the *Smithsonian* article, "The Political History of Cap and Trade," August 2009. The material on Sen. James Inhofe's positions is from several sources: "The Science of Climate Change," James Inhofe, Statement on the Floor of the Senate, July 28, 2003; "Cap-and-Trade: What's Next," in *Human Events*, June 30, 2009; and Jonathan Karl and Z. Byron Wolf, "Amid Heat Wave, Senator Talks 'Global Cooling,'" ABC News, July 23, 2010.

The statistics on the ecological disaster in the Gulf of Mexico is found in Jeremy

Repanich's article, "BP Oil Spill Statistics—Deepwater Horizon Gulf Spill Numbers," *Popular Mechanics*, August 10, 2010. The fact that more subsidies go to dirty fuel companies than to those trying to develop clean energy is reflected in *Scientific American*'s "Should the U.S. Shift More Energy Subsidies to Renewable Power?," August 12, 2012. The amount of stimulus spending going to green initiatives is covered in the October 3, 2012, CNNMoney.com article, "What We Got For $50 billion in 'Green' Stimulus," by Steve Hargreaves.

Wind statistics can be found in an article by Xi Lu, Michael B. McElroy, and Juha Kiviluomac: "Global Potential for Wind-Generated Electricity," *Proceedings of the National Academy of Science* (June 2009). Wind is also discussed on the *Washington Post.com*'s Wonkblog, "Could Wind Power Ever Meet the World's Energy Needs?," September 12, 2012.

Six: Infrastructure Powers Economic Growth

The yearly assessment, "Report Card on America's Infrastructure," is available on the ASCE's Web site, http://www.infrastructurereportcard.org/. The condition of bridges was found in the report by the Federal Highway Administration of the Department of Transportation, "Deficient Bridges by State and Highway System," December 2010. The number of runway incursions was tabulated by the FAA. The FAA stats cited are from the chart "Runway Incursion Totals by quarter," posted on their Web site, www.faa.com. The quote on slumping productivity is from David Alan Aschauer's enlightening article, "Infrastructure and the Economy," *Journal of Contemporary Water Research and Education* 81, no. 1 (1990).

The Global Enabling Trade Report issued by the World Economic Forum is posted on their Web site, www.weforum.com. The cost of improving infrastructure is examined in the *Washington Post* article by Ashley Halsley, "Decaying Infrastructure Costs U.S. Billions Each Year, Report Says." The discussion of the high-speed train is based on several sources, including a map prepared by the Federal Rail Administration of the U.S. Department of Transportation, "High-Speed Rail Corridor Designations," posted online, http://www.fra.dot.gov; Julie M. Fenster, *The Spirit of Invention* (New York: HarperCollins, 2009); Aaron Deslatte, Mark K. Matthews, and Dan Tracy, "Can High-Speed Rail Backers Bypass Gov. Rick Scott?" *Orlando Sentinel*, February 16, 2011; Ted Jackovics, "High-Speed Rail Would Have Been Profitable, State Report Says," *The Tampa Tribune*, February 6, 2012.

The NextGen projections are delineated on the FAA webpage, http://www.faa.gov/nextgen/slides/?slide=1.

Seven: Kids Learn Best When Parents Teach First

More about the two successful programs cited can be seen on YouTube: *Breakthrough Saint Paul*, http://www.youtube.com/watch?v=7q1j2pjvaHs; and *Bridges to a*

Brighter Future, http://www.youtube.com/watch?v=Bqk7ZXXL9oY. The study on charter schools, *Time For Learning: An Exploratory Analysis of NAEP Data* (December 2012) was written by Alan Ginsburg and Naomi Chudowsky. The problems I had with Jeb Bush's programs are reflected in the *Orlando Sentinel* articles "Focus Put on Schools; Bush Touts Successes of A-Plus Plan; Seeks More Funds to Fight Terrorism," January 23, 2002; and "Class Size Cap Goes on Ballot" by Linda Kleindienst, August 2, 2002. Another opinion was offered by William Mathis, in his analysis *Jeb Bush Has Been Overselling Florida Education Policies*" for the National Education Policy Center (June 30, 2011).

The Head Start report referred to in the chapter was reviewed by Grover "Russ" Whitehurst for the Brookings Institute on January 21, 2010. His article was "Is Head Start Working for American Students." The HIPPY program is described at the group's Web site, www.hippy.org. Finland's educational program is the subject of the book by Pasi Sahlberg, *Finnish Lessons: What Can the World Learn from Educational Change in Finland?* (New York: Teachers College Press, 2011). The Center for American Progress Action Fund study, *The Middle Class Is Key to a Better Educated Nation* (November 11, 2011), was written by David Madland and Nick Bunker. The analysis of parents of low-income children, *Basic Facts About Low Income Children* (February 2012), by Sophia Addy and Vanessa R. Right, was published by the National Center for Children in Poverty.

The rise in the cost of tuition is charted in Marybeth Marklein, "Tuition and Fees Rise More Than 8 Percent at U.S. Public Colleges," *USA Today*, October 25, 2011; and in the report by the National Center for Education Statistics, *Price of Attending an Undergraduate Institution* (2012). The NCES "FastFacts" column on its Web site, http://nces.ed.gov/fastfacts, was the source for the figures on college enrolment. The college dropout statistics, based on research by Harvard University and the Pew Institute, appeared in an *Atlantic Monthly* article, "Why Do So Many Americans Drop Out of College?," March 29, 2012, by Jonathan Weissmann.

Eight: Keeping Kids Healthy and Safe

In September 2012, the Department of Agriculture released a report, *Household Food Insecurity in the United States in 2011*, by Alisha Coleman-Jensen, Mark Nord, Margaret Andrews, and Steven Carlson. The study correlating childhood diet and IQ development was described in "Are Dietary Patterns in Childhood Associated with IQ at 8 Years of Age?" by K. Northstone et al., *Journal of Epidemiology and Community Health* (February 7, 2011). The dearth of physical education classes was reported by Al Baker, "Despite Obesity Concerns, Gym Classes are Out," *New York Times*, July 10, 2012.

Statistics and helpful information on pool safety can be found at the CDC Web site, www.cdc.gov/Features/dsSafeSwimmingPool/index.html. The testimony of Alicia Kozakiewicz before the House Judiciary Committee can be seen on YouTube, http://www.youtube.com/watch?v=vGdldKxPock. The study on prisoners and foster care was produced by the California Senate Office of Research: *What Percentage of the State's Polled Prison Inmates Were Once Foster Care Children?* (December 2011).

Nine: Putting the Fight Back in Women's Rights

The words of Abigail Adams are from the book *Familiar Letters of John Adams and His Wife Abigail Adams: During the Revolution*, edited by Charles Francis Adams (New York: Hurd and Houghton, 1876). The Ledbetter case is covered in *The Washington Post* on May 30, 2007, in an article titled "Over Ginsburg's Dissent, Court Limits Bias Suits." Information on the vote in Congress for the Lilly Ledbetter Act can be found at Govtrack, a Web site that tracks legislative activity at many levels of government, www.govtrack.us/congress/votes/111-2009/h37. The income inequality of women is discussed in the *Bloomberg BusinessWeek* article by Frank Bass and Jennifer Oldham, "Wage Gap for Women Endures Even as Jobs Increase," October 25, 2012.

The controversy over Limbaugh's attack on Sandra Fluke has several sources, including Sarah Kliff's *Washington Post* article, "Meet Sandra Fluke: The Woman You Didn't Hear at Congress' Contraceptives Hearing," February 16, 2012; Jim Abrams's coverage for the Associated Press, "Democrats Protest Religious Freedom Hearing," February 16, 2012; "Democrats Hear from Woman Snubbed by GOP Lawmakers," February 24, 2012; Katharine Mangan, "Limbaugh's Name-Calling Puts Georgetown Law Student in an Unexpected Light," *The Chronicle of Higher Education*, March 3, 2012; and Peggy Noonan on an ABC News *This Week* (video), March 4, 2012, retrieved in the posting, "George Will Condemns GOP over Sandra Fluke Response," *Huffington Post*, March 5, 2012.

Olympia Snowe's reasons for declining to run again were covered in the *Bangor Daily News* article "Olympia Snowe Quits Race," February 28, 2012. Meghan McCain's comments came from her piece for the *Daily Beast*, "Meghan McCain on Why the Republican Party Needs to Wake Up," November 16, 2012. Mae Jemison's quote is from Amy Finnerty's article in *The New York Times*, "Outnumbered: Standing Out at Work," July 16, 2000. The Jeane Kirkpatrick quote is from her book *Political Women* (New York: Basic Books, 1974).

Ten: America's Promise to Immigrants

Maria Siemionow's story is recounted in her book *Face to Face: My Quest to Perform the First Full Face Transplant* (New York: Kaplan, 2009). The Department of Homeland Security's U.S. Citizen and Immigration Services' Web site updates H1B quotas and policies. The Census Bureau recorded the number of Americans as of 2000, http://www.census.gov/statab/hist/HS-10.pdf. The effect of immigration policy on skilled workers is the topic of Arlene Holen's report *The Budgetary Effects of High-Skilled Immigration Reform* (March 2009) for the Technology Policy Institute.

The capsizing of the boat carrying the Haitian immigrants was covered in the *Huffington Post*, "Haitian Boat Carrying Migrants Capsized Near Bahamas," June 12, 2012. Information on coyote crashes in Texas is in *The Christian Post*'s "Illiegal Immigration: Crossing the Border Is a Deadly Game of Life and Death," Vincente Menjivar, August 22, 2012.

Statistics on Arizona's Latino population is available at the Census Bureau's Web site, http://quickfacts.census.gov/qfd/states/04000.html. The stripping of SB 1070 can be found in the Fernanda Santos article in *The New York Times*, "Arizona Immigration Law Survives Ruling," September 6, 2012. Daniel Hernandez's quotes are from his February 5, 2013, interview on CNN. Information on the DREAM Act came from several sources, starting with the Web site Dreamact.info; the CBO cost estimate is in its report, *H.R. 6497, Development, Relief, and Education for Alien Minors Act of 2010* (December 7, 2010); see also the Las Vegas *Sun* article by Karoun Demirjian, "Harry Reid Reintroduces Dream Act," May 11, 2011.

Eleven: Civil Rights: A March Without End

Further information on the Terri Schiavo case can be found on my Web site, http://wassermanschultz.house.gov/2005/05/2005May.shtml. Martin Luther King Jr.'s "Letter From a Birmingham Jail" can be found in the book of the same name (New York: HarperOne, 1994). It is also available on the Web, at www.africa.upenn.edu/Articles_Gen/Letter_Birmingham.html. The polling on giving up civil liberties in the fight on terrorism is from American Enterprise Institute's *Political Report*, "The War on Terror: Ten Years of Polls on American Attitudes" (September, 2011).

The Patriot Act provisions that violate civil rights and liberties are listed on the May 26, 2011, blog of the American Civil Liberties Union, www.aclu.org, in an entry titled "Reform the Patriot Act: A Primer." The research by the OIG is covered by Carrie Johnson's article in the *Washington Post*, "Inspector General Cites 'Egregious Breakdown' in FBI Oversight," January 21, 2010.

Some of the details on Edward Snowden and the reactions to the NSA leak are covered in the articles by NBC's Tracy Connor, "What We Know About NSA leaker Edward Snowden" on June 11, 2013, and *The Guardian*'s Daniel Boffey, "Prism Whistle Blower Edward Snowden a Hero to 40% Poll Finds," June 16, 2013.

The Brennan Center for Justice at the New York University Law School has tracked the many efforts to distort elections. It released the report *Ballot Security and Voter Suppression: What It Is and What the Law Says* (updated August 29, 2012) by Wendy Weiser and Vishal Agraharkar. The GOP's motives behind voter fraud legislation and Jim Greer's quote is taken from the November 25, 2012, article in *The*

Palm Beach Post titled, "Former Florida GOP Leaders Say Voter Suppression Was Reason They Pushed New Election Law." The July 17, 2012, *Atlantic* article about voting receipts being turned into lottery tickets is called "The U.S. Should Require All Citizens to Vote" by Norm Ornstein.

Polling on same-sex marriage is found at www.pollingreport.com/civil.htm. The Pew Research Center's Forum on Religion & Public Life released its report *Changing Attitudes on Gay Marriage* in May 2013.

Twelve: Aiming for Sensible Policy on Guns

Research on mass killings is available in the study "U.S. Mass Shootings 1982–2012, Data from Mother Jones' Investigation" (updated February 27, 2012) by Mark Follman, Gavin Aronsen, and Deanna Pan. It is available at www.motherjones.com. The details of Feinstein's bill are at her Web site, www.feinstein.senate.gov/public/index.cfm/assault-weapons-ban-summary. The gun show loophole is discussed in the *New York Times* editorial, "The Yawning Loophole in the Gun Laws," December 18, 2012.

Polls on attitudes about gun laws can be found at CBSNews.com in the January 17, 2012, posting, "Poll: Majority of Americans Back Stricter Gun Laws" by Sarah Dutton, Jennifer De Pinto, Anthony Salvanto, Fred Backus, and Leigh Ann Caldwell. Gabby Giffords's handwritten notes were published in the *Atlantic Monthly* article, "Handwritten Notes for Gabrielle Giffords' Testimony to the Senate Judicial Committee," January 30, 2013.

The NRA opposition to legislation is the topic of William Saletan's article "N.R.A.'s Pathetic Excuses for Opposing Universal Background Checks," February 5, 2013, on *Slate.com*. Mental health parity regarding gun control is debated in Politico.com's "Newtown Renews Panel's Focus on Mental Health" by Paige Winfield Cunningham, January 25, 2013.

Thirteen: Discourse, Not Discord

Sullivan's comment about "killing a couple of Senators" is in Sean Murphy's *Huffington Post* article "John Sullivan, GOP Congressman, Apologizes for 'Killing' Comments," February 24, 2012. The Barbour quote is found in Politico.com's article by Kevin Robillard, "Haley Barbour Apologizes for Obama Remark," September 4, 2012. The California Democratic chairman's remark about Nazis was reported by FoxNews.com in the article "California Dem Offers a Qualified Apology for Comparing GOP Claims to Nazi Tactics," September 4, 2012. Siegel's quote is contained in the *Palm Beach Post* article by George Bennett, "Siegel Resigns as Palm Beach Democrats' Chair," September 7, 2012.

The Tea Party strategy was covered by Lee Fang in ThinkProgress.com's article "Right Wing Strategy Against Dems Detailed in Memo," July 31, 2009. The Lewis quote is from the *Washington Post* article by Paul Kane, "Tea Party Protesters Accused of Spitting on Lawmaker, Using Slurs," March 20, 2010.

For background on the debt ceiling, the best source is the Department of the Treasury's Web page called "Debt Ceiling." The falling credit rating of the United States is covered in the Reuters article by Walter Brandimarte and Daniel Bases, "United States Loses Prized AAA Rating from S&P," August 6, 2011. The S&P's downgrade is explained on that company's Web site in the publication "United States of America Long-Term Rating Lowered to AA+ Due to Political Risks, Rising Debt Burden, Outlook Negative," August 5, 2011.

Fourteen: To Belong to Something

Terri Lannan's story is from the *Omaha World-Herald* article "Red Cross Volunteers Help Those Affected by Sandy," November 24, 2012. The text of George H. W. Bush's inaugural address is available at www.americanpresidents.org/inaugural/40.asp. PTA membership is discussed in the *Huffington Post* article by David Crary, "National PTA Tries to Increase Membership After Numbers Drop," April 6, 2012. More information about joining the group is at the PTA Web site, www.pta.org.

Information on the Peace Corps and the people in it can be found at www.peacecorps.gov.

The study by John Wilson and Marc Musick was introduced in the article "Effects of Volunteering on the Volunteer," *Law and Contemporary Problems* (Fall 1999).

Conclusion: Change . . . What Happens Next Is Up to Us

Further information on the development of the breast cancer EARLY Act is in the article by Alan Peabody, "Breast Cancer Bill Gets Personal for Liberian Woman in the U.S.," WashingtonInformer.com, October 23, 2009. The donations made to anti-gay groups by the Chik-fil-A chain was covered in the *Los Angeles Times* by Tiffany Hsu in "Chik-fil-A Vows to Stop Donating to Anti-Gay Groups," September 19, 2012. Similar news were also in the New York *Daily News* article of the same date by Anthony Bartkewicz, "Chik-fil-A Says It Will Stop Donations to Anti-Gay Groups."

List of Organizations

In the spirit of the book, I encourage readers to reach out to these organizations (and any others that fit your personal interests) to make a difference for the next generation.

Introduction
American Association of Caregiving Youth
1515 N. Federal Highway
Suite 218
Boca Raton, FL 33432
561-391-7401
800-725-2512
www.aacy.org

One:
Consumer Financial Protection Bureau (CFPB)
1700 G Street, NW
Washington, D.C. 20552
202-435-7000
www.consumerfinance.gov

Medicaid and Medicare
Centers for Medicare & Medicaid Services
7500 Security Boulevard
Baltimore, MD 21244

http://cms.gov/apps/contacts/ (Contact Database/ no phone)
www.medicare.gov/index.html

Two:
Social Security Administration
Office of Public Inquiries
Windsor Park Building
6401 Security Boulevard
Baltimore, MD 21235
800-772-1213
www.ssa.gov/OACT/ProgData/funds.html

Three:
American Cancer Society—Cancer Action Network (ACS—CAN)
PO Box 22718
Oklahoma City, OK 73123-1718
800-227-2345
www.acscan.org

The Heritage Foundation
214 Massachusetts Avenue NE
Washington, DC 20002-4999
202-546-4400
www.heritage.org

Four:
The Daniel Cantor Wultz Foundation
318 Indian Trace, Box 654
Weston, FL 33326-2996
www.dcwfoundation.org

Five:
Desoto Next Generation Solar Energy Center (NextGen)
FPL
P.O. Box 025576
Miami, FL 33102
954-581-5668 (Broward—varies from each residential area)
www.fpl.com/environment/solar/desoto.shtml

U.S. Department of Energy
1000 Independence Avenue SW
Washington, DC 20585
202-586-5000
www.energy.gov

Six:
The American Society of Civil Engineers
1801 Alexander Bell Drive
Reston, VA 20191
800-548-2723
703-295-6300 (International)
www.asce.org

Highway Trust Fund
Federal Highway Administration
1200 New Jersey Avenue, SE
Washington, DC 20590
202-366-4000
www.fhwa.dot.gov/highwaytrustfund

Seven:
Bridges to a Brighter Future
Furman University
3300 Poinsett Highway
Greenville, SC 29613
804-294-2000
www.bridgestoabrighterfuture.org

Education is Freedom
2711 N. Haskell Avenue
Suite 2070, LB 18
Dallas, TX 75204
877-642-6343
www.educationisfreedom.com

Education Policy Institute
EPI International/United States
6900 Wisconsin Avenue, Suite 606
Bethesda, MD 20815

202-657-5207
www.educationalpolicy.org

Fund Education Now
P.O. Box 561613
Orlando, FL 32856
No available phone number
www.fundeducationnow.org

Head Start
Administration for Children and Families
Office of Head Start (OHS)
8th Floor Portals Building
Washington, DC 20024
866-763-6481
www.eclkc.ohs.acf.hhs.gov/hslc

Child Care and Development Block Grant
Office of Child Care
Administration for Children and Families,
Department of Health and Human Services
370 L'Enfant Promenade, SW,
5th Floor East
Washington, DC 20447
202-401-4831
www.federalgrantswire.com/child-care-and-development-block-grant.html

Home Instruction for Parents of Pre-School Youngsters (HIPPY)
1221 Bishop Street
Little Rock, Arkansas 72202
501-537-7726
www.hippyusa.org

Teach for America
315 W. 36th Street
New York, NY 10018
212-279-2080
www.teachforamerica.org

Race to the Top Fund
Lyndon Baines Johnson (LBJ)
Department of Education Building
400 Maryland Avenue, SW
Washington, DC 20202
800-872-5327
www2.ed.gov/programs/racetothetop/index.html

U.S. Department of Education
Lyndon Baines Johnson (LBJ)
Department of Education Building
400 Maryland Avenue, SW
Washington, DC 20202
800-872-5327
www.ed.gov

National Parent Teacher Association
National PTA Headquarters
1250 N. Pitt Street
Alexandria, Virginia 22314
703-518-1200
www.pta.org

Center for American Progress Action Fund
1333 H Street, N.W., 10th Floor
Washington, D.C. 20005
Attention: Development
202-682-1611
www.americanprogressaction.org

National Center for Children in Poverty
215 W. 125th Street, 3rd Floor
New York, NY 10027
646-284-9600
www.nccp.org

Council of the Great City Schools
1301 Pennsylvania Avenue, N.W.
Suite 702
Washington, DC 20004

202-393-2427
www.cgcs.org/site/default.aspx?PageID=1

Eight:
YMCA
YMCA of the USA
101 N Wacker Drive
Chicago, IL 60606
Domestic: 800-872-9622
International: 312-977-0031
www.ymca.net

The American Red Cross
2025 E Street, NW
Washington DC 20006
800-733-2767
www.redcrossblood.org

Surviving Parents Coalition
1414 22nd Street, NW
Suite 4
Washington, DC 20037
888-301-4343
www.spcoalition.org

Internet Crimes Against Children Task Force (ICAC)
Broward Police Department
Administration Office
2601 W. Broward Boulevard
Ft. Lauderdale, FL 33312
954-888-5299 (phone number varies by state)
www.icactaskforce.org/Pages/Home.aspx

PACE Center for Girls, Inc.
One West Adams Street, Suite 301
Jacksonville, FL 32202
904-421-8585
www.pacecenter.org

Nine:
National Association of Women Business Owners
NAWBO Institute for Entrepreneurial Development
P.O. Box 826180
Philadelphia, PA 19182-6180
800-556-2926
www.nawbo.org

International Business Federation of Business and Professional Women
BPW International
Rue de Saint-Jean 26
1203 Geneva
Switzerland
No available phone number
www.bpw-international.org

Council on Women and Girls
The White House
1600 Pennsylvania Avenue, NW
Washington, DC 20500
202-456-1111
www.whitehouse.gov/administration/eop/cwg

Ten:
Best Buddies International
Global Headquarters
100 Southeast Second Street
Suite 2200
Miami, FL 33131
305-374-2233
www.bestbuddies.org

Eleven:
The League of Women Voters
1730 M Street NW, Suite 1000,
Washington, DC 20036-4508
202-429-1965
www.lwv.org

The Lesbian, Gay, Bisexual & Transgender Community Center
208 West 13th Street
New York, NY 10011
212-620-7310
www.gaycenter.org

American Jewish Committee
9200 S Dadeland Boulevard
Suite 500
Miami, FL 33156
305-670-1121
www.ajc.org

Twelve:
Americans for Responsible Solutions
PO Box 15642
Washington, DC 20003
No available phone number
www.americansforresponsiblesolutions.org

Thirteen:
Young Survival Coalition (Breast Cancer Advocate Group)
61 Broadway
Suite 2235
New York, NY 10006
646-257-3000
www.youngsurvival.org

Fourteen:
Girl Scouts of America
420 Fifth Avenue
New York, New York 10018-2798
212-852-8000
www.girlscouts.org

Habitat for Humanity
121 Habitat Street
Americus, GA 31709-3498
229-924-6935
www.habitat.org

PeaceCorps
Paul D. Coverdell Peace Corps Headquarters
1111 20th Street, NW
Washington, D.C. 20526
202-692-1470
www.peacecorps.gov

Planned Parenthood
Planned Parenthood Federation of America
434 West 33rd Street
New York, NY 10001
212-541-7800
www.plannedparenthood.org

Corporation for National and Community Service
1201 New York Avenue, NW
Washington, DC 20525
202-606-5000
www.nationalservice.gov

MicroEdge, LLC
619 West 54th Street, 10th Floor
New York, NY 10019
212-757-1522
www.microedge.com

Conclusion
Tigerlily Foundation
11654 Plaza America Drive #725
Reston, VA 20190
888-580-6253
www.tigerlilyfoundation.org
www.workingmother.com

Generations Group Homes, Inc.
PO Box 80009
Simpsonville, SC 29680
864-243-5557
www.generationsgroup.com

Rooted in Community
2150 Allston Way
Suite 460
Berkeley, CA 94704-1375
570-419-3833
www.rootedincommunity.org

League of Conservation Voters
1920 L Street, NW
Suite 800
Washington, DC 20036
202-835-0491
www.lcv.org

Americans for Immigrant Justice
3000 Biscayne Boulevard, Suite 400
Miami, FL 33137
305-573-1106
www.aijustice.org

American Association of Retired Persons
601 E Street, NW
Washington DC 20049
877-434-7598
www.aarp.org

Safe Kids Worldwide
1301 Pennsylvania Avenue, N.W.
Suite 1000
Washington, DC 20004
202-662-0600
www.safekids.org

National Safety Council
1121 Spring Lake Drive
Itasca, IL 60143-3201
800-621-7615
www.nsc.org/Pages/Home.aspx

Index